THE EASY PATH

Gyumed Khensur Rinpoche Lobsang Jampa

The Easy Path

ILLUMINATING THE FIRST PANCHEN LAMA'S SECRET INSTRUCTIONS

Gyumed Khensur Lobsang Jampa

Edited by Lorne Ladner

WISDOM PUBLICATIONS • BOSTON

Wisdom Publications, Inc.
199 Elm Street
Somerville, MA 02144 USA
www.wisdompubs.org

Library of Congress Cataloging-in-Publication Data
Blo-bzaṅ-byams-pa, 1939–
 The easy path : illuminating the first Panchen Lama's secret instructions / Gyumed
Khensur Lobsang Jampa ; edited by Lorne Ladner.
     pages cm
Includes bibliographical references and index.
Includes translation from Tibetan.
ISBN 0-86171-678-7 (pbk. : alk. paper)
1. Blo-bzaṅ-chos-kyi-rgyal-mtshan, Panchen Lama I, 1570–1662. Byaṅ chub lam
gyi rim pa'i dmar khrid thams cad mkhyen par bgrod pa'i bde lam. 2. Lam–rim. 3.
Dge-lugs-pa (Sect)—Doctrines. I. Ladner, Lorne. II. Blo-bzaṅ-chos-kyi-rgyal-mtshan,
Panchen Lama I, 1570–1662. Byaṅ chub lam gyi rim pa'i dmar khrid thams cad mkhyen
par bgrod pa'i bde lam. English. III. Title.
 BQ7645.L35B5333 2013
 294.3'444—dc23

                                        2013009448

ISBN 978-0-86171-678-4
eBook ISBN 978-1-61429-098-8

17 16 15 14 13   5 4 3 2 1

Cover design by Phil Pascuzzo.
Interior design by Gopa&Ted2. Set in Berling LT Std 10/15.

Wisdom Publications' books are printed on acid-free paper and meet the guidelines
for permanence and durability of the Production Guidelines for Book Longevity of the
Council on Library Resources.

Printed in the United States of America.

 This book was produced with environmental mindfulness. We
have elected to print this title on 30% PCW recycled paper. As a
result, we have saved the following resources: 8 trees, 4 million BTUs of energy, 735 lbs. of
greenhouse gases, 3,987 gallons of water, and 266 lbs. of solid waste. For more information,
please visit our website, www.wisdompubs.org. This paper is also FSC® certified. For more
information, please visit www.fscus.org.

Contents

Publisher's Acknowledgment

T HE PUBLISHER gratefully acknowledges the generous contribution of the Hershey Family Foundation toward the publication of this book.

Editor's Preface

THE FIRST PANCHEN LAMA's *Easy Path*, written nearly four hundred years ago, is like a treasure chest that has until now been locked to English speakers. The translation of the root text here with Gyumed Khensur Rinpoche's commentary unlocks that chest of treasures. To gain the greatest benefit from this book, it may be useful to imagine each contemplation and meditation discussed as a precious jewel from that chest being given to you personally. You may want to pause, holding each up to the light to slowly and joyfully examine its facets, beauty, and great value. Khensur Rinpoche was extremely generous in his approach to teaching this text, carefully and precisely revealing many points from the unique, oral tradition that has come down from Lama Tsongkhapa (1357–1419) through Gyalwa Ensapa (1505–66), the First Panchen Lama (1570–1662), and eventually to Rinpoche himself.

If you've read or studied some in the past on the stages of the path to enlightenment, then it may be easy to assume that you already know many of the points explained here. But, if you read carefully, you will discover dimensions not found elsewhere.

At one point in *Easy Path*, when commenting on the resolve "I must at all costs, quickly, quickly attain the precious state of completely perfect buddhahood for the sake of all mother sentient beings," Khensur Rinpoche explains that one way of interpreting the phrase "quickly, quickly" is that the first "quickly" refers to practicing the three lower classes of tantra and the second "quickly" refers to practicing highest yoga tantra. That is of course a profound point. But then Rinpoche shares another interpretation unique to the oral tradition coming through Gyalwa Ensapa. In that interpretation, the first "quickly" refers to practicing the stages of the path to enlightenment, which is explained to be a faster way of attaining full enlightenment than the three lower classes of tantra, and the second "quickly" refers to taking guru yoga as the life of your practice. By reading this book as we might slowly explore jewel treasures, we can gain understanding of how to go about taking guru yoga not just as the heart of our practice but as its very living essence. In this volume, too, we gain a practical understanding of how to integrate visualizations from highest yoga tantra, guru yoga, and other instructions of the oral tradition with our contemplations and meditations on every single step of the stages of the path. In that way, the Panchen Lama's "quickly, quickly" may come to refer not just to practitioners of the past but to us as well!

As you begin reading this book, you'll notice that both the First Panchen Lama and Khensur Rinpoche take a practical approach to transforming the inner life. These instructions are not mere intellectual exercises. They are intended to evoke powerful, visceral responses. Khensur Rinpoche points out how, due to our beginningless familiarity with unrealistic thinking and afflictive emotions, we easily and spontaneously give rise to visceral feelings of desire, anger, jealousy, and the like. As beginners, our experiences of refuge, compassion, or wisdom may seem less heartfelt or "real." That's a sign only that we've not yet familiarized ourselves much with those states. However, if we continue practicing, deeper experiences will come. If we meditate sincerely on our precious human rebirth and on impermanence, we may come to feel as Scrooge did upon waking Christmas morning to find himself still alive, shouting, "I am here . . . I am as light as a feather, I am as happy as an angel, I am as merry as a schoolboy . . . Hallo here! Whoop! Hallo!" As Khensur Rinpoche points out, through training in refuge, we may find ourselves feeling like young children calling out to loving, reliable parents! When meditating on the sufferings of samsara, we may find ourselves utterly disgusted, longing for freedom like a death-row inmate. When meditating on love, we may feel like our hearts have broken open and we're in love with whomever we meet. We may feel that everyone is like our parent, our child, or our dearest friend. When meditating on compassion, each and every sentient being may appear to us as our dear mother drowning and in desperate need of our help. When meditating on emptiness, it may feel like losing everything or like unlocking the secret of the universe! The goal of these meditations is not just to absorb new ideas or information but to gain the tools and skills needed to sculpt ourselves, much as a sculptor might transform a large marble stone into a sacred statue. We can chip away at the clumps of egotism and ignorance, wholly revealing the utterly pure buddha-nature within.

The idea for this book arose when Khensur Rinpoche, in his role as resident teacher at Guhyasamaja Center near Washington DC, agreed to teach on one of the eight great treatises on the stages of the path to enlightenment. After doing some research, I learned that Joshua Cutler of the Tibetan Buddhist Learning Center in New Jersey had made an unpublished translation of the First Panchen Lama's *Easy Path*. Josh generously offered his translation for use during Rinpoche's teachings. The whole of *Easy Path* appears in translation in this book, integrated with Khensur Rinpoche's teachings. Josh's initial translation was revised as we went along to ensure consistency with the commentary, Wisdom's house style, and after checking details with Khensur Rinpoche.

Khensur Rinpoche's commentary here is based on the oral commentary that he gave at Guhyasamaja Center. Those teachings were translated by Rinpoche's excellent translators, Geshe Tashi and Tenzin Buchung. I carefully took notes during those teachings. Based on those notes, Rinpoche, his two translators, and I engaged in many discussions about difficult or complicated points in the teachings. Rinpoche was extremely patient and generous in answering many questions and explaining challenging points from many angles in order to make them clear. The current form of this book arose from my editing those original notes taken during Rinpoche's oral commentary with the further clarifications that came during the discussions. I made every effort to check points of uncertainty; if errors remain it's because I lacked the wisdom to be uncertain when I should have been!

In my experience, whenever Khensur Rinpoche teaches on a given text, he does so by relating what the text itself says, what other great masters have taught on the subject, and also what his own experience has been in contemplating and meditating on those teachings. Some of the related texts and commentaries that Rinpoche reviewed and referred to in the context of these teachings include Tsongkhapa's *Great Treatise on the Stages of the Path*, the First Panchen Lama's *Guru Puja*, Aku Sherap Gyatso's (1803–75) *Notes on "Easy Path,"* two *Easy Path* commentaries by Palmang Pandita Konchok Gyaltsen (1764–1853) called *Clarifying the Vital Points* and *Mirror of the Heart*, the Second Panchen Losang Yeshe's *Swift Path to Enlightenment*, an *Easy Path* commentary by Drakgyap Jetsun Losang Norbu (1903–68), and Pabongka Rinpoche's (1878–1941) *Liberation in the Palm of Your Hand*.

Khensur Rinpoche himself explains in his commentary quite clearly why *Easy Path* is such an important commentary on the stages of the path—particularly for those strongly interested in contemplative and meditative practice. Although *Easy Path* has never before appeared in English, some familiar with English-language books from the Tibetan tradition may find some passages familiar. Because of the seminal role of this text in the Geluk tradition, many versions of the preliminary practices for meditation on the stages of the path to enlightenment quote significant passages from *Easy Path*. For example, Pabongka Rinpoche's *Ornament for the Throats of the Fortunate*[1] contains the descriptions of the refuge and merit fields as well as the "Planting the Stake Prayer" taken directly from *Easy Path*. Kyabje Lama Zopa Rinpoche has composed an extensive version of the preliminary practices combining the *Guru Puja*, sections of *Easy Path*, and other materials.[2] Most versions of the preliminary practices for meditation on the stages of the path in the Geluk tradition written after the First Panchen Lama's time excerpt from *Easy Path*. Also, the commentary on Tsongkhapa's "Three Principal Aspects of the Path" composed by the Fourth Panchen Lama, which has been translated into English by Geshe Lhundup Sopa and Jeffrey Hopkins in *Cutting Through Appearances*, contains significant quotations from *Easy Path*. It is clear that the Fourth Panchen Lama in composing his commentary excerpted relevant sections of the First Panchen Lama's text, adding additional comments.

In terms of our current text, sections of *Easy Path* are indented and set off from Khensur Rinpoche's commentary with distinct type. Headings and subheadings have been added to allow the reader to identify topics more easily and pause for meditation.

This book contains three appendixes. Appendix 1 is an extremely abbreviated version of the preliminary practices. For those with time, many beautiful, extensive versions of the preliminary practices exist in English, such as the two mentioned above. Out of concern for some Western readers who view themselves as extremely busy—perhaps, like myself, due to the laziness of spending lots of time and energy on matters of no spiritual significance—who still may want to engage in practices of the stages of the path to enlightenment, I asked Khensur Rinpoche to explain how to engage in the preliminary practices in the briefest possible way without leaving out what's essential. Consulting the commentaries by Lama Tsongkhapa and Aku Sherab Gyatso, Rinpoche explained a very brief way of doing the preliminaries in accord with what is called the *condensed jewel tradition*. This tradition involves visualizing just one figure, usually atop your head, embodying all your teachers and all other sources of refuge as well. This condensed jewel tradition appears within *Easy Path*, and in the first appendix we provide an even briefer version.

That the lineage of Panchen Lamas became second only to the Dalai Lamas in both spiritual and political importance in Central Asia for the past four hundred years is due largely to the amazing accomplishments of the author of *Easy Path*—the First Panchen Lama. Panchen Losang Chokyi Gyaltsen's activities powerfully impacted the spiritual and political history of Central Asia, and his *Guru Puja* and *Six-Session Guru Yoga* remain the central liturgical staples for Gelukpa practitioners to this day. I share further details of the remarkable life of the First Panchen Lama in appendix 2.

Appendix 3 provides a brief sketch of the life of Gyumed Khensur Rinpoche Lobsang Jampa. "Gyumed Khensur Rinpoche" is actually a title, meaning "precious abbot emeritus of Gyumed Tantric College." Rinpoche graduated as a *geshe lharampa* from Sera Mey Monastic University in 1986, and in 1996 he was appointed abbot of Gyumed by His Holiness the Dalai Lama, a post he held for three years. The great master Ribur Rinpoche, prior to his death, personally requested Khensur Rinpoche to serve as primary teacher to his own next incarnation. Over the seven years I've been close with Khensur Rinpoche, he has almost never spoken about his own life. When I asked him to do so in order to help me compose a brief biography, he replied, "That's not necessary." Only after my repeatedly explaining that the editors at Wisdom Publications and I felt that at least a brief biography would be of interest and benefit to Western readers did Rinpoche agree to speak just a bit about his early life and studies.

Although I've heard high praise of Rinpoche from a number of respected lamas, Rinpoche insisted that I not include those praises in this book. Rinpoche's extreme reticence regarding his own good qualities was a lesson about humility. When Rinpoche spoke about his efforts at memorization during his first couple of years as a monk, I foolishly asked, "When did you turn to your deeper studies, leaving off this focus on memorization?" Rinpoche quite simply replied, "Not yet." Indeed, in his midseventies Rinpoche does continue memorizing texts. Over the course of our discussions about his life, I was also struck by Rinpoche's lack of pretense or drama. When Rinpoche spoke of his escape from Tibet (without any money, food, or belongings) and of his period of recuperation from illness in a hospital after his time at Buxa refugee camp in India, I said, "Those experiences must have been terribly difficult." Again, Rinpoche replied very simply, saying, "I didn't say those things were difficult." Instead Rinpoche expressed gratitude for the help and kindness others had shown to him.

In the section of this book on the preliminary practices, you'll read some about the vast benefits that come from practicing rejoicing. An excellent way to benefit yourself and others is, as you read the biographical sketches of the First Panchen Lama and of Gyumed Khensur Rinpoche, to practice rejoicing in their vast studies, deep contemplative and meditative practices, and extensive compassionate activities.

It is my enormous fortune to have been able to assist in presenting this expression of the wisdom and bodhichitta of these two great masters of the Tibetan Buddhist tradition.

Lorne Ladner

Panchen Lama Losang Chokyi Gyaltsen
From the collection of the Rubin Museum of Art

Introduction

THE SANSKRIT WORD *bodhi* is usually translated into English as "enlightenment." When one attains bodhi, one becomes a *buddha*—an enlightened or awakened being. To attain such an enlightened state, you must purify all negative qualities and fully actualize all good qualities, such as wisdom, love, and compassion. This book explains the essential practices for attaining such an enlightened state in accordance with a seventeeth-century work by Panchen Lama Losang Chokyi Gyaltsen, *Stages of the Path to Enlightenment: Practical Instructions on the Easy Path to Omniscience*—in brief, *Easy Path*. The word "omniscience" in the title is essentially a synonym for enlightenment, or buddhahood. "Practical instructions" indicates that this text provides pragmatic advice that completely reveals the subject.

The Tibetan term *lamrim*, the "stages of the path," describes a genre of literature that was initiated in Tibet by the great Indian master Atisha when he composed his famous *Lamp for the Path to Enlightenment*.[3] In that classic text, Atisha showed how to integrate the vast range of Buddhist teachings into one's own practice of the path by describing how individuals progress through three "scopes" or levels of motivation for spiritual practice. Among the many texts written in Tibet on the stages of the path, there are a set of eight great lamrim texts that are considered especially important. These eight include the extensive, medium, and brief lamrim texts by Lama Tsongkhapa; *Easy Path* by the First Panchen Lama; *Swift Path* by the Second Panchen Lama Losang Yeshe; *Essence of Refined Gold* by the Third Dalai Lama; *Manjushri's Own Words* by the Great Fifth Dalai Lama; and *Path of the Excellent Scriptures* by Dakpo

Ngawang Drakpa. So this book examines one of those eight especially great texts.[4]

The Tibetan term *delam*, here being translated as "easy path," could also be taken to mean a "path to bliss." *De* connotes ease, happiness, well-being, and bliss. As this text involves tantric methods, it does indeed teach a path that can lead you to great bliss. However, the main sense of *delam* in our title is of an easy path—easy because it combines the methods of sutra and tantra—to travel to the state of omniscience. Of the eight great texts, *Easy Path* and *Swift Path* are particularly related to tantra, the Vajra Vehicle.[5] *Swift Path* is a commentary on *Easy Path*. Their titles contain these words—swift and easy—because of their relation to tantric practice, for tantric methods enable rapid progress to enlightenment when employed skillfully.

For example, one special technique explained in this text is the visualization of nectar descending from your spiritual teacher into yourself. Such visualizations are not found in teachings based solely on the Sutra Vehicle. There you may find light rays emanating from buddhas and bodhisattvas but not the descent of nectar blessings from your spiritual teacher. If you can visualize clearly the light rays and nectar of five colors in the context of guru yoga as taught in *Easy Path*, then this leaves powerful imprints that will later ripen as enlightened qualities. Visualizing nectar leaves imprints to realize the illusory body as taught in the completion stage of highest yoga tantra, and visualizing light rays leaves the imprint to realize the completion-stage clear light; visualizing the five colors leaves imprints to realize the five enlightened wisdoms. This is one way that *Easy Path* takes advantage of the techniques of Buddhist tantra.

Because this text contains such elements of tantric practice, it allows you to attain realizations more quickly and easily than you could by practicing only the path of the perfections based solely on the teachings in the Buddhist sutras. If you travel to enlightenment through the path taught in the sutras without engaging in tantric practice, then it takes many lifetimes stretching across eons to attain buddhahood. Five different spans of time are taught in the sutras for the bodhisattva's journey to buddhahood, each with its own simile. Some bodhisattvas travel like a bull cart, taking forty eons; some travel like an elephant, taking thirty-three eons; some travel like the sun and the moon, taking ten eons; some travel like an arhat's magical power, taking seven eons; and some travel like a buddha's magical power, taking three eons.[6]

Buddha Shakyamuni was among this fastest category, attaining enlightenment by training for three eons. This trajectory can be mapped to the Buddhist explanation of the five paths and ten grounds. Such a bodhisattva takes one eon, involving many rebirths, to traverse the first two of the five Mahayana paths—the paths of *accumulation* and of *preparation*. The bodhisattva then takes a second eon to travel from the first bodhisattva ground, which is attained on the path of *seeing*, up to the seventh bodhisattva ground along the fourth path, the path of *meditation*. Continuing on the path of *meditation*, the bodhisattva then takes a third eon to traverse from the eighth bodhisattva ground through the tenth bodhisattva ground, thereby attaining the final path of *no-more learning*, full enlightenment. There are some special cases mentioned in the sutras of bodhisattvas—such as Ever-Crying Bodhisattva[7]—who travel the path more quickly due to extremely powerful guru devotion. But in general it's quite clear that it takes eons to attain full enlightenment when one exclusively practices the Sutra Vehicle.

Practicing the path in a way that integrates the practice of the sutras with the practice of tantra allows one to attain full enlightenment much more swiftly. Through highest yoga tantra, one can even achieve enlightenment in this very lifetime. Of course, doing so requires a lot of effort. But when compared to a path that requires eons, this approach integrating sutra and tantra is indeed much easier!

In addition to integrating tantric practice, *Easy Path* has other special, sacred qualities. One is that it contains secret techniques from the *Tushita Emanation Scripture*. This scripture was given directly to Lama Tsongkhapa by Manjushri, the bodhisattva of wisdom. It is a volume of teachings but not one made of paper and ink; it is visible only to very highly realized masters. Panchen Losang Chokyi Gyaltsen was able to read this *Tushita Emanation Scripture*, and some say that he quoted long sections of it when writing the *Guru Puja*. He also included some special techniques from this scripture in *Easy Path*, which makes this text very essential and effective.[8] *Easy Path* also contains special instructions for practice that were only transmitted orally from teacher to student, from Lama Tsongkhapa down through a line of great masters until they reached Panchen Losang Chokyi Gyaltsen. He was the first teacher to write those instructions down, and they are included in *Easy Path*, making it very special and effective for practice.

Another quality of *Easy Path* is that it belongs to the lineage of Kadampa oral instructions. After the time of Lama Dromtonpa, the great disciple of Master Atisha, there arose three Kadampa traditions— Treatise Followers, Oral Instruction Followers, and Stages of the Path Followers. The Treatise Followers would study the stages of the path in the context of also studying classical Indian treatises such as Maitreya's *Ornament for Clear Realizations*, Chandrakirti's *Entering the Middle Way*, and so forth. Stages of the Path Followers would study extensive texts in this tradition such as Drolungpa's *Great Treatise on the Stages of the Teachings*, Gampopa's *Ornament of Precious Liberation*, and so forth. Geluk practitioners of this style meditate based on the study of texts like Tsongkhapa's *Great Treatise* and *Middle Length Treatise* on the stages of the path. By contrast, this Kadampa lineage of Oral Instructions Followers is the easiest to practice. One engages in practice based upon concise, very clear instructions descending from Atisha's essential oral advice. These essential teachings have been incorporated into *Easy Path*, and this concise work distills all the teachings of Buddha. Those readers who have busy lives and lack time for extensive studies may find instructions like these very useful for practice.

A Summary of the Stages of the Path

The stages-of-the-path tradition shows us how to progress along the entire path to buddhahood step by step. The purpose of these instructions is to lead you to buddhahood. I mentioned earlier that three scopes, or levels of motivation, for spiritual practice are described in this tradition. The small-scope practitioner is motivated to attain good future rebirths. This is the lowest motivation that actually qualifies a practice as genuine spirituality. The middle-scope practitioner is motivated to attain permanent liberation from the samsara, the cycle of suffering rebirth.

And the great-scope practitioner is motivated by great compassion to attain full enlightenment in order to lead all other sentient beings to enlightenment as well. By practicing the stages of the path, you aim for buddhahood for all beings, and along the way, you naturally gain good rebirths and liberation from samsara as well.

The practice of the stages of the path can be summarized in three steps: setting your motivation in accord with one of those three scopes, practicing the eight meditations, and carrying out the practices of the three scopes.

When setting your motivation in accord with the small scope, you renounce the mundane concerns of this life and generate a sincere wish to achieve good rebirths in future lives. For the middle scope, you renounce not just this life's concerns but all of samsara by analyzing the faults of samsara; you then generate the wish to attain liberation— nirvana. For the great scope, you renounce self-cherishing; cherishing others, you strive to attain enlightenment for their benefit.

There are eight meditations or contemplations that accord with those three scopes. Four contemplations accord with the small scope:

1. The precious human rebirth
2. Death and impermanence
3. The sufferings of the lower realms
4. The laws of karmic causality

Two contemplations accord with the middle scope:

5 The faults of samsara
6. The benefits of nirvana

Two contemplations accord with the great scope:

7. Relative bodhichitta
8. Ultimate bodhichitta

Engaging in these contemplations naturally leads you to the third general point of carrying out practices of the three scopes. The small-scope practices are taking refuge in the Three Jewels and making effort at taking up what leads to happiness and abandoning what leads to suffering. The middle-scope practices are generating the wish to achieve nirvana and practicing the three higher trainings. For the higher scope, you generate the awakening mind—*bodhichitta*—and practice the six perfections and the four ways of gathering disciples.

If you've studied the stages of the path before, you may be wondering why relying on a spiritual teacher doesn't appear in this summary. It's because relying on a teacher is the prerequisite for engaging in these practices properly. When you look at broad outlines of texts on the stages of the path, the first section is on how to rely properly on a teacher and second is how to train in the path. Relying on the teacher comes first and is a separate point because it should be carried through all the other practices. A very important point for successful practice is conjoining all your other contemplations and meditations with guru yoga. The Third Panchen, Palden Yeshe, has explained that we should take the lama as the life, the very essence, of our practice by meditating constantly on guru yoga. Integrating such guru yoga with all our practices is an essential instruction for practicing *Easy Path*.[9]

ANALYTICAL AND STABILIZING MEDITATION

The main Tibetan word for meditation, *gom*, literally means "familiarization," and in the case of meditation that means "familiarizing with a virtuous mind." When we focus on some virtuous, positive topic, bringing it to mind again and again and holding the mind on it, that's meditation. For example, focusing your mind on the truth of impermanence is meditating on impermanence. If you're familiarizing your mind with attachment or anger, then that's not meditation because those are not virtuous states of mind.

There are two different styles of meditation: analytical and stabilizing. Analytical meditation entails using reason to contemplate a virtuous topic. We often use faulty reasoning to develop unhealthy states of mind. For example, when we're developing craving we repeatedly exaggerate the good qualities of the desired object, totally neglecting its faults. Through such distorted thinking, we cause our craving to get stronger and stronger. With virtuous objects, however, our thinking is realistic!

For example, if you contemplate how others very much want happiness just as you yourself do but are meeting with suffering, you will generate compassion—a realistic, positive state of mind.

The process of repeatedly running through thoughts about a subject from many angles is similar whether we're cultivating unhealthy or virtuous mental states. When cultivating mental states, reasoning into them repeatedly, familiarizing your mind with them increases their strength. Virtuous mental states are virtuous and lead to happiness because they accord with reality; they are based on reason. As you go through the stages of the path as taught in *Easy Path*, you'll see that all of the meditations aside from calm abiding are analytical meditations. For example, to generate bodhichitta, you first develop an understanding of the teachings on that topic, and then you repeatedly contemplate the correct lines of reasoning until bodhichitta arises.

The other kind of meditation is cultivating stable concentration to develop calm abiding, or *shamatha*. Here you place and then focus your mind on a single object, not letting the mind drift away to any other object of focus. Some scholars say that any concentration practice actually requires analytical meditation. Say the object you are concentrating on is an image of the Buddha. In that case, you first contemplate the details of that image—its colors and shapes—and these scholars view this as a form of analytical meditation. Or say your object of focus is devotion to your spiritual teacher: first you contemplate the reasons for generating a feeling of faith, and then you focus on that single-pointedly. In terms of practice, it's very important for us to combine those two kinds of meditation. This is the most effective approach.

PROGRESSING IN YOUR PRACTICE

I mentioned earlier that the three scopes of practice are differentiated by your motivation. Actually, whether or not what you're doing is spiritual—is Dharma practice—is determined by your intention. If your motivation is spiritual, then every act can become Dharma practice. If you're doing an action motivated toward comfort and happiness in this life, you're not practicing Dharma. When your intention is aimed at benefiting your own future lives, you've entered into the small scope of spiritual practice. At that point, you've not yet entered the path to enlightenment, but you are practicing some Dharma. The middle-scope motivation, wishing to be free from samsara, makes whatever action you are doing a Dharma practice directed into the path to liberation. The great-scope motivation entails doing an action with the intention to overcome self-cherishing and to practice great compassion for others.

It's extremely important to understand this key point: everything depends on your intention. Even if you are giving away money or food to others, if your motive is self-aggrandizement, then you're not doing a spiritual action. Even if you're doing something that looks harmful, if the intention is good, then the action is positive. For example, cutting another person might appear negative and cause him or her pain, but when a surgeon cuts open a patient, the doctor's positive motivation makes that a positive action. Similarly, if a parent scolds her child out of sincere love, this is positive. So if you want to engage in Dharma practice, then you should begin by spending time setting up a pure motivation.

Having set a pure motivation, you then engage virtuous activity. And, when you've completed a particular action, you dedicate whatever virtue or good karma you've created to goals that accord with your spiritual motivation. Having dedicated, your practice becomes complete. Setting a pure motivation, engaging in positive actions, and dedicating should be integrated into all of your practices and ultimately into all aspects of your life.

Now in terms of formally practicing the stages of the path, three major topics appear repeatedly in the text. I'll explain them once here at the beginning. You should then apply them to each of the meditation topics that will come. These three points are what to do before meditating, during the meditation session, and between sessions.

What to Do Before the Meditation Session

Before meditating, very clearly develop a pure motivation and then engage in the preliminary practices. I'll go into detail below about how to do each of the preliminary practices, which are very important for creating fertile conditions for realizations to grow in your meditation. Those preliminary practices are taught in detail for practicing the meditations of the stages of the path, and you also must engage in them when doing tantric practices. They aren't explained in the same way in tantra, but if you do a retreat on a tantric deity, you first have to clean up your place, arrange your cushion, set your motivation, put out offerings, and so forth.

Before doing a preliminary practice such as cleaning your meditation area or setting out offerings, you should set your motivation clearly, making sure that you are actually practicing Dharma as you do the preliminaries. And at the end of the preliminaries, you should dedicate your merit.

If you're doing a few sessions per day, then the preliminary practices should be done in the first session. They are optional for the later sessions of the same day. If your mind is agitated, then you can do some breathing meditation such as the nine-round breathing to settle your mind, visualize your spiritual teacher atop your head, and then simply begin meditating. If you have time to do the preliminaries again, then that's good, but if not then you can just do them in the first session of the day.

Also, if you don't like reciting texts such as those for the generation of the merit field and the preliminary practices, then you can simply see the merit field there and do the preliminaries from your heart without extensive recitations.

The Meditation Session

After the preliminaries comes the actual meditation session. It's good to do two, three, or four meditation sessions per day. The details on how to meditate on each topic will come as we discuss the various sections of *Easy Path*. In general, you practice until you gain some realization. So it's best to review most of the topics from the stages of the path only briefly, spending more time on a single topic until you gain some realization. You might stay with a topic for a month or more until some experience begins to arise. When you practice continuously on a topic such as relying on a spiritual teacher, you'll eventually gain an understanding of it—a sense that "Ah, that's how it is!" This is not yet the realization, but it's a sign you're getting closer.

Then there are two types of realization: contrived and uncontrived. *Contrived realizations* only arise when you make effort, methodically contemplating various reasons and examples to give rise to experience. For example, when you're at the level of contrived realization of properly relying on a spiritual teacher, an intense emotional experience of devotion and faith arise for you when you actively contemplate the lines of reasoning for this topic. *Uncontrived realizations* come vividly and spontaneously without your having to make a conscious effort any longer.

When most people think of an object they desire, genuine craving arises without any delay or effort. Uncontrived realizations are like that in that positive experiences arise vividly, instantaneously, and without any effort as soon as your mind comes in contact with the topic. For example, if you have uncontrived realization of guru devotion, just seeing your spiritual teacher gives rise to strong devotion. You no longer need to bring to mind lines of reasoning, examples, or quotations from scriptures. Instead, through the force of your previous training, the genuine experience arises without effort. So it's good to begin with focusing your meditations mainly on reliance on the spiritual teacher, and then when some realization of that topic has been attained, move on to spending most of your time on precious human rebirth, and so forth, all the way up to meditation on calm abiding and special insight.

To effectively make such progress, it's best to begin with relatively short sessions. Stop your meditation sessions while you're still enjoying meditation, before the mind has become bored or dull. Meditate on one point, then pause and check if you've been focused. Each part of your practice should be done mindfully and well. So meditate a bit, and then pause to see how you're doing. Be sure that your motivation is still clear, that you're deeply engaged in the practice, and that you're enjoying the meditation. It's the same when doing tantric sadhana practices; you shouldn't just recite the words. Check up on yourself, and if you haven't been doing the contemplations and visualizations clearly and mindfully, then pause and go back to redo them. In this way, you can be fully confident that you are doing each part of the practice well and will thereby progress naturally!

What to Do Between Meditation Sessions

Our last general point is what to do between meditation sessions. This includes your time spent eating, sleeping, walking, driving, working, and so forth. Of course, usually we don't meditate much, and so most of our time is spent "between meditation sessions." Therefore, post-meditation time is more important for your spiritual practice than the actual meditation sessions! Also, how you conduct your life between sessions determines your success in meditation itself. So I want to explain in some detail how to keep your mind positive between sessions and in this way illustrate how to both make your meditation support your daily life and make your daily life support your meditation.

In one sense, meditation is like studying in a class, and mindfulness between sessions is like doing your homework. You must work at both to succeed. Of course, if you're with your spiritual teacher, then you can offer service to him or her between sessions, and it's also very beneficial to engage in extensive preliminary practices such as making offerings between sessions. When you're focusing in your meditation practice on a particular topic from the stages of the path, it's good between sessions to read books related to that topic.

But many people are quite busy and don't spend most of their time meditating or reading. Therefore I'd like to share some very profound advice for busy people. During the Buddha's time, King Prasenajit was extremely busy working for his kingdom, so he went to the Buddha to ask for advice regarding how to practice Dharma in that context. The Buddha gave him three instructions: generate bodhichitta, rejoice, and dedicate. This instruction from the Buddha is also excellent for your practice during daily life.

It's a mistake to think that generating bodhichitta, the altruistic mind bent on enlightenment, is only for formal meditation sessions. While it's difficult to realize uncontrived bodhichitta, it's quite easy to generate a bodhichitta motivation any place and any time. You don't need to go on a retreat or have single-pointed concentration. All you have to do is develop a clear intention to attain enlightenment for the benefit of all sentient beings. Practitioners of the past would adopt this motivation when they set out from home in the morning, thinking that all their activities outside that day were directed toward attaining enlightenment for all sentient beings. Then when they came home they'd generate that same intention. When walking or eating, you can think that you're doing that for the benefit of all sentient beings. Even in the restroom you can generate that kind of intention! Generating bodhichitta is very powerful; it makes whatever you're doing into a Dharma practice and a cause of your enlightenment. This excellent and easy practice can be totally integrated into your daily life. Particularly when you're interacting with others, it's easy to make mistakes, harming others or engaging in negative actions. So again at those times, generating bodhichitta is an excellent protection.

The second practice advised by the Buddha for busy people is rejoicing. Rejoicing is also a very important practice that you can do any time, anywhere. Gungtang Rinpoche, a famous lama from eastern Tibet, said that rejoicing is a method for accumulating great merit even while you're lying down to rest. Ordinarily when lying around, you may find yourself worrying about work or craving for objects of your attachment. This is of no spiritual benefit, and even on a worldly level, not getting what you want causes you suffering. Even getting what you want may not bring happiness to your life! So it's much more beneficial to stop thinking such thoughts and to turn your mind to rejoicing. Rejoicing is simply cultivating happiness in the positive actions of others and in the good things that happen to others, thinking "How wonderful for them!" Rejoicing makes you happy while you're practicing it and also generates a great deal of good karma, which will follow you into your future lives. Also, rejoicing in other's good actions and their results is a powerful antidote to jealousy, which otherwise causes so much suffering.

And there's so much that you can rejoice in! You can think joyfully about the marvelous deeds of the buddhas that led them to enlightenment and also their constantly helping other beings. Then you can joyfully think of bodhisattvas who are practicing the six perfections. And you can similarly think of the actions of hearers (*shravakas*) and solitary realizers (*pratyekabuddhas*). Sometimes Mahayana practitioners think of these kinds of Buddhist adepts as lower beings, since their activities are not driven by the bodhichitta intention that characterizes the bodhisattva path. But in reality their activities are similar to those of the buddhas. Their equanimity is so profound that if someone were applying scented water to their right foot while someone else were chopping off their left foot, they wouldn't discriminate, preferring one over the other. Like this, the qualities of hearers and solitary realizers are inconceivable to us, and we can rejoice in the fruits of their practice.

And then you can bring to mind your own good actions and those of other ordinary persons. You can reflect joyfully on everything from great deeds of compassion down to sharing a bit of food with another. There's no end to things we can rejoice in. Having thought extensively of how amazing and wonderful others' good actions are, you can then pray: "May I be able to do as they have done!"

From generating bodhichitta and rejoicing, you'll create lots of good karma. Then you engage in the third practice advised by the Buddha, dedicating the merit from these practices for great purposes. Dedication directs the positive energy of our good actions so that it ripens in line with our bodhichitta motivation—that is, in our own buddhahood, which supremely equips us to secure the happiness of others.

We'll look at some other advice on how to train between meditation sessions when we come to the instructions on this subject in *Easy Path*.

THE GREATNESS OF THE TEACHER

Before we come to the topics discussed in *Easy Path*, there are a few important points that don't appear in this text but are covered in more extensive texts such as Tsongkhapa's *Great Treatise on the Stages of the Path to Enlightenment* and Pabongka Rinpoche's *Liberation in the Palm of Your Hand*. These points should be explained prior to teaching any text on the stages of the path, and so I'll explain them here. The first of them is showing the greatness of the teacher.

The lineage of these teachings on the stages of the path to enlightenment ultimately goes back to the Buddha, the unsurpassed teacher. These teachings derive from the small, medium, and large Perfection of Wisdom sutras, which the Buddha taught on Vulture's Peak in Rajagriha, India. The specific genre of teachings called the *stages of the path to enlightenment* (*lamrim*) began when the great Indian master Atisha came to Tibet in the eleventh century and composed there his *Lamp for the Path to Enlightenment*. The eight great texts on the stages of the path mentioned earlier and all the other many texts on the stages of the path composed in Tibet connect back to Atisha's *Lamp for the Path*, and any text of this type should include all of the essential points of Atisha's text. In his *Great Treatise on the Stages of the Path to Enlightenment*, Lama Tsongkhapa begins with a biography of Atisha. He explains that he does so because one can say that his text is also composed by Atisha—that the entire lineage of teachings on the stages of the path belongs to the great master Atisha. I won't tell Atisha's biography here because you can read about that in other books.[10]

In addition to the Buddha's teachings from the Perfection of Wisdom sutras and Atisha's teachings from the *Lamp for the Path*, texts like this one on the stages of the path are also adorned and informed by the teachings given by Maitreya in his *Ornament for Clear Realizations*, which itself is a commentary on the hidden meaning of the Perfection of Wisdom sutras.

Topics such as the greatness of the teacher and the greatness of the teachings are not topics that you will have to sit on your cushion to meditate upon single-pointedly, but they are very important. Reading the biographies of past great masters like the Buddha, Atisha, and Maitreya expands your faith and enthusiasm. The root of practice is faith, and so understanding these points supports your practice of the path.

THE GREATNESS OF THE TEACHINGS

The next preliminary topic is the greatness of the teachings, which is covered by explaining the three qualities and the four greatnesses of these teachings.

It Contains All the Teachings of the Buddha

The first of the three qualities is that the teachings on the stages of the path contain within them all the teachings of the Buddha. This is particularly true of *Easy Path*. It encompasses all the subject matter of the sutras and of the tantras as well. Lama Tsongkhapa wrote of the stages of the path that:

> It condenses the essence of all scripture.
> By teaching and studying this system for a session,
> one gains the benefit of discussing and studying all holy
>   Dharma.
> Contemplate its meaning, for that is certain to be powerful.[11]

Easy to Practice

The second quality is that it is put into practice very easily. When the practices for a beginning practitioner are given, it shows how to decrease craving for happiness of this life. When the practices of the middle scope are given, it shows how to eliminate craving for happiness of future lives. When the practices of the great scope are given, it shows how to eliminate self-cherishing. More easily than other teachings, it instructs us in a way that allows us to apply the Dharma to our lives.

Adorned by Instructions of Two Gurus

The third quality is that it's superior to other teachings because it's adorned by the instructions of the two great gurus. Atisha's instructions on the stages of the path combine the two great lineages of Mahayana teachings. One of these is the Lineage of Extensive Deeds, which was passed from the Buddha to Maitreya to Arya Asanga; this lineage came down to Lama Serlingpa, who taught it to Atisha. This teaching lineage contains two powerful techniques for realizing bodhichitta—the seven-point cause-and-effect method and the method of equalizing and exchanging self with others; the stages-of-the-path instructions contain both of these, making it superior to teachings that only contain instructions for the paths of hearers and solitary realizers. The other is the Lineage of the Profound View, which was passed from Buddha to Manjushri to Arya Nagarjuna; this lineage came down to Atisha via his teacher Avadhutipa. This lineage contains the instructions on the Prasangika Madhyamaka view of emptiness, which makes it superior to instructions that accord with other philosophical tenet systems.

Recognize Teachings as Free of Contradiction

Next we'll turn our attention to the four greatnesses of these teachings. The first is the greatness of allowing you to recognize that all the teachings are free of contradiction. This is important because it sometimes happens that people develop wrong ideas and prejudices. Sometimes those who exclusively follow the teachings in the sutras discriminate against the Vajra Vehicle, and some Vajra Vehicle practitioners discriminate against those who don't practice tantra. Some meditators wrongly hold that studying and contemplating Dharma texts is unconnected to meditation practice. Actually, every Buddhist teaching is aimed at helping individuals to progress toward buddhahood. Each individual has his or her own unique capacities, and the teachings exist to help them cultivate these. If you study *Easy Path*, then you'll see how the various teachings of the Buddha are not contradictory and are designed for an individual's practice of the path.

See Scriptures as Personal Instructions

The second greatness is allowing you to understand how to take all the scriptures as personal instructions for practice. This point is very important. If you haven't studied the stages of the path, then when you study other texts it's easy to get overwhelmed, feeling that they are too big or that you can't see how they'll help your practice. However, if you study and practice this text, then you'll be able to see all the other texts and teachings of Buddha as related to this teaching. Once you've studied this, you can comprehend all the other teachings of the Buddha, seeing how they function to help lead you to enlightenment.

Discover the Intention of the Conqueror

The third greatness is allowing you to easily discover the intention of the conquerors. *Conquerors* here refers to the buddhas who have conquered all of their inner enemies—the afflictive emotions and negative imprints in their minds. So by studying and practicing *Easy Path*, you will come to understand the thoughts and intentions of the buddhas. In particular, you'll gain an understanding of the three principal aspects of the path—renunciation, bodhichitta, and the correct view of emptiness—and even the meaning of the generation and completion stages of highest yoga tantra. Studying this text allows you to understand all these subjects easily, without much effort. If you study other texts like Maitreya's *Ornament for Clear Realizations*, which is very extensive and requires much effort, you still may not understand the intentions of the buddhas. But if you study this much briefer text, then it bestows the benefit of understanding the thoughts and intentions of the buddhas.

Save from Great Wrongdoing

The fourth greatness is that it allows you to save yourself from great wrongdoing. "Great wrongdoing" here refers to creating the heaviest negative karma of abandoning the Dharma. If you think that the Dharma you yourself practice is the real Dharma and that what others practice is not really Dharma, you are rejecting Dharma teachings. Studying and practicing the stages of the path allows you to appreciate the whole range of Dharma practices.

How to Listen to the Dharma

Benefits of Dharma Study

The next point is the correct manner of listening to or studying the Dharma. Since both the author and the teachings are great, you gain many benefits by studying Dharma. You create much merit through study.

Early in his life, the Buddha gave up his kingdom and family to pursue the Dharma. The Buddha also sacrificed so much in his previous lives in order to receive Dharma teachings. The *Sutra of the Wise and the Foolish* says he was once born as a king and went to ask a brahman meditator for teachings. The brahman told him that he'd teach him the Dharma only if the king agreed to receive one thousand stabs with one thousand iron spikes. The future Buddha agreed, sacrificing his life in that way to receive just four lines of teachings. In another life, he sacrificed himself by jumping into a pit of fire to hear just a few verses of Dharma teachings. While practicing the path, the future Buddha went through so many hardships and sacrifices for the sake of teachings, and he greatly emphasized the importance of the teachings.[12] We too should recognize how precious the Dharma teachings are. We shouldn't be lazy or careless when it comes to listening to teachings!

The *Jataka Tales*, a collection of stories of the Buddha's past rebirths, have a verse on this topic that begins by saying that "Study is a lamp dispelling the darkness of ignorance and a supreme treasure never stolen by thieves." Study dispels the darkness of ignorance in our minds. Also, the wealth of understanding gained by study can never be stolen by others; it will be with you forever. Knowledge is a reliable wealth.

That verse also says that study "is the best friend who teaches you the proper way." Knowledge gained through study is your best friend. When you have difficult times, your understanding will help you and allow you to distinguish between bad choices and good ones to take to build a better life for yourself.

That verse also says that study is an "unchanging friend even for some-one who has fallen on misfortune." Conventional friends, relatives, and partners can leave you when you're going through misfortune. If you have Dharma understanding, it will never leave you even in the worst of times and will give you strength in facing them.

And that verse says that study "is the harmless medicine for the illness of sorrow." It's the real medicine for us who are sick with ignorance, heal-ing our sufferings. Through Dharma you learn how to avoid doing bad karmic actions, which cause suffering, and how to overcome ignorance, which is the root cause of samsara.

Just listening to or studying Dharma is a way to create positive karma. As we listen it may not have an immediate effect, but it brings benefit in the future. You leave imprints as you listen, then those imprints will look for you in the future and will bring benefits. Master Vasubandu recited ninety-nine volumes of texts in a retreat while a pigeon sat nearby. By the power of hearing those teachings recited, the pigeon was reborn as a human being, becoming the scholar Sthiramati.

There's also the story of a man who, when he was quite old, had the opportunity to hear some teachings from the great master Nagarjuna. When the old man died, he took rebirth as a boy in India and, due to the imprints of having heard those teachings, he grew up to become the great scholar Nagabodhi.

During the Buddha's time, there was once an old man walking with a cane to attend a teaching of the Buddha. On his way to the teachings, he accidentally stepped on a frog, injuring it. He picked up the frog and carried it to the teaching place, and the frog heard some teachings of the Buddha. The frog then was reborn in a heavenly realm through merely having heard the teachings of Buddha. These are just a few illustrations of why it's very precious and beneficial to listen to teachings.

Fault of an Upside-Down Cup

When studying Dharma, we must be free from three faults. The first fault to be avoided is to be like an upside-down cup. An upside-down cup cannot retain or hold anything. If you let your mind wander to other places or if you fall asleep during teachings or while studying, then you're like an upside-down cup. Also don't meditate on emptiness, visualizations, or other topics while studying if that may interfere with your hearing all the teachings. Even meditation on the topic your spiritual teacher is teaching on is a mistake if doing so causes you to miss hearing the words of teachings themselves! You should have an attitude bringing your ear and your mind together as one. If your mind drifts away, then you miss some of the teachings. So conjoin your mind with your ear faculty to not miss any of the teachings.

Fault of a Contaminated Cup

The second fault is to be like a contaminated cup. If you have a cup with a bad odor, putting food in it will ruin the food. Listening to teachings with the wrong motivation is similar. If you attend teachings intending to gain fame, accumulate wealth, or heal an illness, this contaminates your mind. If you're of small scope, then motivate to gain a better future life, if you're of middle scope then motivate to free yourself from samsara, and if you're of great scope then motivate to attain buddhahood to liberate yourself and all sentient beings from all kinds of suffering. Don't listen to teachings with counterproductive expectations of samsaric happiness.

As a practitioner of the stages of the path, you should particularly generate great compassion by thinking of each sort of suffering that beings in the six realms of samsara go through. Reflect on the particular sufferings of beings in the lower realms—hell beings, hungry ghosts, animals, and so forth—feeling the greatly compassionate wish to free all those beings from all their sufferings. As you read this book, you should cultivate that sort of motivation.

You should definitely have concern for others while studying these teachings. Keeping in your heart only your own happiness of this life doesn't bring any benefit even in this life, let alone future lives. Keeping a pure mind and a good heart is very beneficial as you study and will definitely lead you to be able to actually benefit others in the future! So simply studying with that motivation benefits others. It creates a cause that will lead to the result of your later being able to directly help others.

If you set up a proper intention for studying this teaching—to bring benefit to all sentient beings—that motivation makes every word you read and even every step you take toward the book a virtuous action. The right motivation makes study itself into virtuous Dharma practice.

Developing such a compassionate motivation is also a way of serving and pleasing the buddhas. The buddhas are omniscient and only want to help all sentient beings. Your cultivating a good heart wishing to benefit others all the time helps to fulfill the buddhas' compassionate wishes. It's also the best offering you can make to them.

Fault of a Leaky Cup

The third fault while studying or listening is to be like a leaky vessel. If you listen to a teaching and understand something at the beginning but then forget before it's over, this is having a mind like a leaky cup. So listen very carefully and then remind yourself again and again so you do not forget.

Six Faults to Avoid

Master Vasubhandu's *Reasoning for Explanations* describes the six faults to avoid when studying. The first is pride, thinking things like, "I'm a genius—I'm so brilliant and I know more than others." The second is lack of respect; if you don't respect your teacher and the Dharma, you cannot digest the Dharma. The third is lack of interest, which stops you from appreciating the teachings. The fourth is having a wandering mind; if you let your mind drift away from the teaching place and you don't focus, then you won't get any benefit. The fifth is narrow-mindedness, which here refers to having a dull mind that doesn't catch any teachings; if you do meditation on emptiness while listening to teaching, that's also a fault of listening. The sixth is displeasure, which refers to occasions like when you attend a long teaching session and get tired or frustrated, which becomes an obstacle to listening to teachings. Sometimes when you listen to teachings, you cannot understand the meaning and you get tired. In that case, reflect on the benefits of hearing a teaching, thinking how it leaves positive imprints on your mindstream, and this will make you happier and give you courage to listen well.

The stages-of-the-path texts teach three faults to avoid and Vasubhandu lists six. If you analyze it, you'll see that all six can be encompassed by the previous three.

Six Helpful Ideas

The next point is to rely on six helpful ideas related to studying the teachings. These are thinking of yourself as a sick person, thinking of the Dharma as medicine, thinking of your spiritual teacher as a skilled doctor, thinking that practicing Dharma intently will cure your illness, thinking of the Tathagata as a holy being, and wishing that the Dharma remains for a long time.

Yourself as a Sick Person

Thinking of yourself as a sick person means to see how you're subject to many kinds of suffering. Tibetan medicine teaches that three factors are the main causes of physical illness—imbalances in your wind element, bile, or phlegm. Similarly, in the mind there are three main causes of suffering—the three poisons of ignorance, desire, and anger. You first recognize that you have these causes in your mind and then that you are subject to suffering because of them and therefore need a cure.

Dharma as Medicine

Dharma practice is the medicine that eliminates those three poisons that are the inner causes of the sickness of samsaric suffering.

Guru as Doctor

If you're diagnosed with an illness by your physician, he or she will prescribe a treatment specifically designed to treat that illness. Similarly, when relying on a guru, view him as a doctor who prescribes specific Dharma practices to cure your sickness and its causes in your mind— your delusions and afflictive emotions.

Dharma Practice as Cure

Even if you receive instructions from your guru, if you don't digest those instructions by putting them into practice, then they won't cure your inner sickness. That would be like filling a prescription from your physician but never taking the medication; it can't help your illness if you leave the medication in the cabinet. The Buddha himself taught, "I cannot take out your suffering with my hands and neither can I transfer my realizations to you; you must understand the nature of reality to attain liberation." We ourselves have to put the teachings into practice; otherwise there's no way to eliminate our faults and our suffering. This point really emphasizes your responsibility for putting what you learn into practice!

The Tathagata as a Holy Being

Tathagata is another name for the Buddha. Seeing the Tatagatha as a holy being benefits us. All these teachings come from the Buddha. Seeing him as a holy being helps us to listen well and to apply his teachings energetically in our lives.

Wish That Dharma May Long Remain

The Buddha went through so many difficulties to share the Dharma in this world. If it remains long in this world it benefits beings more. Our focus on preserving the Dharma is a way of repaying the kindness of the Buddha.

Coordinating Your Study with the Six Perfections

You can coordinate your study of Dharma with the six perfections of generosity, ethics, patience, joyous effort, concentration, and wisdom. If you give your time or even your life to learn Dharma, this is generosity. Offering flowers, water bowls, or a mandala in your study place is also practicing generosity. Abandoning the three and the six faults of listening mentioned earlier is a practice of the perfection of ethics. Bearing others' upsetting words or actions when studying without getting angry is a practice of the perfection of patience. Another kind of patience is voluntarily taking on difficulties to accomplish your goals. A third kind of patience is called "dwelling in the truth of the Dharma," which refers to dwelling on a true understanding, not rejecting it, so as to allow it to counteract your own wrong understandings and negative emotions.[13] All of these can be applied when studying. If you experience fatigue when studying, for instance, bearing that is a way of practicing the perfection of patience. The perfection of joyous effort comes when you take great pleasure and joy in listening to teachings or reading Dharma books. If you are mindful and have stable focus when studying, this is the perfection of concentration. Regarding the sixth perfection, the perfection of wisdom, if you can clearly distinguish between good and mistaken instructions when you are listening, this is a practice of wisdom. Understanding the emptiness of the *three spheres*—how the author, the teaching, and you the reader are empty of inherent existence—is also a practice of integrating your study with the perfection of wisdom. If you have doubts, presenting those doubts to your teacher is another way of practicing the perfection of wisdom.

Regarding listening to the teachings, finally I'd like to note that it's important to have both respect and faith for the teacher and the teachings. Respect and faith each arise in different ways. Respect comes through understanding the kindness of the teacher. Faith in the teacher and in the Dharma itself arises from experience. As you listen to the teachings and then put them into practice, when you experience the pacification of your own afflictive emotions through your practice, this experience naturally gives rise to faith.

How to Teach the Dharma

The outline of how to teach the Dharma has four sections: bringing to mind the benefits of teaching, generating respect for the teacher and the teachings, knowing what to think and do while teaching, and distinguishing between those you should and those you should not teach. These points parallel the ones above about listening.

Bringing to Mind the Benefits of Teaching

When teaching Dharma you should contemplate the great benefits of doing so and not be motivated by afflictive emotions. If while teaching you are craving offerings from your students, that's inappropriate. If you're teaching in a highly visible manner while craving acclaim or more disciples, that's deluded as well. If while teaching others you are hoping they'll notice how wise or learned you are, that's also harmful. Instead of these worldly motives, recall instead the immense spiritual benefits of sharing the Dharma.[14]

Generating Respect for the Teacher and the Teachings

The "teacher" in this context refers to the Buddha himself. The Buddha was initially like us, and then he practiced the Dharma, purifying all his negative qualities, and became a fully enlightened being. Then he gave the Dharma for us. Whatever Dharma we have comes from Buddha. So when teaching Dharma we pay respect to the source of the Dharma—the Buddha.

Since the Dharma is so precious, out of respect for it one usually sits on a throne while teaching. After the Buddha passed into nirvana, when Ananda was collecting his teachings he sat on a throne made of the robes of five hundred monks stacked together out of great respect for those teachings. When the Buddha himself delivered the Perfection of Wisdom discourses on Vulture's Peak, he set up his own throne out of respect for the liberating Dharma. He knew that whatever qualities he'd gained had come from the Dharma, and thus he saw how very precious it was. Following such examples, when we teach we should also pay respect to the Dharma by sitting on a throne, even setting it up ourselves if possible.

Knowing What to Think and Do while Teaching
A verse of advice regarding teaching says:

> Abandon stinginess, singing your own praises,
> sleepiness while teaching, speaking of the others' faults,
> postponing the teachings, and jealousy.
> Have love for your students, and teach properly
> while holding the five attitudes. Think that virtue
> will provide you with happiness.

Abandon stinginess in your teaching—to not give full instructions, holding some back, is a form of miserliness. Also when teaching, don't dwell on yourself, singing your own praises by saying things like "I received this teaching from this person, and then I did this and that." Don't talk about yourself too much. Shake off drowsiness, recollecting the great benefits of teaching so that enthusiasm overwhelms any fatigue. When teaching, voluntarily accept any difficulties, discomforts, or unfavorable circumstances that may otherwise distract you and focus on teaching. Don't give space for jealousy to arise; criticizing other views or religions out of attachment or anger is inappropriate. When you've received requests from students to teach, don't postpone the teachings but follow through in a timely manner. Whenever you give teachings, teach out of love and compassion for your students.

The five attitudes to maintain when teaching are similar to the six helpful attitudes described above in the section on how to study. These five attitudes are to view yourself when teaching as like a doctor, to view the Dharma as medicine, to view the listeners as patients, to see the Buddha as a holy being, and to wish for the Dharma to remain for a long time.

Teach clearly without confusing your disciples. Don't abbreviate too much—give a complete explanation. Don't speak too quickly or too slowly; speak at a moderate pace.

Before teaching, engage in three kinds of cleansing: outer, inner, and secret. *Outer cleansing* means taking a bath or shower and putting on new, clean clothes. *Inner cleansing* refers to doing confession or purification practices if you have committed some nonvirtuous actions. It also refers to restoring your broken vows and commitments. *Secret cleansing* is generating bodhichitta motivation. Another sort of cleansing is *suchness cleansing*, which entails meditation on emptiness.

Before sitting on a throne, make three prostrations to the throne while visualizing all the lineage gurus of that particular teaching stacked one atop the other. After prostrating to those lineage gurus, get on the throne and imagine they all dissolve into you. Then snap your fingers and recite verses about impermanence while bringing impermanence to mind. Once you sit on the throne or cushion, offer a mandala and then reset your motivation. Sometimes lamas will touch the text to their head, honoring the text while re-establishing their motivation.

Distinguishing between Those You Should and Those You Should Not Teach

It is said you should only teach if you've been requested to do so. In general students should request teachings with faith, and teachers should wait to teach until requested. However, if you see someone who's an appropriate vessel and you see that the time is right, then you can make an exception and give the teaching. The texts mention twenty-six behaviors that you should check regarding students' behaviors. For example, if someone is sitting, don't give them teachings while you're standing. If someone is lying down, don't teach while you're sitting. And don't teach someone who is sitting higher up than you.

This concludes the discussion of how to listen to and teach the Dharma. We turn now to the preliminary practices and the beginning of the Panchen Lama's text.

1. The Preliminaries

I always bow down at the feet of the perfect sublime guru, indistinguishable from Shakyamuni Buddha, Vajradhara. Please look after me with great compassion.

E*asy Path* begins with these lines paying homage to the guru. With the phrase "perfect, sublime guru," Panchen Rinpoche is paying respect to his root teacher, Khedrup Sangye Yeshe. He refers to the guru as inseparable from Shakyamuni, the historical Buddha, and also from Vajradhara, which is the exalted form that Buddha takes when teaching tantra. As we'll see later on, this viewing of our spiritual teacher as inseparable from Shakyamuni, who's also inseparable from Vajradhara, has deep meaning for our practice.

Herein is the guide to the stages of the path to enlightenment, the profound method of fortunate persons traveling to buddhahood. This has two sections: (I) how to rely upon the spiritual teacher, the root of the path, and (II) once relying, the stages of mental training.

Relying on the Spiritual Teacher
I. How to rely upon the spiritual teacher, the root of the path
  A. What to do during the actual meditation session
    1. Preparation
    2. The actual session
      a. How to rely in thought

(1) Training in faith, the root [of the practice]
(2) Recollecting the spiritual teacher's kindness and
   being respectful
 b. How to rely in deed
3. Conclusion
B. What to do between meditation sessions

I've already explained why relying on the spiritual teacher comes first and then the various stages of mental training are presented. "Fortunate persons" sometimes refers to actual bodhisattvas, but here it refers to anyone who aspires to buddhahood.

I've also already explained that for each meditation subject, *Easy Path* describes the preparation, how to engage in the actual meditation session, and what to do between sessions. So now, before getting into the actual meditation on relying on the teacher, I'll explain the preliminary practices.

PRELIMINARY PRACTICES

The six preliminary practices are very important, for they contain the essence of the Perfection of Wisdom sutras and of the *Ornament for Clear Realizations*. If you do these six properly, they also transmit the essence of the stages-of-the-path and mind-training instructions. They, and especially the seven-limb prayer, which is the fifth practice, serve as the main source for realizing all Buddhist practices. In particular, the preliminaries as taught in *Easy Path* integrate many profound points from tantra and also from the precious oral tradition coming from Atisha and Lama Tsongkhapa.

> *Preparation*
> In an agreeable place sit upon a comfortable cushion in the eightfold meditation posture or in whatever posture puts you at ease. Then, after examining your mind thoroughly, generate an exceptional virtuous mind.

There are six preliminary practices. *Easy Path* doesn't mention the first two. With its mention of the eightfold posture, *Easy Path* begins from the third preliminary practice. The full list of six are: (1) cleaning your room and arranging symbols of buddhas' body, speech, and mind; (2) obtaining offerings honestly and arranging them beautifully; (3) sitting in the eightfold meditation posture of Vairochana and then taking refuge and generating bodhichitta; (4) visualizing the merit field; (5) practicing the seven-limb prayer; (6) making requests following the oral instructions.

Cleaning Your Room

"Your room" here is the room you meditate in. You first establish your motivation for cleaning, thinking: "In order to attain full enlightenment, I must practice the stages of the path, and to do that I must invite holy beings. Before inviting the holy beings in order to meditate effectively on the stages of the path to enlightenment, I will clean this place with bodhichitta motivation—to attain buddhahood for the benefit of all sentient beings." Whenever we meditate on the stages of the path, we align our motivation with bodhichitta.

Buddhist sutras teach five benefits of cleaning your meditation room: it makes your mind happy, it makes others' minds happy, it makes the gods who delight in virtue (whether worldly or enlightened gods) happy, it creates a karma to have a beautiful form in future lives, and finally it creates karma to be reborn in divine places: cleaning your meditation room clears away obstacles and creates karma to be reborn in the pure land of a buddha.[15]

When cleaning your meditation room, you can extend your visualization and increase your merit by imagining you're also cleaning other holy places, such as Bodhgaya where Shakyamuni Buddha became enlightened and any other sacred place you can remember or imagine. You can create lots of merit by visualizing in that way; it has the same karmic benefit as actually cleaning those places! Your home may already be very neat, but to fulfill this part of your practice, still clean your statues and altar. To clean we usually use a broom; imagine that the broom or other cleaning implement is in the nature of wisdom understanding emptiness.

As you clean with it, imagine that this emptiness wisdom is cleaning away your negative thoughts and emotions.

While cleaning your meditation room, you can recite, "Abandon dirt, abandon stains." This brief verse comes from the story of Panthaka. Panthaka was a dull-witted monk. When he tried to memorize texts, as soon as he went on to the second syllable, he'd forget the first syllable! To help this monk of such low faculties, the Buddha gave him the job of cleaning the monks' sandals and later also of sweeping the temple. The Buddha taught him to recite this very verse as he cleaned. Over time, Panthaka came to understand that the verse was not referring to outer dirt or stains but rather to negative emotions and ignorance. Through the virtues he gained by cleaning with this awareness, he became an *arya*—a noble being who gained a direct perception of the truth of selflessness.

In your clean meditation room, display holy objects representing the Buddha's holy body, speech, and mind. To represent the holy body, you should have a statue of the Buddha and perhaps a statue of Lama Tsongkhapa. To represent the Buddha's speech, you can display a Buddhist text, such as the *Perfection of Wisdom in 100,000 Verses*, the *Perfection of Wisdom in 8,000 Verses*, or the *Vajra Cutter Sutra*. To represent the Buddha's mind, you should display a stupa or a vajra and bell.[16] When you see a vajra and bell, recall that the vajra represents bodhichitta—the method aspect of the path—and the bell represents emptiness—the wisdom aspect of the path. The purpose of having these holy objects is for you to look at them every morning to remind yourself of the holy qualities of the Buddha's body, speech, and mind. Even if you look at holy objects with anger, you still create good karma, creating an imprint to see thousands of buddhas in the future. If you look with faith, then the good karma you create is simply tremendous. It's excellent to look at those holy objects every morning.

Making Offerings

The second preparatory practice is to arrange offerings on your altar. There are two faults to avoid regarding offerings: the origin fault and the motivation fault. The fault of origin is offering something you've acquired through wrong livelihood or through misdeeds, such as stealing, harming others, or cheating someone. If you already have some offerings that were acquired through misdeeds, you can offer them, but in the future you must try hard to avoid such faults. The fault of motivation is making offerings with mundane hopes of gaining wealth, good health, or higher rebirth. Instead of harboring such expectations when making offerings, think that you are making offerings for the benefit of all sentient beings.

When making offerings you can also do extensive visualizations. Even if you're offering just a single flower, picture yourself offering flowers to all the buddhas everywhere, to every stupa that exists, and so forth. In this way you create far more extensive merit. Since the power of your Dharma practice is determined by your motivation, establish your motivation clearly at the beginning.

Your rows of water bowls should be straight, not crooked, and all the offerings should be arranged beautifully.

Sit in the Eightfold Posture

Choose an agreeable place for your meditation cushion. Under your cushion, it's good if you can place durva grass, kusha grass, and a drawing of a swastika. Durva grass, which has many joints, is auspicious for long life. Kusha grass, which is sometimes used in India for making brooms, is auspicious for cleansing contaminants and negativities. The swastika, an ancient symbol from India signifying power and stability, is auspicious for making your practice firm and successful. If you place those materials under your cushion, then you are following the example of Buddha Shakyamuni, who placed those materials under his cushion when he became enlightened. If you're doing a retreat on the stages of the path, then you should have a separate cushion for your retreat and if possible put those objects under that cushion. For regular daily practice, this is not required.

For meditation, the seven-point posture of Vairochana is usually taught, and here breathing meditation is added to make eight points. The first point is the legs, which ideally are placed in vajra posture, with the right foot on the left thigh and the left foot on the right thigh. There is also a half-vajra posture, where only one foot rests on the opposite thigh while the other rests beneath the opposite knee. If you're not comfortable in vajra posture, you can begin by sitting in vajra posture and then change to a regular crossed-leg posture.

The second point is the hands, which rest below the navel in the meditation *mudra*, or gesture, with the left hand below the right and thumbs touching. Touching the tips of your two thumbs creates a triangle shape, symbolizing the three doors of liberation—emptiness, signlessness, and wishlessness.[17] This triangle also symbolizes the body, speech, and mind of the Buddha. Also, the right thumb represents bodhichitta and the left thumb represents wisdom understanding emptiness; their touching represents the union of those two factors.

The third point is that your back should be erect. Keeping your back straight opens up the channels of your body, allowing the subtle wind energies to flow in a smooth and balanced way. As the mind follows these winds, this makes it easier to control your mind. If you lean to the right, this puts pressure on your right channel, through which the wind associated with anger flows, making you more likely to generate anger. If you lean to the left, this puts pressure on your left channel, through which the wind associated with attachment flows, making you more likely to generate attachment. Due to the movements of the winds, leaning back makes you more likely to generate pride, and leaning forward makes it more likely to generate dullness. To avoid those negative factors, try to keep your posture upright when meditating.

The fourth point relates to your mouth: leave your lips, teeth, and tongue however feels natural for you. The fifth point is to keep your head bent slightly forward. The sixth is to keep your eyes open but lowered, so that you're looking toward the tip of your nose. If you find it easier to meditate with your eyes closed, that's acceptable occasionally, but generally it's better to meditate with your eyes open. The seventh point is to keep your shoulders straight but relaxed.

From the perspective of highest yoga tantra, the elements of this posture help you to control the five primary and five secondary wind energies of your body. Having the legs crossed in vajra posture controls the downward-coursing wind, having your hands in the meditation mudra just below the navel controls the equalizing wind, having your back straight controls the all-pervasive wind, having your shoulders straight controls the life-sustaining wind, and having your head bent slightly forward with the tongue touching the palate controls the upward-coursing wind. Having the eyes aimed at the tip of your nose helps control the secondary winds associated with sensory consciousness. There are many profound benefits of this posture, so when you sit down to meditate, scan your body to confirm that your posture includes these seven points.

Having checked your posture, next check your mind. If it's in a negative state, you can do breathing meditation to bring the mind into a neutral state. It's good to begin with the nine-round breathing exercise. For this you begin by inhaling three times through the right nostril, exhaling from the left. Then inhale three times through the left nostril, exhaling from the right. Then inhale three times through both nostrils, also exhaling from both. With each inhalation, imagine breathing in all the qualities, all the compassion and wisdom, of the buddhas. With each exhalation, imagine breathing out all your negative thoughts and emotions. This helps bring your mind to a neutral state. After the nine-round breathing exercise, if your mind is still distracted, worried, or in some other negative state, then just focus on your breathing for a while, perhaps counting up to twenty-one breaths.

After this, *Easy Path* says to generate an exceptional virtuous mind, meaning that you should again generate bodhichitta motivation.

Taking Refuge

Next comes visualizing the objects of our refuge.

> From within that [visualize as follows]: In the space directly in front of me is a high, wide, jeweled throne supported by eight great lions, upon which is a seat of a multicolored lotus, and moon and sun mandalas. Upon that sits my kind root guru in the aspect of the Conqueror, Shakyamuni Buddha. His body is the color of refined gold. His head has a crown protrusion. He has one face and two arms. His right hand presses the earth. In his left hand, which is in the gesture of meditative equipoise, rests an alms bowl filled with nectar. He wears elegantly the

three saffron robes of a monk. He has a body of pristine, luminous light that is adorned by the marks and signs. He sits in the vajra posture amid an aura of light.

Surrounding him is a host of transcendental beings: your direct and lineage gurus, meditational deities, buddhas, bodhisattvas, heroes, heroines, and an assembly of Dharma protectors. In front of each of them upon marvelous thrones sits the Dharma explained by them in the form of texts made of light. The members of the merit field are in the aspect of being pleased with me. By remembering their qualities and kindness, I feel great devotion for them.

In the space before you at a distance of one full-length prostration is a throne upheld by eight lions, representing the eight powers of the Buddha. On that is a multipetaled lotus atop which are moon and sun cushions. These symbolize the three principles of the path—renunciation, bodhichitta, and right view of emptiness, respectively—implying how all in the merit field possess those three qualities. On this main throne, visualize your guru in the form of Shakyamuni Buddha. His right hand touching the earth symbolizes his conquering one of the four obstructing maras—*devaputra*, the divine son. On a gross level, the divine son can be understood as the worldly god of the desire realm who leads other desire-realm gods in efforts to obstruct those practicing virtue. They may do so by causing distractions or, most powerfully, by causing divisions in the Sangha. On a subtle level, this mara can be understood as your own subtle obscurations to omniscience, to achieving the mind of a buddha. The Buddha's begging bowl being filled with nectar having three qualities symbolizes his conquering the other three maras—the mara of the afflictive emotions, the mara of the aggregates, and the mara of death. He has the major and minor marks of a buddha. He sits with legs crossed in vajra posture; visualizing him in that posture leaves an imprint for you to later realize the completion stage of highest yoga tantra.

Around this central throne are four other thrones. On the throne behind Shakyamuni Buddha sits Vajradhara, who's surrounded by the gurus of the lineage of oral instructions. On Shakyamuni's right is

Maitreya and gurus of the lineage of extensive deeds. On his left is Man-jushri and gurus of the lineage of the profound view. In front of Shakya-muni is your root guru and all your personal teachers. Shakyamuni is a bit higher than the others. Each of the four surrounding thrones has the lineage gurus sitting on the throne with their respective central figure, encircling him.

All five of those thrones are themselves on a single, very large throne. On that large throne, other enlightened beings are there in circles sur-rounded the four thrones just mentioned. Closest in is a circle of deities of highest yoga tantra, and then around those deities come circles of deities of each of the other three classes of tantra.[18] Around them is a circle of buddhas such as the eight Medicine Buddhas and so forth. Around them is a circle of bodhisattvas including the eight great bod-hisattvas.[19] Then come circles of solitary realizers, hearers, dakas, daki-nis, and Dharma protectors. In this tradition of the stages of the path, the main protectors are Six-Armed Mahakala for practitioners of great scope, Vaishravana for practitioners of middle scope, and Dharmaraja for practitioners of small scope.

In front of each figure in the refuge field is a table on which sits his or her teachings in the form of a text made of light. Just as a mother is pleased when seeing her child doing well at taking care of herself, the members of this refuge field are pleased because they only care for sentient beings' welfare, and now they see you taking responsibility for yourself by engaging in meditation on the stages of the path.

Next, produce great faith remembering the qualities of the beings in the refuge field, such as their great compassion and altruism equally embracing all sentient beings.

Within that context, think as follows:

From beginningless time up to now, I and all mother sen-tient beings have been experiencing the manifold general sufferings of samsara and especially the sufferings of the three lower realms. Even so, it remains difficult for us to infer the depth and extent of our suffering.

Imagine yourself in front of the refuge field with all your male relatives on your right and all your female relatives on your left. Imagine all enemies, evil beings, demons, and harmful spirits in front of you. Imagine your friends behind you. And all around are the beings experiencing the sufferings of the six realms, such as the hells, but visualized in human form.

This practice of taking refuge is very important. Even if you can't do other practices intensively, practicing refuge is sufficient. Here I'll give a brief explanation of how to take refuge, and then more details will come at the section of *Easy Path* on refuge practice.

The verse above evokes one of the two essential, causal factors for taking refuge: fear of samsara. You must be afraid of something to sincerely seek a refuge. The verse mentions how we've been suffering from beginningless time. Here you can bring to mind the three, six, or eight types of suffering. For example, the eight types of suffering include the sufferings of being born, aging, sickness, death, separation from what is attractive, meeting with disagreeable things, seeking but not obtaining what you desire, and having a body and mind created by delusions and karma. Here, as the verse says, you can particularly think of the sufferings of the three lower realms—those of hell beings, hungry ghosts, and animals. Particularly focus on the sufferings of the hot hells, the cold hells, and the neighboring hells. Recognizing that you could very easily come to experience those sufferings in the future, you generate fear of samsara.

> At this time I have obtained an exceptional human birth, which is difficult to find and, once found, so valuable. At this time, if I do not obtain at once the high state of a guru buddha, the superior liberation wherein one has abandoned all the sufferings of samsara, I will experience again either the suffering of samsara in general or that of the three lower realms in particular.

If you recognize the rarity and preciousness of your human life and see the danger of falling into lower realms, then you will generate fear of not engaging in Dharma practice!

My guru and the Three Jewels, who are sitting in front of me, have the ability to protect me from those sufferings. Therefore I must at all costs attain the precious state of completely perfect buddhahood for the sake of all mother sentient beings. In order to do that, I will go for refuge from the depths of my heart to my guru and the Three Jewels.

This verse is for generating the second of the two essential, causal factors for taking refuge: faith in the objects of refuge, which include your gurus and the Three Jewels. Based on your fear of samsaric suffering, it's this faith that leads you to turn to them for refuge and protection. To generate faith in the Three Jewels, contemplate four of their qualities: they are free from suffering, they have unique methods to overcome suffering, they don't discriminate between sentient beings who honor or don't honor them, and they offer their help to every sentient being, neither discriminating nor excluding.

Regarding refuge, it's important to recall that among the Three Jewels, the Buddha is the teacher who gives instructions on how to overcome our sufferings, while the Dharma that he taught is the actual refuge that protects you. If you don't keep from the ten nonvirtuous actions, then the Buddha cannot protect you from suffering. Your own Dharma practice is what really protects you. If you practice Dharma then you can achieve buddhahood. The Sangha refuge are like friends or companions—examples you can see. The great pandits such as the six ornaments and the two supreme ones were human beings who realized the Dharma.[20] So you can take them as examples, thinking that you can do likewise.

Going for refuge involves getting closer to and more familiar with the Three Jewels, making it easier to receive their blessings. Your refuge shouldn't be half-hearted. You should develop a relationship of total trust and reliance, relying on them completely in all your activities. Reciting refuge verses is conventional refuge; actual refuge happens in the mind when you've developed fear of samsaric suffering as well as faith in the Three Jewels. Always coordinate your refuge practice with bodhichitta, remembering that you're practicing for the sake of all sentient beings.

So having contemplated to give rise to both fear of samsara and faith, you can recite:

> I go for refuge to the Guru.
> I go for refuge to the Buddha.
> I go for refuge to the Dharma.
> I go for refuge to the Sangha.

Another verse that can be recited while taking refuge is: "I go for refuge to the guru, the deity, and the Three Jewels." A third alternative for recitation is:

> I go for refuge until I am enlightened
> to the Buddha, Dharma, and Sangha.
> Through the merits I create by practicing generosity and
>   the other perfections,
> may I attain the state of a buddha
> to be able to benefit all sentient beings.

There's a practice of meditating on refuge while reciting a refuge verse one hundred thousand times. If you wish to do that practice, you can choose any one of these three verses according to your own preference. The last of the three also includes bodhichitta practice. For your daily practice, you can also choose any or all of these verses. As a minimum practice, you can recite the first verse, saying each line seven times while specifically meditating on that object of refuge.

While reciting such verses, continue visualizing all sentient beings around you in front of the refuge field. As you recite "I go for refuge to the guru," you can visualize light rays and five-colored nectars descending into you and all sentient beings. First they descend from Shakyamuni Buddha, who is inseparable from your own teachers. Then they descend from each of the other main figures—your root guru, Vajradhara, Maitreya, and Manjushri—each of whom is viewed as inseparable from your gurus. Then they descend from all five simultaneously. Finally, all five streams of light and nectar coming from all five combine into one that dissolves into you. As you do this, imagine purifying all negative karma created in relation to your gurus, such as by not putting their advice into practice, and also imagine receiving all the realizations and good qualities of the path. If you have time, you can do more recitations while individually thinking of each of your personal teachers.

Then, while reciting "I go for refuge to the Buddha," visualize that light and nectar come from the two categories of buddhas appearing in the refuge field. One category is buddhas of the Sutra Vehicle context, such as Shakyamuni Buddha, the eight Medicine Buddhas, and the thousand buddhas of this fortunate eon. The other category is buddhas of the Vajra Vehicle context, such as Guhyasamaja, Chakrasamvara, and all the other deities of the four classes of tantra. As you recite "I go for refuge to the Buddha," imagine the light and five-colored nectars entering through your crown and purifying all negative karma created in relation to the Buddha, such as putting Buddha statues on the ground, selling Buddha statues, injuring a buddha causing him or her to bleed, or discriminating judgmentally between Buddha statues based on the materials they're made from. Then also imagine you receive all good qualities.

While reciting "I go for refuge to the Dharma," visualize the light and nectar coming from texts that you previously visualized on tables in front of all the figures in the refuge field. This light and nectar purify negative karma created in relation to the Dharma by doing things like criticizing other religions, selling Dharma books for money, going against the advice of Dharma, such as by not helping and instead harming others, and so forth. After this purification, again imagine receiving all realizations and good qualities.

While reciting "I go for refuge to the Sangha," visualize light rays and nectar coming from bodhisattvas, solitary realizers, hearers, dakas, dakinis, and Dharma protectors. Remember and purify any negative karmic actions you've done in relation to the Sangha, and then also imagine receiving all the qualities as before.

Generating Bodhichitta and the Four Immeasurables
Next, *Easy Path* says:

> Cultivate refuge, bodhichitta, and the four immeasurables.

As mentioned above, one often cultivates refuge and bodhichitta in tandem through reciting this verse:

> I go for refuge until I am enlightened
> to the Buddha, Dharma, and Sangha.
> Through the merits I create by practicing generosity and the
>   other perfections,
> may I attain the state of a buddha
> to be able to benefit all sentient beings.

Here one generates both aspiring and engaged bodhichitta. *Aspiring bodhichitta* is a compassionate wish to attain enlightenment for the benefit of all sentient beings; as a wish it doesn't involve an actual commitment to action. *Engaged bodhichitta* includes that same wish along with a firm commitment to actually practice the path to enlightenment, which includes practicing generosity and the other five bodhisattva perfections.

In terms of your practice of the six perfections, it's essential to dedicate your practice to fully actualizing bodhichitta and progressing to full enlightenment. Again, the six perfections are: generosity, ethics, patience, joyful effort, concentration, and wisdom. The first three are especially emphasized for laypeople. Master Chandrakirti says in *Entering the Middle Way*, "Buddha said that the layperson's form is superior for practicing generosity and so forth." Giving things to those in need—this is generosity. You do such virtuous actions naturally in your life. Laypeople have more wealth and possessions than monks or nuns, so they can practice more generosity. For training in ethics, laypeople meet with more challenges that could provoke immoral actions. If you meet those challenges and remain ethical, then you create more good karma. Also you can take vows such as to avoid killing, lying, and so forth. Whether you take such vows for a day, a month, a year, or for your whole life, by keeping them you practice ethics. When you voluntarily meet hardships and challenges for your Dharma practice, you're practicing patience. When others harm you and you don't react angrily, again you're practicing patience. Monks and nuns meet with fewer occasions for developing patience than laypeople do, so it's easier for laypeople to create more good karma of patience. In general, these first three perfections are easier to practice as they don't require elaborate study or meditation. The practices of concentration and wisdom require intensive meditation, but sincerely giving to someone in need doesn't require study or meditation; anyone can do it. Patience is similar—if you don't react with attachment or aversion when someone harms you, this is a genuine practice of patience, whether or not you have developed the final two perfections.

Easy Path also teaches a third kind of bodhichitta called *taking-the-result bodhichitta*. This kind of practice usually appears in tantric sadhanas and is a form of taking the result as the path. Once you've generated aspirational and engaged bodhichitta, you see the Buddha in the refuge field in front of you. He's pleased with you and as a blessing sends an identical Buddha that dissolves into you. You transform into a buddha, and then you send out light rays transforming all realms to divine realms and all beings to buddhas. Since actual buddhas do send out light rays to fulfill the wishes of sentient beings, here you're imagining your future buddhahood, doing the activities of a buddha! This practice is really unique and precious. Imagining light rays transforming all places to divine realms and beings to divine beings allows you to create a lot of virtuous karma quite easily.

Next comes meditation on the four immeasurable attitudes—immeasurable equanimity, compassion, love, and joy. You cultivate each of these immeasurable attitudes by meditating on four different levels of engagement or commitment to that attitude. For example, with love first you think how wonderful it would be if everyone were happy. Then you actually develop the loving wish for everyone to be happy. Then you bravely develop an attitude committed to making this come about yourself. And finally you request the blessings of the guru-deity to help you become able to accomplish that aspiration. Those same four levels of engagement apply to the other immeasurable attitudes as well.

Then produce the following thought seven, twenty-one, or however many times:

> In particular, I must at all costs quickly, quickly attain the precious state of a completely perfect buddha for the sake of all mother sentient beings. In order to do that I will meditate on the instructions on the stages of the path to enlightenment through the profound path of guru-deity yoga.

This verse is for generating unique, special bodhichitta. This phrase, "quickly, quickly" comes when generating special bodhichitta in tantric practice. This verse is similar to another verse by Panchen Losang Chokyi Gyaltsen in the *Guru Puja* that says, "For the sake of all mother sentient beings I shall quickly, quickly, in this very life, attain the state of a primordial buddha, the guru deity."

There are a number of interpretations of the meaning of "quickly, quickly." A general interpretation is that the first "quickly" refers to engaging in tantric practice in general, which is a faster path than relying only on the vehicle of the perfections and which can lead one to attaining enlightenment in one lifetime. In this interpretation, the second "quickly" refers to engaging in particular in the practice of highest yoga tantra, through which one can attain enlightenment in one brief lifetime of this degenerate era. Another interpretation of "quickly, quickly" comes from Gyalwa Ensapa, who attained full enlightenment in one lifetime and who was the previous incarnation of the Panchen Lama who wrote *Easy Path*. Gyalwa Ensapa's interpretation comes from the Ganden Oral Tradition practice lineage. In this interpretation, the first "quickly" refers to practicing the stages-of-the-path tradition. There are special qualities of the stages-of-the-path tradition that make it an even faster path to enlightenment than the three lower classes of tantra. And then the second "quickly" refers to taking guru yoga as the very life of your practice.

In general, tantric practitioners take guru yoga as their primary practice. But here Gyalwa Ensapa refers to something unique to the Ganden

Oral Tradition, which is taking guru yoga as the *life* of your practice. Taking guru yoga as your primary practice is not the same as taking it as the life of the practice. It is said that this is faster than highest yoga tantra and can lead to the attainment of enlightenment in just twelve years or even in just three years! Just practicing the stages of the path is quite different from practicing the stages of the path with guru yoga. Taking guru yoga as the life of your practice of the stages of the path and also as the life of your tantric practices such as those of Yamantaka and Guhyasamaja make those practices far more powerful.

The Panchen Lama is revealing something very profound in *Easy Path* from the oral tradition that came down from Gyalwa Ensapa. You'll note as we go along that the meditations on the stages of the path will be presented in the form of prayers, requesting blessings. This is to help you to integrate this practice of taking guru yoga as the life of your practice into all of your meditations.

Visualizing the Merit Field

Next comes visualizing the merit field, which is the fourth of the six preliminary practices. The merit field is different from the refuge field described above. After reciting the preceding prayer, you dissolve the refuge field. There are three ways of doing this. The first is to have the whole refuge field all dissolve into one figure—in this case Shakyamuni Buddha—who dissolves into the point between your eyebrows. The second is to have the entire refuge field dissolve into space-like emptiness. The third is to first generate the merit field and then dissolve the refuge field into the merit field.

> Next [visualize the field for assembling merit as follows:] In the space directly in front of me is a high, wide, jeweled throne supported by eight great lions, upon which is a seat of a multi-colored lotus, and moon and sun mandalas. Upon that is my kind root guru in the aspect of the Conqueror, Shakyamuni Buddha. His body is the color of refined gold. His head has a crown protrusion. He has one face and two arms. His right hand presses the earth. In his left hand, which is in the gesture

of meditative equipoise, rests an alms bowl filled with nectar. He wears elegantly the three saffron robes of a monk. He has a body of pristine, luminous light that is adorned by the marks and signs. He sits in the vajra posture amid of an aura of light.

[In all directions the following beings are seated] upon lotus, moon, and sun cushions. Behind and above the guru-buddha is the conqueror Vajradhara, who is surrounded by the gurus of the lineage of the blessings of practice. To the guru-buddha's right is the venerable Maitreya, surrounded by the gurus of the lineage of extensive deeds. To his left is the venerable Manjushri, surrounded by the gurus of the lineage of the profound view. In front is your own kind root guru, surrounded by those gurus with whom you have a teaching connection. Encircling those are a host of transcendental beings—meditational deities, buddhas, bodhisattvas, heroes, heroines, and an assembly of Dharma protectors. In front of each of them upon marvelous thrones are their own verbal teachings in the form of texts with a nature of light.

The figures all send outward into the ten directions inconceivable arrays of emanations, which are taming disciples each according to [his or her individual capacity]. The principal and the accompanying members of the field have a white *Om* at the crown of their heads, a red *Ah* at their throats, a blue *Hum* at their hearts, a yellow *Sva* at their navels, and a green *Ha* at their secret regions. Light of these five colors radiates forth.

Rays of light from the *Hum* at the heart of Lord Guru Shakyamuni Buddha radiate in the ten directions. This light invites the wisdom beings corresponding to those upon whom you are meditating from their natural abodes. These [wisdom beings] dissolve into each commitment being. Thereby you should believe [each member of the merit field] to be a composite object of refuge.

There are numerous options for how to visualize the merit field. *Swift Path*, the *Easy Path* commentary by the Second Panchen Lama, says that one option is to use the merit field from the *Guru Puja*, so if you're familiar with that practice, then you can visualize like that. Since that merit field is also related to tantric practice, it's quite suitable to use with your meditations on *Easy Path*. If you do that, then when the guru comes to the crown of your head later in the practice, he will be in the form of Lama Tsongkhapa with Shakyamuni Buddha in his heart and with Vajradhara in the heart of Shakyamuni.

Another option is to use the merit field described here. For that, visualize a high, wide, jeweled throne at eye level one full prostration's length in front of you. Eight lions support the throne, upon which sits your root guru in the aspect of Shakyamuni Buddha. Behind this main figure is Vajradhara with the lineage gurus of the four classes of tantra sitting in a circle around him. On Shakyamuni Buddha's right is Maitreya surrounded by Asanga and the other gurus of the lineage of extensive deeds. On his left is Manjushri surrounded by Nagarjuna and the other gurus of the lineage of the profound view. Your own root guru is in front of Shakyamuni Buddha. Your root guru is a teacher who has given you profound Dharma teachings that have brought about some positive changes in your mind. When you do tantric practices such as Yamantaka, you think of the guru who gave you that initiation, commentary, or personal instructions on that practice as your root guru. Here you can visualize whichever teacher most helped change your mind for the better. Encircling these teachers, visualize meditational deities, buddhas, bodhisattvas, heroes, heroines, and protectors as you did for the refuge field.

Each figure in the merit field has a white *Om* at the crown, a red *Ah* at the throat, a blue *Hum* at the heart, a yellow *Sva* at the navel, and a green *Ha* at the secret place. Light rays of five colors radiate from those five syllables. The beings you've visualized up to this point are the commitment beings, the *samaya sattvas*. The light rays invite the wisdom beings, the *jñana sattvas*, to come and dissolve into the commitment beings, making them more powerful. The wisdom beings are the actual enlightened beings who come, so here you convince yourself that the actual guru-buddha is there.

When you invoke and visualize buddhas, they are actually there.

Buddhas are omniscient and omnipresent. When the full moon is out, it appears effortlessly reflected in any body of water. Your faith is like the water; when you have the water of faith, the moon of the buddhas' presence will arise.

If you cannot visualize all the figures of the merit field clearly, then it is sufficient simply to imagine that they're there and to cultivate faith. Aku Sherap Gyatso taught that if you are not capable of elaborate visualizations, then you can simply imagine that all the enlightened beings are there in front of you like massed heaps of clouds.

Another option for the merit field is called the condensed-jewel method. That visualization comes later on in *Easy Path*, when all the other figures of the merit field dissolve into your own root guru, who comes atop your head in the form of Shakyamuni Buddha with Vajradhara in his heart. The condensed-jewel method entails visualizing just one figure atop your head embodying all your gurus, meditational deities, buddhas, bodhisattvas, heroes, heroines, and protectors. It's very effective to visualize one figure embodying all. If you find elaborate visualization difficult, you can apply that condensed-jewel method here, doing the remaining preliminary practices in relation to your guru in that form atop your crown.

The condensed-jewel method is a profound visualization that comes from Gyalwa Ensapa. Shakyamuni Buddha's form is the commitment being, and in his heart is Vajradhara as the wisdom being. In Vajradhara's heart is a syllable *Hum* that serves as the concentration being, or *samadhi sattva*. This is a tantric approach to visualization for guru yoga. This same visualization of the guru as a three-tiered being comes in the *Guru Puja*, all visualized inside the outer form of Lama Tsongkhapa.

The Seven-Limb Practice

> Then offer the seven limbs of worship along with the mandala and make fervent and sincere prayers in accordance with your quintessential instructions.

Next offer a condensed practice of the seven limbs and a mandala offering. The seven practices are prostration, offering, confession, rejoicing, requesting the wheel of Dharma be turned, requesting the field of merit to not depart to nirvana, and dedication. Mandala offering is a separate practice from these seven. In some other texts it says "practice accumulating merit and purification"; this is a reference to the seven limbs. Confession is primarily for purification, and the other six are primarily for accumulating merit.

This practice of the seven limbs is very important, so I'll explain how to engage in it in some detail here. In the Tibetan tradition, nearly every prayer and sadhana has these seven limbs near the beginning. Doing these practices well is the source of all realizations. For us beginners these are very important, and high bodhisattvas also do these practices. They're an easy, convenient way of creating vast good karma. Every sentient being, including you, has buddha nature. But you have to activate it, to make it workable. To make a seedling grow into a tree, you have to water and fertilize it. Doing these practices functions like that in relation to your buddha nature. By purifying negativities and generating great merits, you activate your buddha nature, making it easier to achieve realizations such as bodhichitta.

The first limb is **prostration**. The Sanskrit *namo* means "respect," and prostration is an expression of respect. There are three kinds of prostration—physical, verbal, and mental. Bowing your head, folding your hands, and so forth are physical forms of prostration. There are also physical prostrations that engage your whole body. These can be short, with five points touching the ground, or long, with your whole body flat on the ground.[21] When physically prostrating, you make the jewel-holding mudra by bringing your hands together in a gesture of prayer and inserting your two thumbs between your palms to represent a wish-granting jewel. This space between the palms represents selflessness and is unique to Buddhism. You imagine the jewel radiating light, and those light rays become clouds of offerings. Your right hand symbolizes method, and your left hand symbolizes wisdom; touching them symbolizes the union of method and wisdom.

With your hands in this mudra, you touch the crown of your head. This has many different meanings: it purifies negative karmas of body such as stealing, sexual misconduct, and killing; it leaves an imprint to untie the knots at your crown chakra on the completion stage of highest yoga tantra; it leaves an imprint to achieve the enlightened body of a buddha; and it leaves an imprint to attain a buddha's crown protrusion. Next, touching your throat purifies negative karmas associated with speech, such as lying, divisive speech, harsh words, and gossip; it leaves an imprint to untie the knots at the throat chakra; and it leaves an imprint to achieve the enlightened speech of a buddha. Next, touching your heart purifies negative karmas created with your mind, such as ill will, covetousness, and wrong views; it leaves an imprint to untie the knots at the heart chakra; and it leaves an imprint to achieve the omniscient, enlightened mind of a buddha.

Before prostrating, you can recite the mantra *Om namo manjushriye namo sushriya namo uttama shriye svaha*. Having reciting this mantra three times at the beginning, the merit created by each prostration is increased one thousand times. Again, keep in mind that you can do short prostrations touching five points to the ground or full prostrations touching the whole body.

If you understand the deep meanings behind prostrations, then they bring many powerful benefits. For beginners on the path, the main goal is typically to avoid rebirth in the lower realms and attain good rebirths so as to continue progressing toward buddhahood. Prostrating is the best practice for attaining rebirth in the higher realms. When you prostrate, each atom of earth your body covers during each prostration grants you that many rebirths as a wheel-turning king. You can count the atoms beneath you from all the layers below the earth's surface down to what we call the Vajra Ground. So from each prostration you'll be reborn as a Dharma king countless times! Since you create the causes for rebirth in lower realms through actions of body, speech, and mind, when you touch those three points on your body as you prostrate, you purify those three "doors" through which you've created such negative karmas.

From the perspective of highest yoga tantra, prostrations can also leave the imprint for achieving the illusory body. You can think of your five right fingers as the five root winds of your subtle body and the five left fingers as the five branch winds, which are manipulated in tantra as the basis for attaining realizations. Touching your hands to your heart then symbolizes drawing all these ten winds into the central channel inside the heart chakra. On tantra's completion stage, you have to be able to bring them inside the heart chakra. By thinking in this way you leave with each prostration the imprint to achieve the illusory body, the basis for the form body, the *rupakaya*, of a buddha! And once you achieve the illusory body, you will attain enlightenment in that very lifetime. Also, you can associate the five fingers of your right hand with the five sense powers and those of your left with the five sense objects; touching those at the crown, throat, and then the heart signifies dissolving those ten energies at the heart chakra, which leaves the imprint for achieving clear light, the basis for a buddha's *dharmakaya*, or truth body. Also, you can think that the right hand is the illusory body and left hand is clear light; bringing those two to the heart symbolizes the union of clear light and the illusory body, which is the attainment of enlightenment itself!

It's also very good if you can integrate your practice of prostrating with what are called the *four infinites*—the infinite sentient beings for whom you're prostrating, the infinite buddhas and objects of refuge, infinite bodies in front of those infinite objects, which you imagine are making infinite prostrations. The amount of merit or good karma you create when doing an action such as prostrating depends on your mind— on your intention—and so by integrating the four infinites into your practice of prostrating, you create infinite, inconceivable merit! In terms of infinite sentient beings, recall that the purpose of doing prostrations is for the sake of numberless, mother sentient beings who are exactly like you in wanting happiness and not wanting suffering. This wish is universal. As you prostrate, imagine purifying all their negativities and accumulating all virtues for them to be happy and free from suffering. Doing each prostration with the idea that it's not only for yourself but for all sentient beings creates the same amount of merit as the number of sentient beings you're prostrating for—which is infinite. In terms of infinite buddhas, if you have a statue in your home you can prostrate in front of it, but in your mind, visualize prostrating to numberless buddhas. Buddhas do in fact pervade the entirety of space, so visualize prostrating to all of them. You can also think of prostrating to all the buddha statues and stupas in this world. If you imagine numberless buddhas as objects of your prostrations then this again creates limitless merit. In terms of infinite selves, as you prostrate, visualize emanating numberless avatars of yourself, who all prostrate together. Imagine all your past selves—a self for each previous year of your life, each previous day of your life, and each previous second as well; then imagine all your previous lives as well prostrating together in human form. You can also imagine emanating these past selves to other realms where there are buddhas, prostrating to them too.

That covers physical prostration. You can also pay homage with your voice by reciting verses aloud as you prostrate. Any verses of praise to the enlightened beings can be used here. The verses for prostrating to the thirty-five buddhas from the *Sutra of the Three Heaps* are very good.[22] Generating faith is the essence of mental prostration. By integrating physical, verbal, and mental prostration together, you simultaneously purify negative karmas of your body, speech, and mind.

The second limb is **offering**. There are two general categories of offerings—surpassable and unsurpassable offerings. Surpassable offerings can include offering water for drinking, water for cleansing feet, flowers, incense, light, pleasing scents, food, and music as well as offering the eight auspicious symbols, the objects of the five senses, the seven royal emblems, and so forth.[23] Each of these offerings has its own qualities and benefits. For instance, water's quality of moisture helps you to generate bodhichitta. Its cleansing quality helps you purify your negativities. Water's clarity, which reflects objects, helps you to understand the illusory nature of things—their emptiness. Offering flowers creates the karma to have a beautiful form, for just as flowers bring pleasure when seen, offering them creates karma to have a body that brings pleasure when seen. It also creates the karma to achieve a buddha's holy form. Offering incense creates karma to keep your ethics and vows purely. Just as lights eliminate darkness in a room, offering them creates karmic imprints to gain wisdom eliminating the darkness of ignorance. Offering lights particularly helps you to abandon the misconception grasping at a truly existent self and thus to attain the realization of emptiness. According to the tantric teachings, particularly those of Chakrasamvara, extensive light offerings also create the karma to realize inner fire and clear light. Offering scented water to the chest eliminates bad odors and has similar qualities to offering water generally. Food is required for survival, and offering food extends your lifespan. Offering music creates karmic imprints to attain the sixty qualities of Buddha's speech. In general you can offer whatever makes your mind joyful. Compassion for those who are suffering is also an offering to the buddhas, bringing them pleasure.

As with prostrations, you can integrate your practice of offering with the four infinites. Even if you're offering just a single piece of incense in your room, you can imagine offering every beautiful fragrance that exists. When offering even just one flower, imagine offering every beautiful flower in the world. You can apply this to the other offerings in this same manner. Recall that the purpose of making offerings is for the benefit all sentient beings and imagine making those offerings to numberless buddhas. You can also engage your body, speech, and mind together when making offerings—as you physically offer things you can recite mantras or verses while generating bodhichitta and so forth with your mind. This is how to go about making ordinary, surpassable offerings.

Unsurpassable offering is also called the *Samantabhadra offering*. Samantabdhara here refers to the bodhisattva Samantabhadra, to bodhichitta, and to the union of bliss and emptiness. The bodhisattva Samantabhadra is one of the eight great bodhisattvas. Though these eight are equal in their level of realization, due to the power of their prayers, each has his own unique qualities: developing wisdom for Manjushri, enhancing compassion for Avalokiteshvara, power for Vajrapani, increasing the fertility of earth for Ksitigharbha, holding the lineage of extensive deeds for Maitreya, purifying proscribed and naturally negative actions for Akashagharbha, purifying obscurations in general for Sarvanivaranav-ishkambhin, and making extremely extensive offerings and prayers for Samantabhadra.

There are a number of different ways to make unsurpassable Samanta-bhadra offerings. For one, you imagine yourself in the form of Samanta-bhadra holding a wish-granting jewel at your heart. Light radiates from all your pores, and on the tip of each ray is a Samantabhadra holding a jewel radiating light from all his pores, and you imagine that happening countless times, so that infinite Samantabhadras fill the expanse of space. Then light rays emanate from all their wish-granting jewels with countless flowers and other offerings. Alternately, you can imagine yourself as Samantabhadra in the center of a thousand-petaled lotus with a Samantabhadra on each petal. You all hold wish-granting jewels from which light rays emanate to all buddha realms, filling them with offerings.

As *Samantabhadra* can refer to bodhichitta, any offering made with the extensive motivation of bodhichitta can also be considered a Samantabhadra offering. This point is taught in the *Sutra Requested by [the Bodhisattva] Ocean of Wisdom*, which also says that holding the supreme Dharma is an unsurpassable offering. The *White Lotus of Compassion Sutra* similarly explains the benefits of the unsurpassed offering of putting whatever Dharma you've learned into practice. So the meaning here is that if you learn some Dharma and then put it into practice, you're holding that Dharma, and there is no better offering than that. Say you take up the practice of cleaning your meditation place as described earlier; that is a genuine offering of practice. You can do this with any teachings you've studied, and nothing pleases the gurus and buddhas more than offering your own practice. One way of offering your practice is to imagine the virtues you've created taking form—as a flower, for instance, or as an ocean of nectar—and then offering that form to your gurus.

Finally, according to tantra, *Samantabadhra* refers to a union of the wisdom of great bliss and emptiness. Actually, in tantric practice all offerings are thought of as being in the nature of great bliss and emptiness. They take the aspect of various offering objects, but their function is to give rise to the pristine awareness of the single taste of great bliss and emptiness united.

The third of the seven-limb practices is **confession**. As I mentioned earlier, we can divide the seven limbs into two things: accumulation and purification. The practice of confession is specifically for purifying. There are various things to be purified, but the main thing to be purified is negative karma. Anyone can create bad karma, but only those who've taken vows and commitments can transgress those. If you've taken individual liberation vows, bodhisattva vows, or tantric vows or commitments, you should purify any mistakes you've made regarding those. You can also purify other obstacles to enlightenment like fundamental ignorance and the subtle imprints that are obscurations to omniscience that even arhats and arya bodhisattvas have before they become fully enlightened buddhas. When you practice confession, your intention is to purify all these negativities of the past and present.

The main thing to be purified, negative karma, has two definitions—actions that bring suffering generally and actions that brings the suffering of rebirth in the lower realms in particular. Whereas positive karma naturally brings pleasure and happiness, negative karma by definition is what makes you uncomfortable and unhappy. We've all performed lots of negative actions in this life. And although you can't remember your previous lives, you can infer that you've accumulated huge stores of negative karmic actions in previous lives. The very fact that you meet with many difficulties in this life is proof that you created many negative actions in previous lives.

One good quality of bad karma is that no matter how heavy it is, it can be purified using these four powers! During the Buddha's time, Angulimala killed 999 people, cutting off each of their little fingers to make a finger-rosary. Yet in that very lifetime he engaged in purification and became an arhat! Also, King Deche Sangpo created one of the heaviest of negative karmas by killing his mother, but he then generated strong regret, becoming overcome with grief and dismay. He practiced the four opponent powers and became an arya in that very life. Another king, Maketa, killed his father but then practiced purification and became an arhat. Any negative karma can be purified through confessing in the context of practicing the four opponent powers.

You begin practicing the four opponent powers by generating bodhichitta. The power of *reliance* has two aspects, and this initial generation of bodhichitta fulfills one of those. Next you focus in the second power: *intelligent regret*. To generate intelligent regret for your negative actions, you have to understand which actions are negative and contemplate what sorts of bad results they bring until you become afraid or terrified. Each negative action brings three kinds of karmic results: the ripened result, the result similar to the cause, and the environmental result. For example, with killing, the *result similar to the cause* is that when you're reborn as a human you have a short life, which is similar to the cause as you shortened others' lives by killing. The *environmental result* of killing is being reborn in a violent place where lots of killing occurs. The *ripened result* of heavy negative karma is rebirth in hell realms, of medium negative karma is rebirth in hungry ghost realms, and of small negative karma is rebirth in animal realms.

It's easy to see the suffering of animals. Animals are always afraid, constantly alert to danger. Some animals can't find enough food or water. Even domestic animals suffer from inability to express themselves, lack of intelligence to avoid some problems, and so forth. We can help them with some obvious sufferings, but there are many other kinds of suffering they experience about which we cannot do anything. The sufferings of the hells and hungry ghost realms are hidden to us, but you can imagine them. You can read about the eight hot hells, the eight cold hells, and the neighboring hells, as well as the specific sufferings of hungry ghosts. By contemplating in detail, repeatedly, on these various suffering results of your negative actions, you'll generate pure, reasonable regret, the opponent power from which the rest develop naturally.

This intelligent fear of suffering leads you to sincerely look to the three objects of refuge for help in purifying. So the second aspect of the power of reliance—refuge—develops naturally from regret itself. You sincerely turn to the Three Jewels for protection from that suffering. And your regret and refuge give rise to a natural enthusiasm for following the advice of the Three Jewels by applying the power of the *antidote*, engaging in recitations or practices to counteract the force of your negative actions. Six practices in particular are emphasized for the power of the antidote—reciting the names of tathagatas such as those of the thirty-five confession buddhas; reciting mantras such as the hundred-syllable mantra of Vajrasattva, the mantra of Akshobhya, or the mantra of Samayavajra; reciting sutras such as the *Vajra-Cutter Sutra* or the *Sutra of Golden Light*; meditating on emptiness; making intensive offerings; and making statues of buddhas. Generally speaking, any virtuous action can serve as an antidote to your negative actions. If you generate the other three opponent powers, then even offering one piece of incense or doing your sadhana can serve as the power of the antidote.

Lama Tsongkhapa practiced intensive purification by reciting the names of the thirty-five buddhas of confession.[24] This practice from the *Sutra of the Three Heaps* includes both reciting a sutra and reciting the names of buddhas. It is profound because each of those thirty-five buddhas when they were still bodhisattvas made special prayers and dedications to help others to purify, so when you recite their names, you receive benefit from their past dedications. Even just reciting the name of one of those buddhas can purify many eons of negative karma, and if you combine your recitation with physical prostrations, it becomes extremely powerful. If you prostrate reciting just one name today and then the next name tomorrow, then after thirty-five days you will have purified a great deal of negative karma and will also naturally begin memorizing the names! Master Shantideva advised reciting this practice three times each day and three times each night to purely keep one's bodhisattva vows; this is a powerful practice for purifying transgressions of those vows. It's best if you can prostrate while reciting, but if you can't do that, then it's sufficient to simply recite the prayer.

The final opponent power is *restraint*. Once you've sincerely contemplated the consequences of negative actions and generated fear, you'll voluntarily want to refrain from such actions in the future. If an action is not very difficult to give up, then it's good to commit to forgoing it for the rest of your life. With negative actions to which you're quite habituated, however, you can begin by committing to avoid them for shorter periods of time—say a day or two—and gradually build up to longer periods.

Engaging in those four opponent powers as part of your daily practice is essential for generating realizations. For those who cannot engage in intensive Dharma practices, it's excellent to focus on purification. Since negative karma causes all suffering, this will protect you from suffering. The mahasiddhas, or great adepts, of the past engaged in purification throughout their whole lives. You'll find it's not difficult and it's very helpful if you do likewise.

The next of the seven limbs is **rejoicing**, which is a really wonderful practice. In the *Collection of Sutras*, it says that it's possible to measure the weight of Mount Meru but that the weight of the merits you gain by rejoicing in others' good deeds is immeasurable. Lama Tsongkhapa said rejoicing in others' merits is a way to accumulate lots of merit without much effort. You can rejoice in the virtues of five different kinds of beings: buddhas, bodhisattvas, solitary realizers (*pratyekabuddhas*), hearers (*shravakas*), and ordinary beings. Rejoicing in the buddhas' virtues can include thinking of their first generating bodhichitta, of their many practices while on the path, and also in their infinite virtues as buddhas. Rejoicing in the virtues of the bodhisattvas includes rejoicing in their practices of abandoning self-interest and cherishing others, of practicing the six perfections, of engaging in the four ways of gathering disciples, and so forth. Solitary realizers and hearers have many amazing virtues and good qualities as I described earlier. There are so many positive actions that holy and ordinary beings have done, and you can rejoice in all of them. Don't discriminate when rejoicing: if someone lower than you or from a different religious tradition does something positive, rejoice! Rejoicing is such an easy practice. You can engage in it through your three doors: you can rejoice physically by folding your hands at your heart to pay respect; verbally by praising their actions aloud; mentally by understanding their actions, feeling joy about them, and wishing to act similarly. When participating in a gathering where virtuous deeds are done, you accumulate the same merits as others just by rejoicing in what they're doing. If you just go around seeing others do good things and rejoicing, this allows you to create a lot of merit without much effort.

Jealousy is the opposite of rejoicing. Jealousy makes us miserable and rejoicing makes us happy. Also, rejoicing makes sense. If you have compassion, and particularly if you've taken the bodhisattva vows, then your intention is for others to be happy and free from suffering. When you see others doing positive, virtuous things, you should recognize that they're liberating themselves from suffering and leading themselves to happiness. Strive to feel like a parent who sees her child doing the right things—doing well in school and so forth—and so is joyful!

Only rejoice in positive deeds, not negative ones. Rejoicing in others' virtues allows you to create as much merit as they are creating, but rejoicing in others' harmful deeds causes you to create a similar amount of bad karma. If someone kills a person and you rejoice in that, you create the same amount of negative karma as the murderer! When you watch television or read the news, it's very easy for negative rejoicing to arise. Such negative rejoicing doesn't help anybody and harms you. So take care to only rejoice in the positive actions of others.

The fifth limb is *requesting the wheel of Dharma be turned*. There are numberless buddhas. During the first of his three eons of practicing the path, Buddha Shakyamuni accumulated merit in the presence of 75,000 buddhas, in his second eon 76,000 buddhas, in his third eon 77,000 buddhas. When Buddha achieved enlightenment he remained silent for a while. Then the god Brahma came to him and offered a Dharma wheel, requesting him to teach. So you can imagine yourself in Brahma's form approaching thousands of buddhas, requesting them to turn the wheel of Dharma. Doing this practice purifies the negativity of abandoning the Dharma. Through this also you won't be separated from the Dharma in the future.

The sixth limb is *requesting the field of merit to not depart to nirvana*. You ask them to remain in the world to benefit all sentient beings. This practice purifies any negativities committed by disturbing the buddhas or your gurus. It serves as a long-life prayer for your gurus, and it also creates the cause for your own long life.

The final limb is *dedication*, which is crucial. Through your practice of the previous six limbs you created merit. Now that merit is the object of your dedication. Merit is like gold. Dedication is like a goldsmith making gold into objects; how you dedicate determines what shape your virtues will take. A goldsmith can fashion a sheet of raw gold into a Buddha statue or into any other object he wishes. He can turn the gold into a sacred statue or a toilet depending on his wish. Similarly, if you dedicate your merits for your future enlightenment, they become causes for that. But if not then they take some other form. Dedication is also like directing a horse by pulling the reins one way or another. Your virtues are like the horse, and dedication is like pulling the reins right or left. How you dedicate will determine where they take you.

There are many dedications for different purposes. Some people dedicate virtues for the welfare of just this life, which is not a good way to dedicate. Others dedicate just for future lives. Hinayana practitioners dedicate for their own personal liberation. Mahayanists dedicate for full enlightenment. You can control where your merits will take you. Of the many dedications, three are superior: dedicating for Buddha's teachings to increase and remain forever, because if these teachings remain in this world then we can study and practice them; dedicating for remaining inseparable from your guru so as to receive his or her teachings continually and put them into practice so as to become enlightened; and dedicating for your achievement of full enlightenment for the benefit of all beings.

It's also very good if you can seal your dedication with awareness of the emptiness of the dedicator, the object dedicated, and the goal dedicated toward. Emptiness is a direct antidote to self-grasping, which causes all the other afflictive emotions, so sealing your dedication with emptiness applies the direct antidote to all bad qualities. Merits dedicated with awareness of emptiness will never be destroyed by other afflictive emotions because emptiness is the direct antidote to all afflicted states of mind.

At the beginning of an activity you must set up a pure motivation, and at the end you must dedicate your merits. If you don't dedicate, it's like receiving valuable goods and then throwing them away. If you do one of those superior dedications, then other forces such as anger cannot destroy your virtues. If you dedicate virtues to buddhahood, then other forces cannot destroy your virtues.

If you know how to think, then the practice of Dharma is really quite simple. As was explained above in the context of Buddha's advice to King Prasenajit, the practices of rejoicing, generating bodhichitta, and dedicating are so easy to do at any time and create an enormous amount of merit, and these involve just altering your normal ways of thinking. But if you don't think properly and do not create a good motivation, then nothing you do becomes Dharma. If you're offering to Buddha or monks just to defeat your enemy, for instance, that's not Dharma practice! Since you do have buddha-nature, the potential to become enlightened, however, if you purify negativities and accumulate virtues then your buddha-nature will become activated and you will become enlightened. This is why practicing the seven limbs is so important. Even if you cannot practice the entirety of the stages of the path to enlightenment, if you do the various preliminary practices being discussed here, then you are holding the essence of the entire practice. Just doing the six preliminary practices is sufficient for maintaining the essence of Dharma practice.

Offering the Mandala

Next comes the practice of offering the mandala—offering a visualized version of the entire universe in a pure form. There are different versions of the mandala offering. The shortest version represents the cosmos with seven "heaps"—Mount Meru, the four continents, the sun, and the moon. In the Kalachakra tantra there's a version with nine heaps—the above seven with two planets called Kalagni and Rahu added. The long version of the mandala offering has twenty-five heaps. In Guhyasamaja tantra there's a mandala with twenty-three heaps, which is similar to the long one but without the golden ground and the vajra fence. In brief, you can offer any beautiful objects in your mandala offering practice. The great yogi Drupkon Gelek Gyatso made offerings all the time. Whenever he saw beautiful objects, he'd recite the verse for the short mandala offering.

Making Prayers and Requests

After offering the mandala, *Easy Path* says to make fervent and sincere supplications. Here, there are four kinds of supplications you can make: the prayer for the three great purposes, the prayer for opening the door of supreme fields, the prayer of heaps of blessings, and the planting the stake prayer.

The *prayer for the three great purposes* is made particularly after you offer the short mandala prayer with seven heaps. This prayer is as follows:

> I prostrate and go for refuge to the guru and the precious
> Three Jewels. Please bless my mind. Please pacify immediately
> all wrong conceptions—from incorrectly devoting to the guru

up to the subtle dualistic views of the white, red, and black
visions—that exist in my mind and in the minds of all mother
sentient beings. Please generate immediately all the correct
realizations, from devotion to the guru up to enlightenment
within my mind and within the minds of all mother sentient
beings. Please pacify immediately all outer and inner obstacles to actualizing all the stages of the path to enlightenment
within my mind and within the minds of all mother sentient
beings.

The request to pacify the subtle dualistic view of the white, red, and
black visions refers to an advanced level of the completion stage of
highest yoga tantra; in that context those are obstacles that must be
abandoned to realize the clear light, the illusory body, and the state of
union, thereby becoming a buddha. If one is practicing Sutrayana exclusively, then one prays instead that all obstacles may be removed up to the
realization of the two selflessnesses—of persons and phenomena—so as
to attain the path of no-more learning. You can see by this that the first
great purpose is to pacify all incorrect states of mind, the second is to
generate all the qualities from relying on the teacher up to buddhahood,
and the third is to pacify all obstacles to your own and others' achieving
those realizations. If you don't want to pray with these more extensive,
poetic words, you can just pray as follows:

By offering this mandala may I be able to abandon all bad
qualities, generate all good qualities, and eliminate all outer,
inner, and secret obstacles.

Outer obstacles are things like enemies, demonic hindrances, and political, economic, or social problems; inner obstacles involve sicknesses;
while secret obstacles are such things as the three root delusions in your
own mind.

A second kind of prayer you can do here is the *prayer for opening the
supreme fields*, meaning fields of merit. Extensive versions of this prayer
have been translated into English.[25] In this prayer, you call on your guru

and to each of the lineage gurus by name, asking them to bless you. It's called a prayer for opening the supreme fields because it includes prayer to Lama Tsongkapa followed by receiving his blessings to receive his knowledge and realizations, which are supreme.

The third kind of prayer you can do here is the prayer of heaps of blessings. For this you recite the brief prayer summarizing the stages of the path to enlightenment by Lama Tsongkhpa entitled "The Foundation of All Good Qualities." Each verse ends with requesting your guru to "bless me," and you recite that final line of each verse twice, receiving heaps of blessings from your guru.

> Next rays of light radiate from the *Hum* at the heart of Guru Shakyamuni Buddha. They penetrate all the infinite fierce and peaceful deities who are seated around him. Those deities thereby transform into light and, condensing, dissolve into Shakyamuni Buddha; your root guru also dissolves into him, and he comes to the crown of your head. From that transformation you observe on the crown of your head a lion throne with a variegated lotus, moon, and sun mandalas. Upon that is my kind root guru in the aspect of the Conqueror, Shakyamuni Buddha. His body is the color of refined gold. His head has a crown protrusion. He has one face and two arms. His right hand presses the earth. In his left hand, which is in the gesture of meditative equipoise, rests an alms bowl filled with nectar. He wears elegantly the three saffron robes of a monk. He has a body of pristine, luminous light adorned by the marks and signs. He sits in the vajra posture amid an aura of light.
>
> Offer a condensed version of the seven-limb practices along with the mandala. Then think that you are praying in unison with all mother sentient beings, who surround you:
>
> Embodiment of the four bodies, guru supreme deity:
> to Shakyamuni Vajradhara I make requests.
>
> Embodiment of the truth body, free of obscurations,

guru supreme deity:
to Shakyamuni Vajradhara I make requests.

Embodiment of the great-bliss enjoyment body, guru
    supreme deity:
to Shakyamuni Vajradhara I make requests.

Embodiment of the various emanation bodies, guru
    supreme deity:
to Shakyamuni Vajradhara I make requests.

Embodiment of all gurus, guru supreme deity:
to Shakyamuni Vajradhara I make requests.

Embodiment of all meditational deities, guru
    supreme deity:
to Shakyamuni Vajradhara I make requests.

Embodiment of all buddhas, guru supreme deity:
to Shakyamuni Vajradhara I make requests.

Embodiment of all holy Dharma, guru supreme deity:
to Shakyamuni Vajradhara I make requests.

Embodiment of all Sangha, guru supreme deity:
to Shakyamuni Vajradhara I make requests.

Embodiment of all dakinis, guru supreme deity:
to Shakyamuni Vajradhara I make requests.

Embodiment of all Dharma protectors, guru supreme
    deity:
to Shakyamuni Vajradhara I make requests.

In particular [beseech]:

Unity of all objects of refuge, guru supreme deity:
to Shakyamuni Vajradhara I make requests.

All mother sentient beings and I have been born in samsara and have endured a host of intense sufferings over a
long time. This is a result of not relying properly upon
the spiritual teacher in both thought and deed. Therefore,
guru deity, please bless me and all mother sentient beings
to now rely properly upon the spiritual teacher in both
thought and deed.

The other three kinds of prayers don't appear in *Easy Path*, but the
planting the stake prayer does. Before reciting this prayer, visualize light
rays radiating from the *Hum* syllable at the heart of the central figure
of the merit field—your guru in the form of Shakyamuni Buddha with
Vajradhara in his heart. Those light rays cause all the lineage masters
of the profound view to dissolve into Manjushri, those of the lineage
of extensive deeds to dissolve into Maitreya, those of tantra to dissolve
into Vajradhara, and all your personal teachers to dissolve into your root
guru. These four figures then dissolve into the central figure, Shakyamuni
Vajradhara. Shakyamuni Vajradhara, inseparable in essence from your
root guru, then comes to the crown of your head. He is a three-tiered
being: Shakyamuni Buddha with Vajradhara at his heart, who himself
has a *Hum* syllable at his heart.

Focusing on your root guru in this form atop your head, again do a
brief seven-limb prayer, a short mandala offering, and this prayer called
"planting the stake" because it's like when you stick a dagger into the
ground when putting up a tent—you have to hit the dagger again and
again on one point to make it go deep. You are similarly here praying
again and again to the one guru atop your head. The meaning of this
prayer is very similar to the verse in the *Guru Puja* that says:

You are my guru, you are my deities, you are the dakinis and
Dharma protectors.

From this moment until enlightenment, I need seek no refuge
    other than you.
In this life, the bardo, and all future lives, hold me with your
    hook of compassion.
Free me from samsara and nirvana's fears, grant all attainments,
    be my unfailing friend, and guard me from interferences.

This prayer in *Easy Path* and most of the *Guru Puja* comes from the text I mentioned earlier called the *Tushita Emanation Scripture*, which is not made of paper and ink. It was received by Lama Tsongkhapa from Manjushri and was then passed down from master to disciple by highly realized masters of the Ganden Oral Tradition. Panchen Losang Chokyi Gyaltsen was the first master to write these verses and prayers down so that now we can use them in our practice.

In terms of the meaning of this prayer above, "embodiment of the four bodies" means that the root guru atop your head is an expression of the four bodies, or *kayas*, of a buddha—the truth body and nature body, which fulfill one's own purposes, as well as the enjoyment body and emanation bodies, which fulfill the purposes of others. The "truth body," the *dharmakaya*, "free of obscurations" refers to the buddha's mind, which is purified of all temporary stains of the afflictive emotions and also of all natural stains or impurities of grasping at true existence. Having purified those two is the truth of the cessation of suffering. The next two verses are requests to the guru as the enjoyment body, or *sambhogakaya*, which manifests to benefit arya bodhisattvas, and the emanation bodies, or *nirmanakayas*, which manifest to benefit all different kinds of sentient beings. The next line is for recognizing your root guru as the embodiment of all your gurus—not seeing them as different in essence. The next is for recognizing your guru as the embodiment and source of all meditational deities, referring to all the deities of the four classes of tantra. The next is for seeing your guru as embodying all the buddhas, including the thousand buddhas of this eon, the seven Medicine Buddhas, the thirty-five buddhas of confession, and so forth. The next refers to your guru as embodying of all the holy Dharma—both the transmitted Dharma and the Dharma borne of inner realization. The actual cessation of all negativities is also the Dharma. Thus, your guru embodies all these. The verse next is for seeing your guru as embodying the entire Sangha, including bodhisattvas, solitary realizers, and hearers. The next verse refers to the dakas and dakinis, such as those abiding in the twenty-four holy places of this earth, seeing all of them as embodied in the guru. The next verse refers to the guru as embodying the Dharma protectors, referring to Six -Armed Mahakala, who protects great-scope practitioners, Vaishravana, who protects middle-scope practitioners, and Yamaraja, who protects small-scope practitioners. In the merit field for *Easy Path* or for the *Guru Puja*, we generally only include those three protectors, though some people also include other enlightened protectors as well.

Earlier we visualized all these various figures in the merit field, and then they all dissolved into the guru atop your head. He thus embodies the essence of all those beings. This is an essential point for practicing guru yoga—seeing all enlightened beings as emanations of your guru and seeing your guru as the embodiment of all enlightened beings. The last line requests the guru as "unity of all objects of refuge." We prayed to guru as embodying each of those qualities individually, and now we pray to the guru as the source of protection who embodies all qualities in one. We especially pray for our wishes to be fulfilled, particularly requesting blessings to gain the realization of guru devotion. At then end of your prayer, five-colored nectars and lights dissolve into the crowns of your own and others' heads. This descent of lights and nectars completes the preliminaries.

The Absorption of Light Rays and Nectars

> With this supplication, streams of five-colored nectars together with rays of light descend from the body of your guru deity upon your crown. These streams enter the bodies and minds of all sentient beings and yourself, thereby purifying all misdeeds and obstructions accumulated from beginningless time. In particular they purify all the misdeeds, obscurations, sicknesses, and spirit possessions that prevent the ability to depend properly upon the spiritual teacher in both thought and deed. [Your

and all others'] bodies transform into the nature of pristine, luminous light. All [your and others'] good qualities, such as a long lifespan and merit, are increased and expanded. In particular, think that these streams have produced in the minds of yourself and all others the special realization that enables you to rely properly upon the spiritual teacher in both thought and deed.

I mentioned visualizing the descent of light rays and five-colored nectars in the context of refuge practice. Here this appears in detail in *Easy Path*. This visualization is very profound, and you'll encounter it again below, integrated with each meditation topic. So I'll explain how to visualize and the meanings here, and you should apply your understanding as you progress through the various meditation topics throughout the rest of the book.

This visualization is extremely important; it doesn't appear in earlier texts on the stages of the path. It is a unique, profound instruction for integrating tantric visualization with the meditations on the stages of the path that was passed down orally from guru to disciple until Panchen Losang Chokyi Gyaltsen wrote it here.

Receiving blessings through visualizing light rays descending into you is found in the exoteric tradition of Sutrayana, but receiving blessings from your gurus through the descent of nectars is unique to tantra, to Vajrayana. This practice has many levels of meaning and leaves important imprints for actualizing the path to enlightenment quickly.

In terms of how to visualize, imagine five rays each of a different color emanating from your guru, who is inseparable from the Buddha atop your crown. These rays are white, yellow, red, green, and blue. On each ray flows nectar that's the same color as that ray, coiling along the ray and dripping into you. There are three kinds of nectar—wisdom nectar destroying the afflictive emotions, nectar of deathlessness, and medicinal nectar. The nectars flow along the rays much like water in a heavy rain flows along a taut rope that's holding up a tent. These nectars and light rays of five colors flow into you and all sentient beings, who you're visualizing around you, totally cleansing all your bodies and minds. As your bodies are filled, they become utterly purified, pristine, and luminous. They no longer appear solid; they are clear like rainbows or like holograms.

As the text says, the nectars purify all of your misdeeds, the afflictive emotions obscuration, the obscuration to omniscience, sicknesses, spirit possessions, and particularly all obstacles to fully realizing whichever meditation topic you're contemplating. Then the nectars increase qualities such as lifespan, merit, and realizations of all the stages of the path, including whichever topic you're meditating on.

The light rays descending symbolize your being blessed to realize clear light. The nectars descending symbolize your being blessed to realize great bliss and the illusory body. Their coming down together symbolizes your being blessed to realize great bliss unified with the wisdom understanding emptiness as well as the union of clear light and the illusory body. The text says that through this blessing, your and all others' bodies transform into the nature of "pristine, luminous light." Here the meaning is similar. "Pristine" means that your body takes on the appearance of being totally pure and clear, like an extremely clean mountain lake. It's utterly without stain or impurity. This pristine quality also symbolizes the illusory body. As I mentioned, your body takes on an appearance like a rainbow; *rainbow body* is a synonym for *illusory body*. "Luminous" refers to the fact that your body is radiant, symbolizing clear light. Light has both of these qualities—it is utterly pristine and luminous by its very nature. So your and others' bodies being light symbolizes your own and all others attainment of the state of union.

On the path of highest yoga tantra, one who has received the initiation and keeps the vows and commitments begins by practicing the generation stage. The first of two stages, the generation stage involves the visualizations of deity yoga (seeing oneself and others as deities and the environment as a mandala) in the context of taking death as one's path to the truth body, the intermediate state as one's path to the enjoyment body, and rebirth as one's path to the emanation body.

Having completed the generation stage, one progresses to the completion stage, on which one is able to control the subtle wind energies of the body, bringing them into the central channel and thereby manifesting subtle states of mind. At a very advanced level of the completion stage, one becomes able to fully channel all the winds into the indestructible drop in the heart chakra, thereby actually manifesting the most subtle mind of innate clear light—a level of mind usually only manifest at the time of death. Using this subtle mind to meditate on emptiness, one realizes the example clear light. One then arises from this realization of emptiness in an impure illusory body, or rainbow body, which is not made of flesh and blood but of the most subtle wind energy that accompanies that most subtle mind. Having gained this level of realization, one has overcome ordinary death and will attain full enlightenment in that very lifetime.

By continuing to practice, one eventually again manifests that most subtle mind of innate clear light, and this time one is able to realize emptiness directly, thereby realizing the meaning clear light. One arises from that in a pure illusory body. The most subtle wind acts as the substantial cause of the pure illusory body, while the mind of the meaning clear light directly realizing emptiness acts as the cooperative condition for its arisal. At this point, one has achieved the *union of abandonment*—the union of the pure illusory body with the abandonment of all afflictive emotions. Having thus abandoned all afflictive obscurations, one has simultaneously become an arhat, completely liberated from all suffering, and has entered the path of meditation as taught in highest yoga tantra. Although one is an arhat, one has not yet abandoned the obscuration to omniscience; one is not yet a buddha. So one again gives rise to the most subtle mind of innate clear light directly realizing emptiness, thereby attaining the *union of realization*. This union of realization is a union of the pure illusory body and the meaning clear light. This is the principal union for a trainee still on the path who is progressing toward the state of omniscience. Such a trainee practices conduct with elaboration, without elaboration, and/or completely without elaboration until achieving the *union of no-more learning*, buddhahood itself, in that very life. You can see, can't you, that receiving blessings and creating imprints for these realizations is something very precious! It is so very beneficial to contemplate the meaning of these qualities of the visualization.

The five colors also represent the five wisdoms associated with the five tathagatas—or the five buddha families. The five tathagatas are the ultimate purity of the five aggregates, and the five wisdoms are the ultimate purity of their corresponding afflictive emotions. So as these nectars and rays descend, you should feel great joy thinking that you are transforming your five aggregates into the five tathagatas and the five afflictive emotions into the five wisdoms.

Color	Tathagata	Wisdom Attained	Aggregate Purified	Affliction Transformed
White	Vairochana	Mirror-Like Wisdom	Form	Ignorance
Red	Amitabha	Discriminating Wisdom	Perception	Desire
Blue	Akshobhya	Dharma-Sphere Wisdom	Consciousness	Hatred
Yellow	Ratnasambhava	Equanimity Wisdom	Feeling	Pride & Miserliness
Green	Amoghasiddhi	All-Accomplishing Wisdom	Compositional Factors	Jealousy

Another symbolism of the five colors relates to your body's five subtle energy winds, which naturally have the radiance of those five colors. When you gain enlightenment and create your own buddhafield in the form of a celestial mandala with a divine mansion surrounded by a ring of fire, fences, and so forth, that pure mandala along with the fire and so forth will all be made up of those five colors. This is because your five subtle energy winds will serve as the substantial causes of that mandala. These five subtle energies are the foundation of your current physical and mental experiences, and when you gain enlightenment, the divine mandala will be a natural expression of the enlightened forms of those five basic energy winds. So your visualizing the nectar with five colors has a special significance for purification.

Resultant Bodhichitta Practice

While you're engaging in the practices of the stages of the path, your guru in the form of Shakyamuni Vajradhara remains atop the crown of your head. At the end of your practices, you can absorb him through the practice of taking resultant bodhichitta as the path as follows. You begin with a prayer such as "I prostrate to my Guru Buddha, to the Dharma, and to the Sangha." Imagine that Guru Shakyamuni Vajradhara dissolves into your body. You then transform into Guru Shakyamuni Buddha. Think that your mind has become the truth body free from any conceptual elaborations and your body has taken on the aspect of Shakyamuni Buddha. This is taking resultant bodhichitta as the path, a skillful method for swiftly creating extensive merits that is part of the oral tradition from Gyalwa Ensapa.

In your heart center, visualize a white *Ah* syllable with a yellow *Hum* inside it. Light rays emanate from that *Hum* transforming all sentient beings into Shakyamuni Buddha's form, each with an *Ah* and a *Hum* at their hearts. Around the *Ah* syllables is the mantra of Shakyamuni Buddha: *Tadyatha om muni muni maha muniye svaha.* Next you recite that mantra ten, twenty-one, or more times, imagining that all sentient beings, as vast as infinite space, are reciting it along with you.

When your session is done, don't just jump up from your cushion. Pause to review and rejoice sincerely in the positive actions you've done and the merits you've created! Then dedicate those virtuous merits, reciting any verses you like. One such verse is:

Through these virtuous merits,
may I quickly attain the state of a guru buddha
and thereby lead all sentient beings
to that enlightened state.

2. Relying on a Spiritual Teacher

E*asy Path* teaches how to rely on a spiritual teacher based on two main points—how to rely on the teacher in your thoughts and how to rely through your actions. Other texts discuss this subject through either six or four main points. If four main points are given, then two preliminary points—the benefits of relying on a teacher and the disadvantages of not relying on the teacher—are taught before the two points in our current text. Those two preliminary points are important because understanding the benefits gives us the courageous energy to rely well, and understanding the disadvantages makes us cautious about avoiding negative karma and mistakes.[26]

BENEFITS OF PROPER RELIANCE

Although *Easy Path* doesn't mention the benefits of properly relying on a spiritual teacher, *Swift Path*, which is a commentary to this text, does teach these points, so I'll cover them here as they're important for practice. Eight benefits are taught.

The first is that you'll get closer to buddhahood. One reason for this is that your teacher gives you all the instructions of the three scopes of practice, and by practicing those you come closer to enlightenment. Another reason is that doing two things—serving and pleasing your teacher—brings you closer to your teacher and closer to enlightenment. In his *Five Stages*, Nagarjuna says, "If you take the guru as the life force of your practice, you will quickly attain omniscience." The measure of taking the guru as the life force of your practice is visualizing the guru atop your head and practicing devotion in every practice you do. The

Source of Vows says that if you rely properly on a teacher then you will become enlightened, attaining the state of great bliss in one lifetime, and so it advises paying homage to the guru, who is like a precious jewel.

As mentioned above, Ever-Crying Bodhisattva attained enlightenment especially quickly due to his powerful guru devotion. The Perfection of Wisdom sutras teach how Ever-Crying Bodhisattva was on the path of accumulation when he took Supreme-Dharma Bodhisattva as his teacher. Ordinarily it takes one eon to go from the path of accumulation to the first bodhisattva ground and another eon to go from the first to the eighth ground. By relying well on his teacher, Ever-Crying Bodhisattva skipped those and went from the path of accumulation to the eighth ground in that one lifetime. Commenting earlier on the phrase "quickly, quickly," I mentioned that the first quickly refers to practicing the stages-of-the-path tradition and the second quickly refers to taking guru yoga as the life of the practice; Ever-Crying Bodhisattva's practice was like that. Even if your teacher is not physically present, you can imagine him or her atop your head, pay homage, make offerings, and especially make the offering of putting the teachings into practice.

The second benefit is that our relying on the teacher pleases the buddhas. The reason is twofold. First the buddhas will be pleased because all they want is to benefit sentient beings, and if they manifest an enjoyment body or a supreme emanation body with the marks and signs, you won't have sufficient good karma to see them. You can only benefit from teachers you can see and relate with, such as when they manifest in ordinary, human bodies. When the buddhas see you practicing properly in relation to such teachers, they're pleased because you're receiving benefit. Secondly, when you offer to a guru, the buddhas come into the guru and receive the offerings, and this also pleases them. The Tibetan master Lopon Sangye Yeshe wrote that when you're devoted, the buddhas enter the body of your spiritual teachers and receive your offerings, thereby purifying your negativities, allowing you to quickly become enlightened.

The third benefit is that by relying properly you won't be harmed by spirits or negative friends. The *Extensive Enjoyment Sutra* explains how you create extensive merits by relying well and so cannot be harmed by demons or negative friends.

The fourth benefit is that your delusions and negative actions will naturally decrease.

The fifth is that your insights and realizations of the path to enlightenment will increase. When Atisha analyzed the levels of realization of three of his disciples—Dromtonpa who served as his secretary, Ame Jangchup who served as his cook, and Mahayogi who was always in retreat—he found that the two who'd been serving him had gained more insight and experience of the path than the one who'd been meditating continually. Master Shonuwa didn't get ordained as a monk because he was worried that if he got ordained he wouldn't be able to serve his guru. By serving his guru he gained high realizations.

The sixth benefit is that you won't be deprived of virtuous spiritual guides in all your future lives. In the *Blue Scripture*, Geshe Potowa said:

> As long as we have not examined our relationship with a
>   teacher, there is not much [we need to observe],
> but once we have examined and adopted a guru, we must
>   respect him.
> This is the true way to not be without our guru in the future,
> since the effects of our karma are inexhaustible.

Examine a potential teacher very thoroughly at the beginning, and once you've decided to take someone as your guru, then never show disrespect. If you check carefully first and then rely properly with devotion, you won't be disappointed. Through this you'll always meet qualified teachers in future lives.

The seventh benefit is that you won't fall into the lower realms. The *Sutra of Kshitigarbha* teaches that by devoting well to your guru, you can very quickly purify karma that would otherwise have caused you to suffer in the lower realms for millions of eons. Through proper reliance, such karma may instead be purified by manifesting in this life as some small problem, like a bad dream or brief headache.

The eighth benefit summarizes all the others: you will achieve all your mundane and supramundane aims. The supramundane aim referred to here is buddhahood. Lama Tsongkhapa said, "The kind and venerable guru is the foundation of all good qualities"—everything from having a happy life, good health, and good companions, to attaining realizations on the path, up to achieving full enlightenment.

The disadvantages of not devoting properly are also explained in eight points that are just the opposite of the eight benefits. I won't cover those in detail here. Next come the two points covered in *Easy Path*: training in faith, the root of the practice, and remembering your teachers' kindness and developing respect.

How to Rely on Your Teacher in Your Thoughts

Training in Faith, the Root of the Practice

> Visualize the gurus with whom you have a direct teaching connection emanating from the heart of Guru Shakyamuni [seated upon a lotus, moon, and sun cushions upon the crown of your head and] sitting in the empty space before you. Observing them, think:

>> These spiritual teachers of mine are actually buddhas. The completely perfect Buddha said in the precious tantras that in the degenerate time Conqueror Vajradhara would show the physical form of a spiritual teacher and work for the welfare of beings. Accordingly, even my spiritual teachers are not just Conqueror Vajradhara showing different physical forms, but they are Vajradhara showing the physical form of a spiritual teacher for the sake of looking after us beings who did not have the fortune to see Buddha directly. Therefore, guru deity, please now bless me and all mother sentient beings to directly perceive these spiritual teachers as Shakyamuni Vajradhara.

> With this supplication, streams of five-colored nectars together with rays of light descend from the body of your guru deity upon your crown. These streams enter the bodies and minds of

all sentient beings and yourself, thereby purifying [all misdeeds and obstructions accumulated from beginningless time. In particular these streams purify all the misdeeds, obscurations, sicknesses, and spirit possessions] that prevent [the ability to directly perceive your spiritual teachers as Shakyamuni Vajradhara. Your and all others' bodies have the nature of pristine, luminous light. All your and others' good qualities, such as long lifespan and merit, are increased and expanded. In particular], think that these streams have produced in the minds of yourself and all others the special realization [that enables you to directly perceive your spiritual teachers as Shakyamuni Vajradhara].[27]

Here you cultivate faith in your gurus. To begin this contemplation, focus on your guru in the form of Shakyamuni Buddha atop your head with Vajradhara at his heart. Light rays emanate from the *Hum* at the heart of Vajradhara, manifesting the actual forms of each of your spiritual teachers in the space in front of you, looking down at you. If you've received even a single Dharma talk from someone with the intention of learning Dharma from that one—of having him or her guide you spiritually—then he or she should be included in this visualization of your teachers.[28] You have to contemplate in order to give rise to the view that all these teachers of yours are actual buddhas.

Training to see your gurus as buddhas is for your own spiritual benefit. It's a mental training that allows you to receive the blessings of the buddhas through your gurus. It allows you to create vast merits of offering to all the buddhas when you make offerings to your gurus. It allows you to more easily bring the buddhas to mind and to feel closer to them. In the tantric context you don't just view your gurus as Vajradhara, you view all appearances as divine. Everyone you encounter you view in the form of whichever deity you're practicing. So there's no flaw in viewing your teachers as buddhas! It's a skillful way to open the door to blessings and to speed your progress on the path.

Of course, a person can be a teacher without being a buddha, so some of your teachers may not actually be buddhas. Some may even be ordinary beings who've yet to see emptiness directly. Atisha was an *arya*—someone who has seen emptiness directly. But his teacher Serl-ingpa was a follower of the Mind-Only school who had not yet gained even a perfect inferential understanding of the ultimate nature of reality. Whether any one of your teachers is truly a buddha is an extremely hidden phenomenon that you cannot know for certain. This training is not about the object; it's about the subject: your own mind receives the benefit.

Easy Path refers to faith in your teacher as the "root" of your training on the path. This can mean two things. One is that faith itself is the root from which all the other practices grow and develop. The other is that the teacher himself or herself is the root of all the practices, as they all come from the teacher.

"Faith" as it's being used here doesn't just refer to belief in something religious. When you watch advertisements or go to the mall, you see objects and develop faith that they'll bring you some happiness, so then you aspire to have them. Our minds work like that all the time. It's similar in Dharma practice. First, you have to see good qualities in your teachers, and this naturally leads to the aspiration to practice in order to attain those qualities yourself. You pursue something when you have faith that doing so will bring good results.

One sort of faith is *pure faith*, seeing good qualities in an object (in this case your teachers, the buddhas, and the bodhisattvas) and then quickly developing a strong aspiration to be like them. Just having such faith purifies your mind, as a murky pond clears when the dirt in it settles. Seeing our teachers' good qualities brings such peaceful purity. Another sort of faith is the *faith of belief*, which comes from seeing how things work and developing confidence based on that. If you see how angrily harming others brings lots of problems and you therefore have faith that such actions are bad for you, this is the faith of belief. In relation to your teachers, the faith of belief is like when a child has repeatedly been helped by her mother and so has complete trust and faith in the mother's love. When you've developed that sort of trust and faith in your teach-ers, you have faith of belief. A third sort of faith is *supreme faith*, which definitively understands how one thing serves as the cause of another.

When someone completely understands how buddhahood is attainable through the practice of the six perfections, they have supreme faith in those practices. For an ordinary person, you already have supreme faith in the power of water to allay your thirst. When you feel toward your teacher like a dehydrated person longing for water who has no doubt that water will quench that thirst, you've developed supreme faith in your teacher.

Without faith, no aspiration to practice will arise. As *Lamp on the Three Jewels Sutra* says, "Faith is the preparation, giving birth like a mother: it protects all good qualities and increases them."[29] Faith nurtures your practice and allows it to grow. Once a man asked Atisha for instructions and Atisha remained silent. When the man asked again, Atisha shouted, "Have some faith! Faith!" Atisha was indicating how without faith to motivate taking them to heart, spiritual instructions can't bring much benefit. Faith is the doorway through which we enter into Dharma practice. It's the gateway to all knowledge and understanding. Jetsun Milarepa, who attained enlightenment in one lifetime, said, "The faith of many people is just words in their mouths; my faith is in my heart." Gyalwa Ensapa, who also attained enlightenment in one lifetime, said:

> Whether our realizations are great or small depends on whether we have meditated with great or small faith. Therefore, may I keep as my heart practice the instruction to reflect only on the qualities of the kind guru, source of all realizations, and not look at faults. May I fulfill this commitment without any obstacles.

As this verse indicates, focusing on your teachers' good qualities and not on faults is the root from which realizations grow.

Thus, having recognized that it benefits you to develop faith, there are four contemplations for enhancing faith in your teachers. The first is that Vajradhara stated that the guru is Buddha. *Easy Path* notes how in the tantras themselves, the Buddha in his form as Vajradhara promised that in degenerate times such as the present, he would manifest in the form of ordinary teachers to lead sentient beings like you. In these degenerate times, beings don't have the merit to see and interact with Vajradhara in the form of a deity, so he must manifest in the form of ordinary humans who teach the path. Aside from these spiritual teachers of yours, how else could Vajradhara manifest to guide you? In the *Hevajra Tantra*, Vajradhara says, "In future times, my physical form will be that of masters . . . in the last five centuries, I will take the form of masters. Think that they are me and develop respect for them . . . In future degenerate times, my form shall be that of churls, and through various means I will show my forms."[30] The Buddha says in a sutra, "In times to come I will show myself bodily as abbots. I will abide in the form of masters."[31] So while visualizing each of your gurus in space before you, think about Buddha Vajradhara's promise to manifest in ordinary forms to guide people like you and how your teachers are indeed those manifestations.

The second contemplation is on how the guru is the agent of all the Buddha's good works. Thousands and thousands of buddhas have vowed to benefit sentient beings. To benefit bodhisattvas, they come in the form of bodhisattvas. To help solitary realizers, they come in the form of solitary realizers. To help ordinary persons like yourself, they come in the form of ordinary persons. When the buddhas engage in enlightened activities, they come in a way that accords to the capacities of those to receive benefit. The main enlightened activity is teaching Dharma. For ordinary people like us, the only way to access Dharma talks is through our teachers. This is why the guru is the agent of all the buddhas.

The third contemplation is that the buddhas and bodhisattvas are still working for the sake of sentient beings; they never stop doing so. It's their very nature to compassionately benefit suffering beings like us. As you visualize your personal gurus in space before you, think about how these very teachers are the only answer to how the buddhas are still working today for your benefit, leading you along the path to enlightenment.

> Should you think, "Well, buddhas have eliminated all faults and attained all good qualities, but I can see that my spiritual teachers have faults motivated by the three poisons. Thus they are not exactly buddhas," then [your response should be]:

That is due to my impure perceptions. Previously as well Bhikshu Upadhana saw, through the influence of his impure perceptions, all the activities of the teacher Buddha as only deceit. Asanga saw Venerable Maitreya as a female dog. Maitripa saw the yogic master Shavaripa as doing wrong, such as killing pigs and so on. Similarly the appearance of the fault is not from my spiritual teachers but is due to my own impure perception. Therefore, guru deity, please bless the minds of all sentient beings and myself to not produce for even a mere instant the mind that conceives faults in these spiritual teachers and to produce easily the great faith that sees whatever they do as beneficial.

The fourth contemplation is that you cannot be sure of appearances. Even if it appears quite certain to you that someone is not a buddha, you cannot be certain that you are correct. Maitreya first appeared to the great master Asanga as a sick, wounded dog. And Bhikshu Upadhana couldn't even see the vast good qualities of Shakyamuni Buddha despite having served the Buddha for twenty-four years! When the Buddha would go for alms and tell people particulars about their past karma, Upadhana saw the Buddha as a charlatan. Even the great master Naropa initially saw his guru Tilopa as someone doing negative actions. So when you see faults in your teachers, you shouldn't put complete trust in your own perceptions. For though you seem to be perceiving flaws outside you, it's quite possible the problem lies inside you—that you're projecting your own internal flaws onto the external teacher. When practicing tantra, we train our minds to forgo ordinary appearances in order to cultivate divine appearance. It's similar here. You block your own perception of faults to develop a pure view.

Another traditional story related to this final contemplation is of Sudhana, who traveled to the realm of King Anala to receive a very secret instruction from him. When Sudhana arrived at King Anala's place, he saw piles of dead bodies. King Anala seemed to be punishing criminals by chopping up their bodies and piling the corpses! Sudhana lost his faith and decided to leave when a voice came from the sky, saying "Great sage, remember those instructions!" Inspired by this voice, he went to the king to ask about the secret teachings. The king, aware of Sudhana's doubts, told him how he had the power to emanate many magical forms. "Those people who you're seeing punished are not really beings. I've gained the magical power to emanate forms. Those people being cut and piled up are my own magical emanations. I'm doing that activity to control my people, preventing violence and crime." The appearance was bad, but things weren't as they appeared.[32]

In ordinary life, children often misperceive their parents as being mean or unreasonable when they set boundaries, such as making the child do her homework, not eat too many sweets, or stay in at night to keep safe. As adults, we also often misunderstand other people's intentions, thinking that they are negative when they're actually being kind. If you bring such everyday experiences to mind, then it shouldn't be difficult for you to recognize that your perceptions of faults in your gurus are not entirely trustworthy.

> With this supplication streams of five-colored nectars together with rays of light descend from the body of your guru deity seated upon your crown. These streams enter the bodies and minds of all sentient beings and yourself, thereby purifying [all misdeeds and obstructions accumulated from beginningless time. In particular these streams purify all the misdeeds, obscurations, sicknesses, and spirit possessions that develop the mind that conceives faults in these spiritual teachers and] that prevent [the ability to produce easily the great faith that sees whatever they do as good. Your and all others' bodies have the nature of pristine, luminous light. All your and others' good qualities, such as long lifespan and merit, are increased and expanded. In particular], think that these streams have produced in the minds of yourself and all others the special realization [that enables you to not produce for even an instant the mind that conceives faults in these spiritual teachers and to produce easily the great faith that sees whatever they do as beneficial].

Visualizing your gurus in front of you and engaging in these four contemplations, develop the types of faith described earlier, concluding with the descent of nectars and light rays.

Remembering Your Teachers' Kindness and Developing Respect

Visualize the spiritual teachers in front of you. Then think:

> These spiritual teachers are extremely kind to me. By their kindness I have understood the profound path that bestows easily the precious high state of a completely perfect buddha, the supreme liberation that abandons all sufferings of samsara and the lower realms. Therefore, guru deity, please bless the minds of myself and all mother sentient beings to produce easily the great respect that remembers the kindness of these spiritual teachers.

With this supplication streams of five-colored nectars together with rays of light descend from the body of your guru deity seated upon your crown. These streams enter the bodies and minds of all sentient beings and yourself, thereby purifying [all the misdeeds and obstructions accumulated from beginningless time. In particular these streams purify all the misdeeds, obscurations, sicknesses, and spirit possessions] that prevent [the ability to produce easily the great respect that remembers the kindness of these spiritual teachers. Your and all others' bodies have the nature of pristine, luminous light. All your and others' good qualities, such as long lifespan and merit, are increased and expanded. In particular], think that these streams have produced in the minds of yourself and all others the special realization [that enables you to produce easily the great respect that remembers the kindness of these spiritual teachers].

You develop feelings of respect and devotion for your gurus by contemplating their profound kindness to you. You can contemplate the gurus' kindness by reflecting on four points: that your guru is much kinder to you than all the buddhas, that your guru is kind in teaching you the holy Dharma, that your guru is kind in blessing your mental continuum, and that your guru is kind in attracting you by giving you gifts.

I won't go through these points in great detail, but in brief the guru's most important kindness is in teaching you the Dharma. Every happiness up to the ultimate happiness of full enlightenment comes from practicing the Dharma you've learned from your teachers. There is no greater kindness than giving Dharma teachings! As far as the guru being kinder to you than all the previous buddhas, though those buddhas were greatly compassionate, you yourself didn't have the merit to be able to hear the Dharma from them. It's only your teacher who guides you along the path. If you take a long-term perspective, then it's clear that no one anywhere is kinder to you than your spiritual teachers. If you think about this in detail, you will naturally develop much gratitude, respect, and devotion.

The goal of these contemplations is not to develop an inferential valid cognition that your teacher is Buddha Vajradhara. Rather it is to have your perception of your teachers' kindness and good qualities overwhelm any perceptions of faults that arise. It's similar to when you really adore someone—you focus so wholeheartedly on their good qualities that any perception of their faults is totally overshadowed. This naturally makes you feel closer and closer to that person. So for your practice it's excellent to read the lines from *Easy Path* and then to contemplate the reasons and quotations given here. In that way, your experience of faith and devotion will grow naturally and organically. When the appearance of faults arises to your mind, again apply those lines of reasoning and use them to gradually transform your way of thinking. This is how you gradually train in devotion.

You should understand that with this point and the later contemplations on the stages of the path to enlightenment, you have to analyze the lines of thinking again and again to train your mind. It takes many sessions to gradually familiarize your mind with a new way of thinking. So you repeatedly think through the contemplations described, occasionally also imagining the descent of nectars and light rays.

Also, to effectively familiarize yourself with the contemplations on the stages of the path to enlightenment, it's very helpful if you gradually memorize the outline for each major contemplation. If you memorize just one benefit of relying on the spiritual teacher each day, then after ten days you'll know all of those by heart. In the same way, it won't take very long to memorize the other points for developing faith and respect. *Easy Path* presents things in a somewhat condensed way, so you can conjoin the outlines here with those from *Swift Path* or from Je Tsongkhapa's *Great Treatise on the Stages of the Path,* or from Pabongka Rinpoche's *Liberation in the Palm of Your Hand* when you go about memorizing outlines.

How to Rely on the Spiritual Teacher in Deed

Visualizing the spiritual teachers in front of you, think:

> For the sake of these spiritual teachers, who are actually buddhas, I'll freely give my resources, body, life, and so on. I'll especially please them through the offering of practicing according to their instructions. Guru deity, please bless [me and all others] to be able to do this.

With this supplication streams of five-colored nectars together with rays of light descend from the body of your guru deity seated upon your crown. These streams enter the bodies and minds of all sentient beings and yourself, thereby purifying [all the misdeeds and obstructions accumulated from beginningless time. In particular these streams purify all the misdeeds, obscurations, sicknesses, and spirit possessions] that prevent [the ability to give up freely your resources, body, life, and so on for the sake of your spiritual teachers, and to please them through the offering of practicing according to their word. Your and all others' bodies have the nature of pristine, luminous light. All your and others' good qualities, such as long lifespan and merit, are increased and expanded. In particular], think that these streams have produced in the minds of yourself and all others the special realization [that enables you to give up freely your resources, body, life, and so on for the sake of your spiritual teachers and to please them by the offering of practicing according to their word].

"Giving your body" in this context refers to physically offering service to your guru. "Giving your life" in this context refers to not turning back from or giving up your Dharma practices even at those times when you encounter real dangers while practicing. Risking your life to benefit others in your practice is also an example of this. "Giving your resources" means making offerings from things that you own. The best offering to your gurus is practicing the instructions you've learned from them. Giving up negative actions that your teacher has advised against while doing Dharma practices according to his instructions is a real offering pleasing to the mind of your guru.

PRACTICING BETWEEN MEDITATION SESSIONS

Conclusion [of Your Session]
Meditating on the guru deity seated upon the crown of your head, make supplications, recite mantras, and dedicate the roots of virtue that come from those actions with strong aspiration to achieve the temporary and final objectives of yourself and others.

What to Do Between Meditation Sessions
Furthermore, in between sessions, look at the scriptures and commentaries that show the way to rely on the spiritual teacher, restrain the doors of your senses through mindfulness and introspection, eat moderately, make effort in the yoga of sleeping, do what should be done at the time of going to sleep, and make effort in the yogas of bathing and eating.

Easy Path here gives some specific advice for how to conduct yourself between meditation sessions. This advice appears repeatedly throughout the text. I'll explain it once, and you should apply the same understanding to the later occurrences.

Generally you should restrain the doors of your senses by being mindful and introspective. *Mindfulness* here means always remaining aware of the Dharma that you're practicing—in this case developing faith and respect for your spiritual teachers. *Introspection* refers to guarding the doors of your own six senses—being aware of how you are relating to sights, sounds, smells, tastes, tactile sensations, and thoughts. "Guarding" means not following thoughts or feelings of attachment when you experience desirable objects or people, and not following thoughts or feelings of aversion and hatred when you experience objects or people you find undesirable. Thus you should be introspective, notice such thoughts, and let them go while returning your mindfulness to training your mind in the path. It's also good between sessions to read books related to what you're meditating about. For example, if you're meditating on relying on the spiritual guide, then between sessions you may read books like the biographies of Ever-Crying Bodhisattva or of Milarepa.

Easy Path advises eating moderately—not too much or too little. Tibetan medicine advises thinking of the four quarters of the volume of your stomach and then at mealtime filling two quarters with food and one with water, leaving the last quarter empty. The food you eat should be healthy, easily digestible, and fresh. Food should be acquired ethically, which means not purchasing it with money obtained through wrong livelihood or by selling holy objects. *Easy Path* also advises to "make effort in the yoga of sleeping." Technically, the meaning is that you divide the period of darkness at any given time of year into thirds. Then try to stay awake and practice Dharma during the first third and last third of the night, only sleeping in the middle third. If you find this too difficult, then perhaps you can sleep around six hours, doing Dharma practice in the morning and again before bed.

Easy Path also mentions practices to be done when going to sleep. For positioning your body, it's best to point your head to the north, which is auspicious for Buddha's teachings to remain long in the world; face west, which is auspicious for being reborn in Amitabha's western paradise; point your feet south, which is auspicious for long life; and have your back to the east, which is auspicious for being free from attachment to samsaric pleasures. Lie on your right side when going to sleep. This is called the *lion posture* and is how the Buddha slept. By lying in this posture like the Buddha and recalling his enlightened qualities, you accumulate much merit. Sleeping in other positions may bring obstacles to your meditation; face down is the way animals sleep and may increase ignorance, while sleeping face up may increase your desire. While you are going to sleep, generate a positive mind by meditating on emptiness, love, compassion, and bodhichitta. If you fall asleep with such positive thoughts, then your whole time sleeping becomes virtuous.

Next, *Easy Path* mentions the yoga of bathing. All your normal, daily activities are to be integrated into your practice of Dharma. As *Easy Path* is related to tantric practice, when you bathe, imagine Vajrasattva pouring purifying nectar onto you. You can also recite his mantra while bathing. While you're cleaning the dirt off your body, think also of cleansing your mind—your negative karma as well as your broken vows and commitments.

The yoga of eating can be performed in various ways. In the Vinaya tradition focused on individual liberation, you think of food as you would medicine, consuming it without attachment in order to keep yourself healthy. A verse you can recite for this practice is: "Viewing this food solely as medicine, I enjoy it without craving or aversion. Driven neither by vanity nor the pursuit of physical prowess, I eat simply for sustenance." In the bodhisattva tradition, you think of the many tiny beings—germs and so forth—living inside your body, giving food to them to benefit them now and also so that later they can become your disciples so you can lead them to enlightenment. You also think that you are eating to live so as to complete your practice of the path in order to become a buddha for the benefit of all sentient beings. A verse you can recite for this practice is: "Now I gather the small creatures inside my body by giving food; in the future I will gather them by giving Dharma. May I enjoy this food and drink in order to achieve the state of enlightenment for other sentient beings."

In the tantric tradition, you can recite *Om Ah Hum* to bless the food. Ordinarily people recite this mantra three times. You think that with the first recitation the food is cleansed and purified, with the second it is transformed into nectar, and with the third is becomes inexhaustible. Alternatively, you can recite this mantra seven times, thinking that the first three purify the three negative karmic actions of body, the next four purify the four negative actions of speech, and your pure motivation while reciting purifies your mental negative karma. Then offer it to your guru, the buddhas, and the bodhisattvas. A verse you can recite for this practice is, "I gather this magnificent food of a hundred tastes, offering it to the buddhas and bodhisattvas out of devotion. May all sentient beings enjoy as a result the inexhaustible food of meditative concentration."

You can use that verse for offering food in the traditions of the lower tantras or of highest yoga tantra. Each deity of highest yoga tantra has its own mantras and visualizations for blessing food. You can apply those if you wish. And you can think of the food as nectar in celestial containers at a ritual feast, or *tsok*, offering to yourself in the aspect of the deity and to your guru and all holy beings.

Actually in tantric practice, you can recite *Om Ah Hum* three times to bless and offer almost anything. For example, you can recite it to bless your clothes and then offer them to yourself in the form of the deity. You can recite it to bless your home, with the first recitation purifying all bad qualities of the house, the second transforming it into a mandala, and the third making it inexhaustible. Then you offer that divine mansion to yourself in the form of a guru deity. This mantra is the essence of the body, speech, and mind of all the buddhas. Reciting it to bless objects and then to offer them is a very skillful method to easily accumulate vast merit.

3. Precious Human Rebirth

Contemplating the Human Life of Freedoms and Opportunities
II. After relying on the spiritual teacher, the stages of mental
   training
   A. The exhortation to utilize the essence of freedoms and
      opportunities
      1. What to do during the actual meditative session
         a. Preparation
         b. Actual session
            (1) Thinking about the great importance of free-
                doms and opportunities
            (2) Thinking about the difficulty of finding them
         c. Conclusion
      2. What to do between sessions

Preparation
The preparation is the same as in the previous session, all the
way down to the supplication:

> I pray to you, unity of the objects of refuge,
> my guru supreme deity, Shakyamuni Vajradhara.

Then:

> All mother sentient beings and I have been born in sam-
> sara and have endured a host of intense sufferings over a
> long time. This is due to not generating in our minds the

special realization of the great importance and difficulty
of finding freedoms and opportunities. Therefore, guru
deity, please bless all mother sentient beings and me now
to produce the special realization of the great importance
and difficulty of finding freedoms and opportunities.

With this supplication streams of five-colored nectars together
with rays of light descend from the body of your guru deity
seated upon your crown. These streams enter the bodies and
minds of all sentient beings and yourself, thereby purifying all
the misdeeds and obstructions accumulated from beginningless time. In particular these streams purify all the misdeeds,
obscurations, sicknesses, and spirit possessions that prevent the
development of the special realization of the great importance
and difficulty of finding the freedoms and opportunities. Your
and all others' bodies have a nature of pristine, luminous light.
All your and others' good qualities, such as long lifespan and
merit, are increased and expanded. In particular, think that
these streams have produced in the minds of yourself and all
others the special realization of the great importance and difficulty of finding the freedoms and opportunities.

In terms of the general outline for this meditation subject, after the
preliminaries, *Easy Path* has two sections: the great importance of the
freedoms and opportunities and the difficulty of finding them. Most
texts on the stages of the path have an additional section prior to these
two on identifying the eighteen qualities of freedom and opportunity
that characterize a precious human rebirth. After discussing the preliminaries, I'll discuss those eighteen qualities, because you have to be
able to identify a precious human rebirth in order to appreciate its great
importance and rarity.

The preparation is generally the same as I described earlier: you
engage in the six preliminary practices, the nine-round breathing exercise to balance the wind elements in your body, and so forth. You must
do those at the beginning of your first meditation session of the day.

If you are doing two or more sessions per day, then you don't have to repeat the six preliminaries. Instead, at the end of your first session, you don't dissolve Guru Shakyamuni Buddha atop your head; you keep your guru there throughout the day. So then, when you sit down for subsequent meditation sessions, you simply reassert the visualization of your guru deity atop your head and do the seven-limb practice in relation to him. If your mind is disturbed, then you can also do the nine rounds of breathing. Then you can simply begin meditating.

One small difference in the preliminaries that does come with each meditation topic is the brief prayer to the guru that relates to the specific meditation you'll be engaging in. Here the prayer relates to human life of freedoms and opportunities. This prayer describes how you continue circling in samsara because you don't recognize how meaningful and important your human life is. Therefore you waste this rare and precious opportunity. So pray to your guru to bless you to realize the great benefits of a human life of freedoms and opportunities so that you can take its essence. Having made such requests, visualize the descent of five-colored nectars and light rays as described earlier.

IDENTIFYING A LIFE OF FREEDOMS AND OPPORTUNITIES

Having a precious human rebirth of freedoms and opportunities entails having eight freedoms and ten opportunities. Having freedom means the freedom to pursue and achieve your goals. The eight are freedom from each of the eight states of bondage. The first four are freedom from four kinds of nonhuman rebirth—as hell being, hungry ghost, animal, or long-lived god. In the hells, beings are totally overwhelmed by pain and suffering and so have no freedom at all to practice Dharma or pursue spiritual goals. Hungry ghosts experience extremely intense, chronic hunger and thirst; constantly suffering and searching for food and drink leaves them as well with no leisure for practicing Dharma. Animals are clouded by ignorance and so have a very difficult time learning anything; even if you try for a long time you cannot teach them to train their own minds in the path to enlightenment. Some long-lived gods or goddesses remain absorbed in deep states of meditation, blocking all sensory perceptions, and so cannot train in compassion or do other Dharma practices. Other gods and goddesses are too caught up in the sensory pleasures of heavenly realms to find any time for developing their minds in the path. Thus these four nonhuman states are extremely unfavorable for practicing the path to enlightenment.

Next come four unfavorable conditions in the human realm. One of these is being reborn human but in a time when no Buddha has come and so the Dharma doesn't exist on the planet where you're living. Of course, you cannot practice Dharma under such circumstances. Another obstacle is when the Dharma has been taught but you are born and live in a remote region where that Dharma has not spread. This second obstacle can also include your being a barbarian, which means having no understanding of spiritual matters and only focusing on worldly wealth, comfort, power, and the like. Another is being reborn without the ability to understand language or to speak; under such circumstances you cannot study or contemplate Dharma. The final freedom is being free from having wrong views; even if you are born as a human where Dharma is flourishing, if you do not believe in karma or in the possibility of enlightenment, then this is very unfavorable for practicing the path to enlightenment! Right now you are free of those eight unfavorable conditions, and that is extremely precious.

Next come the ten opportunities. Five of these are personal and five are related to others. The first of the five personal opportunities is being a human being. Having a human body and brain is the best life form in the universe for practicing Dharma. As a human you can generate really intense, pure compassion and bodhichitta. Other life forms cannot generate such strong bodhichitta. The second personal opportunity is being reborn in a central land. There are various ways of defining a central land, but in brief it's said that there are four planets in this region with human beings living on them, and of those planets Earth is the most favorable for Dharma practice. The third personal opportunity is having all six of your senses—sight, hearing, smell, taste, touch, and mental sense—working properly. Of these, having the ability to hear and read Dharma and then having your mind working well so you can understand what you've heard or read are especially important. The fourth is not having done any of the five immediate negative actions. This means you have not killed your own mother or father, killed an arhat, drawn blood with malice from a buddha, or caused a schism in the Sangha community. Someone who has committed one of those five especially negative actions does not have a fully qualified precious human rebirth unless he or she purifies this heavy negative karma. The next is having faith in the Buddha's teachings. Some scholars describe this endowment as "having faith in the Vinaya," holding that it means specifically having faith in the Buddha's teachings on the vows as taught in the Vinaya. Others describe it as "having faith in the three baskets," which includes the Vinaya teachings, the Sutra collection, and the Abhidharma as well. And finally, some scholars say that these two positions are not contradictory because the real meaning of Vinaya in this context includes the teachings on overcoming transgressions as taught in the Vinaya itself as well as the teachings on overcoming the afflictive emotions, which are taught in detail in the other two collections.

The five opportunities related to others are that a Buddha has come, that that Buddha has taught the Dharma, that the teachings remain, that those teachings are being followed and are leading beings to gain realizations, and that others have love in their hearts so that they help and support practitioners. Actually, we do not have a fully qualified form of the first four of these. A fully qualified form means that the Buddha is still present, that that Buddha or his arhat students are teaching the Dharma, that their teachings remain without degeneration, and that there are still significant numbers of practitioners gaining realizations of those teachings. The Buddha passed to parinirvana in India long ago, the arhats who were his direct disciples have also long since passed away, and we live in a degenerate time when the teachings are in decline and we doesn't see large numbers of practitioners attaining the fruits of the practice. But the essential lineages of the Buddha's teachings do remain, there are beings in this world who have gained realizations, and we can study with them. So we do have a facsimile of those four endowments. The fifth of these relational endowments is that there are people who lovingly serve as benefactors. As there are people who kindly organize Dharma teachings, offer robes and food to the ordained

Sangha, and so forth, we do have this endowment in a fully qualified manner.

You should thus contemplate those eighteen qualities in order to understand your current situation, which is extremely precious and meaningful! Just being alive today as a human being is wonderful, and then you also have these special qualities that give you so much opportunity to practice Dharma. If you think deeply about this, you'll feel genuine joy. You'll want to take the essence of your life.

THINKING ABOUT THE GREAT IMPORTANCE OF FREEDOMS AND OPPORTUNITIES

Meditating on the guru deity seated upon the crown of your head, contemplate as follows:

"Freedom" is having the time to practice the holy teaching. "Opportunity" entails having the complete inner and outer favorable conditions for practicing the teaching.

In short, this life of freedoms and opportunities that I have obtained is very important. Depending on it I am able to practice generosity, ethics, patience, and so forth, which cause the marvelous resources and bodies of high status. In particular, generating the three vows within this life, I can attain easily even the high state of a buddha within one short lifespan in this degenerate age.

Therefore I will not waste this life of complete freedoms and opportunities, which is difficult to find and once found so important, but will take its essence. Guru deity, please bless me to be able to do that.

With this supplication streams of five-colored nectars together with rays of light descend from the body of your guru deity seated upon your crown. These streams enter the bodies and minds of all sentient beings and yourself, thereby purifying [all the misdeeds and obstructions accumulated from beginningless time. In particular they purify all the misdeeds, obscurations, sicknesses, and spirit possessions] that prevent [the development of the special realization of the great importance of freedoms and opportunities. Your and all others' bodies have a nature of pristine, luminous light. All your and others' good qualities, such as long lifespan and merit, are increased and expanded. In particular], think that these streams have produced in the minds of yourself and all others the special realization [of the great importance of freedoms and opportunities].

Here contemplate how you yourself have achieved something extremely important and meaningful. This sort of life form that you have right now, qualified by those eighteen qualities, is unbelievably precious. You can achieve anything with this kind of life!

It's important for you to understand the great benefits you can extract from your current situation—the benefits you can gain from this human rebirth. By using this opportunity well, you can achieve good future rebirths, permanent liberation from samsara, the realization of bodhichitta, or even the state of a fully enlightened buddha—you can even achieve buddhahood in this one brief lifetime!

If you wish to achieve a good future rebirth, you can definitely do so by practicing ethics now. If you wish for wealth, you can definitely achieve that by practicing generosity in this life. If you wish for good friends and family in your future lives, you can achieve that by practicing patience. You can use this life to create the causes for whatever kind of wonderful future lives you wish for. Of course, those are temporary benefits. You can also achieve ultimate benefits with this life. If you wish to achieve the state of individual liberation from samsara, you can achieve that by practicing the three higher trainings in ethics, concentration, and wisdom now. If you wish to achieve buddhahood, you have the freedom so long as you still have this precious human rebirth to progress toward that goal by practicing bodhichitta any time you like. If you wish to achieve buddhahood very quickly, you can even do that by engaging in the generation stage and completion stage practices of highest yoga tantra, which exist in this world! Lama Tsongkhapa said that if you contemplate these benefits of freedoms and opportunities, then you'll feel very sorry to use your time for small or meaningless purposes.

Since you may not find a human body or get the chance to study Dharma again, you should at least use this precious opportunity to take refuge and take vows to not kill, steal, lie, and so forth. Anyone can gradually progress in avoiding the ten nonvirtuous actions, which are described below. Thus, you should at the very least take this chance to engage in the small-scope practices so that you don't leave this jewel-filled island of your precious human life empty handed.

THINKING ABOUT THE DIFFICULTY OF FINDING THE FREEDOMS AND OPPORTUNITIES

Meditating on the guru deity seated upon the crown of your head, contemplate as follows:

Besides being very important, this life of freedoms and opportunities is also so difficult to obtain. For the most part beings—humans and so forth—engage very strongly in the ten nonvirtuous deeds and so on, preventing the attainment of the freedoms and opportunities.

In particular, in order to obtain a life of complete freedoms and opportunities, you need a basis of pure ethics, assisted by giving and the other perfections, conjoined with pure aspirational prayers. Thus very few beings will even achieve such causes. Relative to the bad transmigrations—as animals and so on—the attainment of merely a good transmigration seems impossible. Even relative to good transmigrations, this attainment of a life of complete freedoms and opportunities is extremely rare, like a daytime star.

Therefore I will not waste this one-time attainment of a life of complete freedoms and opportunities—which is difficult to find and, once found, so valuable—but will take its essence.

Moreover, the method of taking its essence is to rely on the guru who is inseparable from Buddha and then to practice the essence of the Mahayana instructions given by him or her. Having done so, I will easily obtain the high state of a buddha in this very lifetime. Guru deity, please bless me to be able to do that.

With this supplication streams of five-colored nectars together with rays of light descend from the body of your guru deity seated upon your crown. These streams enter the bodies and minds of all sentient beings and yourself, thereby purifying [all the misdeeds and obstructions accumulated from beginningless time. In particular they purify all the misdeeds, obscurations, sicknesses, and spirit possessions] that prevent [the development of the special realization of the difficulty of finding the freedoms and opportunities. Your and all others' bodies have a nature of pristine, luminous light. All your and others' good qualities, such as long lifespan and merit, are increased and expanded. In particular], think that these streams have produced in the minds of yourself and all others the special realization [of the difficulty of finding the freedoms and opportunities].

It would be a big mistake to let this life pass by assuming that you'll find another precious human rebirth qualified by the freedoms and opportunities again in the future. Such a rebirth is extremely difficult to encounter! Stages-of-the-path texts generally discuss the rarity of such a rebirth by discussing its causes, providing examples, and looking at its nature. In *Easy Path*, the Panchen Lama particularly focuses on its causes. He notes that to achieve such a life, one must practice very pure ethics, which is very rare. But that's not sufficient. One must also practice generosity, patience, and so forth. And then one must conjoin those practices with heartfelt, pure prayers. If you look around, it's easy to see that sentient beings rarely engage in creating the combination of such causes.

The great Tibetan yogini Machik Lapdron said if you compare those who do practice Dharma with those who don't, practitioners are as rare as the *udumvara* flower, which only blooms when at the time of a Buddha. It's very hard to come across people practicing genuinely. Lama Tsongkhapa said if you contemplate the difficulty of finding a human form with the freedoms and opportunities, then you won't remain lackadaisical about spiritual practice.

If you contemplate deeply and sincerely the great meaning of this life and the difficulty of finding another like it, then you will naturally be more and more intent on not wasting your precious time! Think again and again about the eighteen special qualities of your life, of how amazingly beneficial it can be for you, and about the extreme difficulty of finding such a situation again in the future. Then you will want to take its essence by practicing the small, medium, or great scope of spiritual practice. Particularly when you contemplate how you can achieve buddhahood itself, you will naturally want to make use of your life and won't take waking up each day for granted! You will feel so happy to be alive and to be able to practice Dharma.

Conclusion
It is the same as before.

What to Do Between Sessions
In between sessions look at the scriptures and commentaries that reveal the part of the doctrine on freedoms and opportunities, just as described above.

I explained these points earlier, so you can refer to those explanations and apply them here.

4. Small-Scope Mind-Training Practices

How to Use the Essence of the Freedoms and Opportunities
1. Training the mind in the stages of the path shared with
   small-scope beings
   a. What to do during the actual meditative session
      (1) Preparation
      (2) Actual session
         (a) Contemplating impermanence and death
         (b) Contemplating the suffering of the lower realms
         (c) Practicing going for refuge to the Three Jewels
         (d) Developing the faith of conviction in karmic
            cause and effect
      (3) Conclusion
   b. What to do between sessions

Preparation
The preparation is the same as in the previous session, all the
way down to the supplication:

> I pray to you, unity of the objects of refuge,
> my guru supreme deity, Shakyamuni Vajradhara.

Then:

> All mother sentient beings and I have been born in sam-
> sara and have endured a host of intense sufferings over a
> long time. This is due to not having contemplated imper-
> manence and death; not having gone wholeheartedly for

refuge to the Three Jewels after fearing the sufferings of the lower realms; and not having engaged properly in adopting virtue and rejecting nonvirtue after having developed the faith of conviction in karmic cause and effect. Therefore, guru deity, please bless all mother sentient beings and me now to be able to be aware of impermanence and death, to fear the sufferings of the lower realms and then go wholeheartedly for refuge to the Three Jewels, and to adopt virtue properly and reject wrongdoing after having developed the faith of conviction in karmic cause and effect.

With this supplication streams of five-colored nectars together with rays of light descend from the body of your guru deity seated upon your crown. These streams enter the bodies and minds of all sentient beings and yourself, thereby purifying all the misdeeds and obstructions accumulated from beginningless time. In particular they [purify all the misdeeds, obscurations, sicknesses, and spirit possessions] that prevent the development of the special realizations of [the awareness of death and impermanence, refuge in the Three Jewels after fearing the lower realms, and the adoption of virtue and rejection of wrongdoing after developing the faith of conviction in karmic cause and effect]. Your and all others' bodies have a nature of pristine, luminous light. All your and others' good qualities, such as long lifespan and merit, are increased and expanded. In particular, think that these streams have produced in the minds of yourself and all others the special realization of [the awareness of death and impermanence, refuge in the Three Jewels after fearing the lower realms, and the adoption of virtue and rejection of wrongdoing after generating faith of conviction in the effects of actions].

NEXT COME four practices shared with beings of small scope. "Shared" here means that even if you're aspiring to practice the middle or the great scope, you must also train well in these practices. Success in those practices is completely dependent upon doing these practices well.

As noted in the outline from *Easy Path* above, there are four general topics to meditate upon in common with the persons of small scope. First come meditations on impermanence and death, then on the sufferings of lower realms, then on refuge, and then finally on generating conviction and faith in the infallibility of the laws of karma.

The Vinaya teachings divide small-scope beings into three types: ordinary, middling, supreme small scope. Ordinary small-scope persons only wish for happiness in this life and for that purpose engage solely in negative actions. Middling small-scope persons wish only for happiness of this life and then engage in both negative and positive actions to achieve that. Supreme small-scope persons only wish for happiness of future lifetimes and therefore engage in wholesome, positive actions. This Vinaya classification's supreme small-scope person corresponds with the small-scope person as described in the stages-of-the-path tradition. The ordinary and middling small-scope persons described by the Vinaya are not yet practicing Dharma. Only the person who is performing wholesome actions aimed at the happiness of future lives has begun practicing spirituality; such a person has entered the door of Dharma practice.

Thus a small-scope practitioner engages in virtuous actions to attain higher rebirths in the human or god realms. "Higher" rebirth means having a better body, better friends, and more wealth or enjoyments than those in the lower realms. Being ethical is the karmic cause for a better physical body, being patient is the cause for better relationships, and being generous is the cause for better wealth. Human and divine realms are called "higher" realms because these things are better there than they are in the lower realms.

Meditations on impermanence and death are the first mind training of this small scope, inspiring us to enter upon the practice of Dharma.

CONTEMPLATING IMPERMANENCE AND DEATH

Just prior to meditating on impermanence and death, it's good to contemplate the disadvantages of not meditating on impermanence and death and the benefits of meditating on them. This brings enthusiasm for the meditation itself. Six disadvantages of not contemplating those topics are that if you don't deeply understand impermanence then you won't really study the Dharma; even if you do study some Dharma you won't practice it; even if you engage in some practice your practice won't be pure; you won't be able to generate the effort required for successful spiritual practice; you'll engage in many negative actions; and you may die with regret. The six benefits of engaging in contemplations on impermanence and death are that they are highly beneficial for your mind, especially in helping you to take the essence of your life; they are powerful in helping you to overcome afflictive emotions; they are helpful at the outset of your practice by motivating you to start out on the path; they are helpful in the middle of your practice by motivating you to continue on your journey; they are helpful at the end of your practice by inspiring you to reach the end of the path to enlightenment; and they allow you to die with joy and peace. These points are quite straightforward.

There are many ways to contemplate impermanence and death. One tradition is to contemplate external impermanence, internal impermanence, and moment-by-moment impermanence. Another tradition is to meditate using many examples and scriptural quotations. The unique tradition Lama Tsongkhapa taught his disciples is to contemplate the three roots, nine reasons, and three certainties. This is the approach followed in *Easy Path*.

Death Is Certain

Meditating on the guru deity seated on your crown, contemplate as follows:

This life of freedoms and opportunities is difficult to find; once found, it is so valuable; and it perishes quickly. For certain, the Lord of Death will come. That is, I will definitely die because (1) there is no turning away death by any internal or external conditions; (2) my lifespan decreases without interruption and cannot be increased; and (3) even when I am alive, there is no time to practice the teachings.

As before, you begin by meditating on the guru deity atop your head, engaging in either a long or brief version of the preliminaries ending with the descent of nectars and light rays to bless you particularly to gain the realization of impermanence and death. First of the three roots is certainty of death referred to in the text by the phrase "For certain, the Lord of Death will come"—the grim reaper of death comes for everyone. This first root has three reasons that you contemplate to bring your mind to awareness of death's certainty: there is no turning away death through outer or inner conditions, the nature of things is that our lifespans diminish continually and cannot be increased, and even while we're alive we have little time to practice Dharma.

In terms of outer conditions, it's quite clear that wealth, possessions, and power cannot stop death. Inner conditions refer to special practices to give rise to the *vidyadhara*, or "knowledge holder," state of immortality. Even people who do such practices and achieve this state of immortality also die! Nothing anywhere can free you from the fact of your own mortality.

That your lifespan decreases means it's continually slipping away, second by second. Karmically, there's a maximum length of time your life can last; your body will naturally fall apart at some point. You cannot add to this maximum no matter what you do. And if you do some activity for an hour, then at the end of that hour you are definitely one hour closer to the time of your death! Even if you're idly spending your time distracted, your lifespan is being used up. If you do something for a month, then a month of your life is totally gone. If you do something for a year, then a year of your life is finished. Your time is a waterfall, pouring down without ever pausing.

For the third reason, you contemplate how even while you're alive there's little time for spiritual practice. Mentally divide your life into three periods. The first is from your conception up to age twenty; during this time you were too immature and inexperienced to practice Dharma.

Then during your prime, adult years much of your time is spent sleeping, and when you're awake you're usually very busy working, parenting, eating, driving, shopping, doing chores, talking with friends, watching sports or videos, surfing the internet, and so forth. Then you find yourself in old age, when even if you feel urgency about spiritual matters, your physical and mental limitations keep you from being able to do much. If you consider all of this, you find that there are perhaps just five or six years in total when you can effectively engage in Dharma practice. Kelsang Gyatso, the Seventh Dalai Lama, expressed it powerfully when he wrote:

> Right from the moment of your birth, you have no freedom
> to stop for a moment your race toward the Lord of Death.
> What you call "living" is a journey on the great highway to
>   death.
> The mind of the criminal being led to the place of his execu-
>   tion is not content!

So if you contemplate the first root—the certainty of death—by way of these three reasons, you'll come to the first certainty: I must engage in Dharma practice.

The Time of Death Is Uncertain

> While death is certain, the time of death is completely uncertain, because (1) there is no certainty in regard to my lifespan in this world, (2) so many conditions bring about death and few conditions foster life, and (3) my body is fragile like a water bubble.

The second root is uncertainty of the time of death, which again has three reasons to contemplate. The first is that the lifespan on this planet is totally uncertain. On other planets there is a fixed lifespan, but on this earth one can die while still in the womb, as an infant, as a young child, or at any age. If you check around, it's obvious that this is true. People your present age die every day. The second reason is that there are so many conditions that bring about death and few that sustain life. Even the things that you use to sustain your life can cause your death. People take medicines to sustain their lives, for instance, but medicines also kill people. You have to eat to live, but there are many stories of people dying from eating certain foods. Even houses sometimes collapse on their occupants. The third reason is the fragility of your own body, which is like a water bubble. Even a tiny factor like a virus, bacteria, blood clot, or aneurism can ruin your fragile body and cause your death.

If you contemplate the second root—the uncertainty of the time of death—by way of these three reasons, you'll come to the second certainty: I must engage in Dharma practice right now!

Only Dharma Helps at the Time of Death

> When I die nothing whatsoever is helpful except for Dharma practice because (1) although I am surrounded by friends and relatives, I cannot take even one with me, however greatly they are loved; (2) however abundant the wondrous riches I have, I cannot take even a mere atom of them with me; and (3) I must separate from even the flesh and bones born with me.

The third root is that at the time of death, only Dharma practice helps you. Again this root has three reasons: friends and relatives cannot help, wealth cannot help, and even your own body cannot help you at the time of death. Actually, your attachment to friends, loved ones, and possessions not only doesn't help, it causes increased grief, sorrow, and fear at the time of death. These contemplations lead to the third certainty: I must engage in pure and perfect Dharma practice.

> Then what is the use of being attached to the marvels of this life? The enemy, death, will certainly come, and there is no certainty as to when it will come. As there is a risk that I might die even this very day, I must prepare for death. Furthermore, as preparation, I will practice the teachings right now purely,

without attachment to any of the marvels of this life. Bless me,
guru deity, to be able to do that.

This verse summarizes the three roots and three certainties. The "marvels of this life" are friends, relatives, reputation, wealth, and so forth.

Buton Rinpoche expressed the importance of meditating on impermanence and death by saying that if you don't think of this one thing, then that will block hundreds of other positive thoughts. If you don't think about this subject, you won't be able to think about hundreds of positive things that can bring about your full enlightenment. In a sutra, Buddha says, "Even if one has wealth and food to last for a hundred years, at the end of that one must depart empty handed. Even if one has clothing to last a hundred years, at the end of that one has to go on alone." Gungtang Rinpoche writes, "Even if the entire country is filled with gold, at death you cannot carry even one atom of gold with you. But if you've recited even one syllable of a mantra, then that can be your travel budget to the next life."

If we think carefully, there's no external phenomenon that doesn't teach us of impermanence. The changing of the seasons, the rising and setting of the sun and stars, the passing of days, months, and years, the changes in your own and others' bodies, the changes in your mind—all these teach impermanence. All outer phenomena teach of impermanence. Everything in your life teaches impermanence.

> With this supplication streams of five-colored nectars together
> with rays of light descend from the body of your guru deity
> seated upon your crown. These streams enter the bodies and
> minds of all sentient beings and yourself, thereby [purifying
> all the misdeeds and obstructions accumulated from begin-
> ningless time. In particular these streams] purify [all the mis-
> deeds, obscurations, sicknesses, and spirit possessions] that
> prevent [you from practicing the teachings right now purely,
> without attachment to any of the marvels of this life. Your and
> all others' bodies have the nature of pristine, luminous light.
> All your and others' good qualities, such as long lifespan and

merit, are increased and expanded. In particular], think that these streams have produced in the minds of yourself and all others the special realization [that enables you to practice the teachings right now purely, without attachment to any of the marvels of this life].

After contemplating the three roots, nine reasons, and three certainties, pray to your guru atop your crown for blessings to realize these points in meditation. Then imagine the descent of nectar and rays as before, remembering the various levels of meaning for the five colors, the nectars, and the rays and for visualizing your body as made of pristine, luminous light.

Contemplating the Sufferings of the Lower Realms

Meditating on the guru deity seated upon your crown, contemplate as follows:

This life of complete freedoms and opportunities—which is difficult to find and, once found, so valuable—also perishes quickly. After it's destroyed, I don't become nonexistent; I must be reborn.

Furthermore, my place of rebirth is not other than either a happy or bad transmigration. If I am reborn in a lower realm, as a hell being I will suffer from extreme heat, cold, and their effects; as a hungry ghost I will suffer acutely from hunger, thirst, and their effects; and as an animal I will have the inconceivable sufferings of stupidity, ignorance, and being eaten. I have no way of bearing these sufferings of the lower realms.

Therefore, at this time of obtaining a life of complete freedoms and opportunities—which is difficult to find and, once found, so valuable—I will attain the high state of a guru buddha who has abandoned all the sufferings of the lower realms. Bless me, guru deity, to be able to do that.

With this supplication streams of five-colored nectars together with rays of light descend from the body of your guru deity seated upon your crown. These streams enter the bodies and minds of all sentient beings and yourself, thereby [purifying all the misdeeds and obstructions accumulated from beginningless time. In particular these streams] purify [all the misdeeds, obscurations, sicknesses, and possessions] that prevent [your developing the special realization of the sufferings of bad transmigrations. Your and all others' bodies have the nature of pristine, luminous light. All your and others' good qualities, such as long lifespan and merit, are increased and expanded. In particular,] think that these streams have produced in the minds of yourself and all others the special realization of [the sufferings of bad transmigrations].

The second of the four practices for a person of small scope is contemplating the suffering of bad rebirths. You begin as before with the guru deity atop your own and all sentient beings' heads, making fervent prayers for blessings to be able to realize the suffering nature of the lower realms. Then contemplate on how death does not spell the end of your mindstream. You don't go out of existence at death; you must take rebirth either in higher or in lower realms. Which of these occurs for you is not a matter of choice; it depends on your actions—your karma. So visualize the specific sufferings of various lower realms. Think of the extreme cold and heat of the hell realms, of the extreme hunger and thirst of the hungry ghost realms, of the extreme ignorance of animals as well as of their being eaten by others. Thinking of and imagining the suffering of these realms in meditation motivates you to avoid negative actions and do positive actions.

Here, it's important to understand that death is not like a clump of hay being consumed by fire, leaving nothing behind. Death is not a mere cessation. Your mental continuum is beginningless and endless, so death is a transition. Your consciousness will continue on, leading you to take rebirth either in a happy place or in one of the three lower realms.

Negative actions lead to lower rebirths; positive actions lead to higher rebirths.

In *Manjushri's Own Words*, the Great Fifth Dalai Lama explains the causes for taking rebirth in the hell realms. Performing the ten negative actions very intensely is one such cause. Those ten are killing, stealing, sexual misconduct, lying, harsh speech, divisive speech, gossip, covetousness, ill will, and wrong views. Engaging in those ten actions intensely means doing them with the four qualities of a complete negative karma: doing the action intentionally, doing it motivated by a strong afflictive emotion, carrying it to conclusion, and feeling satisfied when you've completed it. If you do any negative action with these four factors present, it makes that action very powerful and can send you to a hell realm. The five immediate misdeeds—drawing blood from a buddha with ill intent, creating a schism in the Sangha, killing an arhat, killing one's mother, or killing one's father—also serve as causes for hell rebirth. The first three are grave due to the level of spiritual attainment of the object; the last two are grave due to the kindness one's parents have shown to oneself. Another such cause is intentionally holding to wrong views, which means strongly asserting that there's no such thing as karma, that enlightenment isn't possible, that the Three Jewels don't exist, and so forth. Taking individual liberation vows and then breaking them also creates a cause for rebirth in a hell realm. For example, if monks or nuns commit one of the four root downfalls—killing, stealing, sexual misconduct, or lying—they commit such an action. Taking the root bodhisattva or tantric vows and breaking them also serves as a cause for rebirth in a hell realm. Disrespecting bodhisattvas or one's own gurus with an attitude of hatred is also a cause for rebirth in hell.

Recognizing that you yourself have created some such causes, it's good to contemplate the sufferings of specific hells in detail. The eight hot hells are Continual Reviving, Black Line, Assemble and Be Crushed, Crying, Wailing, Hot, Extremely Hot, and Hell Without Respite. You visualize these eight in the center surrounded in the four cardinal directions by the four neighboring hell realms. When you gain freedom from the hot hells, you wind up in the neighboring hells—they are the hell of burning ashes where you're submerged to the knees in burning ashes, molten mud pool hell, plain of razor blades hell, and the hell that's a deep torrent of boiling water with no bridges. All the hot hells have a ground, walls, and ceiling of burning iron.

One scripture says it may be difficult to imagine such a place, but these are karmic results of having meted such harm to others. In some countries people cook chickens inside a steel box; they put a live chicken in thru a hole in the top, and the chicken plucks its own feathers and puts them under its feet to try to protect itself from the heat. It plucks itself. When the chicken tries to put its beak out the top for cooler air, the person pours the oil and spices inside the chicken's beak. If we can see that kind of suffering in the human realm, then it shouldn't be hard to imagine the sufferings of hells.

The causes for rebirth in the cold hells are taught in *Swift Path*. The eight cold hells are called Cold Blisters; Bursting Cold Blisters; "Achu," which expresses suffering from intense cold like shouting "Brrr"; "Gehue," which is a way of crying out even more intensely; Chattering Teeth, Bursting Like an Utpala Flower, Bursting Like a Lotus, and Greatly Bursting Like a Lotus. The last three names describe how the cold blisters of the beings reborn there burst open.

Next come the nature and causes for rebirth in hungry ghost realms, which are also taught in *Swift Path*. One cause of such rebirths is engaging in the ten negative actions described above but to a moderate degree, with a moderate amount of afflictive emotion. Additional causes of such rebirths include having afflictive emotions of craving and desire, miserliness, stealing, covetousness, not properly feeding one's workers, changing one's mind after dedicating part of one's wealth to a person or institution, stealing wealth and food from others and thereby causing them to starve, or calling a person who has gained Dharma realizations by the nickname "hungry ghost." Any of these can lead to rebirth as a hungry ghost. The three types of hungry ghosts are those with external obstructions, with internal obstructions, and with both outer and inner obstructions.

Causal factors for animal rebirth are engaging in the ten negative actions with little intensity and a small amount of afflictive emotion. Other causes for animal rebirth include abandoning the Dharma, disrespecting the Dharma, and disrespecting or criticizing spiritual teachers. The animal realm is divided into those who dwell "in the depths"— referring to those who live in the depths of the ocean or under the earth—and those who live in sunlight. We can easily see many of the kinds of sufferings experienced by animals, including lack of intelligence, cold, heat, and being eaten by others.

Some people don't like discussions of the intense sufferings of the lower realms. But Nagarjuna wrote in his *Precious Garland* that awareness of the horrific sufferings of the hells, the hunger and thirst of the hungry ghosts, and the stupidity and other sufferings of the animals should be cultivated on a daily basis. Contemplating these sufferings brings many benefits to your spiritual practice. First, thinking deeply of such sufferings helps propel you to stop engaging in negative actions. By generating an appropriate fear of harming others and of the pain it will cause, you generate the energy to be able to honestly assess your own actions, to purify your negativities, and to avoid committing harmful actions again.

Also the generation of renunciation of samsara begins with recognizing the terrible sufferings of the lower realms in which you've been reborn countless times. Renunciation is the gateway to Dharma practice; you only begin the spiritual path when you face our own and others' suffering. Through generating renunciation you begin seeking liberation. First you generate genuine renunciation of the lower realms, and then you progress to renouncing samsara as a whole.

Facing the oceans of real misery that exist in the universe also helps us to put our own problems in a realistic perspective. Once you've really contemplated the sufferings of the lower realms, you can face your own difficulties with greater bravery and perseverance. Another benefit of such contemplations is that they give rise to empathy for others. As you think of these sufferings, imagine yourself into the experience of beings suffering in those realms. This empathy is necessary for generating compassion. You cannot realize universal compassion or bodhichitta if you're not willing to empathically face the sufferings others undergo! You may find thinking of these sufferings frightening. But such fear is healthy. You have to face dark truths if you want to make progress in giving up your faults, generating positive qualities, realizing renunciation, and developing great compassion.

You can directly perceive the sufferings of animals by looking at the animals around you and also by watching films of animals in the wild. To understand the sufferings of beings in the other lower realms, you have to rely on descriptions given by the Buddha. You cannot see them directly, but you can use logic to understand them. If you see the Buddha as reliable by logically analyzing his teachings on suffering, impermanence, emptiness, and so forth, then you can rely on his descriptions of those realms.

In terms of how to meditate, it's helpful to recall that although you're not in the lower realms right now, you don't know what karma you created in the beginningless past. You can be very confident that you have created causes for such rebirths. Contemplate that you yourself may very well be reborn in those suffering realms just after you die. Of course, you'll feel that you couldn't possibly tolerate such sufferings! You can't even tolerate the much milder sufferings that come along in your daily life. If you think like this while recalling the causes of such rebirths, a sincere motivation and resolve to purify your negativities and engage in positive actions will naturally arise.

Once you've given rise to such sincere feelings, you should engage in the practice of the four powers of purification as they were explained above in the section on the preliminaries, resolving very strongly not to repeat those actions in the future. Also engage in various wholesome actions such as rejoicing, cultivating compassion, and so forth dedicated to gaining higher rebirths.

As before, complete your meditations by visualizing the descent of nectars and rays, cultivating a conviction that you and all others purify all obstacles to realizing these topics and then gain perfect realization of them.

GOING FOR REFUGE TO THE THREE JEWELS

Next comes the practice of going for refuge from your heart, which is extremely important and beneficial. When Atisha came to Tibet, he often taught on refuge. One of his disciples came to see him and told him that Tibetans were calling him "Refuge Lama." Atisha was very pleased by this, thinking that even his nickname would bring some benefit!

The Kadampa lama Chengawa was simply doing refuge practice. He said that because of his guru's blessings, he could realize calm abiding along with the concentrations of the generation and completion stages of highest yoga tantra, but leaving those aside, he focused instead on refuge practice.

Kadampa lama Neusurpa was about to realize the concentrations of the generation and completion stages of highest yoga tantra involving, respectively, complex visualization practices and the control of the subtle wind energies, but he said that instead of pursuing those, he just focused on refuge practice.

Lama Dromtonpa said that if someone asked him whether he'd choose someone with great philosophical knowledge of the three vehicles who lacked the practice of refuge or someone who simply practiced refuge but had no other knowledge, he'd choose the uneducated one who only practiced refuge.

So don't underestimate the importance of refuge practice. For ordinary people like us, the most pressing danger is falling into the lower realms, which totally blocks our chances for progress on the path to enlightenment. Practicing refuge at the time of death is the best way to insure that this won't happen. Even if you're a great scholar of Buddhist scriptures and philosophy, if you don't take refuge from your heart and avoid doing the ten nonvirtuous actions, your knowledge cannot protect you from falling into the lower realms. But taking refuge and avoiding the ten nonvirtuous actions can!

Actual refuge practice is not the recitation of verses; actual refuge takes place in your mind. If you rely wholeheartedly on the Three Jewels when you are facing good times or bad, that is taking refuge.

Of the three objects of refuge, the Dharma is the actual refuge. Some other religious traditions believe in a creator who to them would be their actual refuge. We do not believe in an external creator, and neither is the Buddha the actual refuge. Buddhists believe that karma is what leads to happiness and suffering; the Buddha cannot force us to be happy or free from suffering. The Buddha is a teacher who explains how suffering and happiness as well as samsara and enlightenment arise. The Dharma taught by the Buddha, which shows us how to think, meditate, and behave, is the actual refuge. The Sangha are those who experientially hold the Dharma instructions. They've gained some realizations through their practice, so by looking at them we can see that the Dharma works. Some Sangha members have become arhats, some have become stream enterers, and so forth. Their examples can inspire us by showing the sorts of results that we ourselves can also attain by practicing the Dharma.

As I mentioned earlier, the two causal factors necessary for actually taking refuge are fear and faith. You have to fear some sort of suffering and also have faith that the Three Jewels can help you to be free from that suffering. For practicing the small scope, contemplating the sufferings of the lower realms as just described gives rise to a healthy, realistic fear of such suffering. So you can see why refuge practice comes just after the contemplation of the sufferings of the lower realms. The middle-scope practitioner also fears the sufferings of the lower realms but then fears the sufferings of remaining in samsara more generally as well. The great-scope practitioner fears these things, too, but then also fears the continued suffering in samsara of all other sentient beings, who such a bodhisattva cherishes like her own mother or children.

Having generated such healthy fear, next you must generate faith that the Three Jewels can protect you from such sufferings. To generate such faith, you can bring to mind how engaging in the ten nonvirtuous actions and the other negative actions described above lead to rebirth in the lower realms. You can think about the various sorts of suffering results that come from specific negative actions and also about how the Buddha taught clearly on how to avoid such causes. In this way, you'll develop faith that practicing the Dharma can indeed protect you from falling into the lower realms. Similarly, if you contemplate the teachings that will come in the next chapter on the causes of remaining in samsara and the nature of the path to liberation, you'll develop genuine faith that practicing the Dharma can protect you from the sufferings of samsara in general. Your faith here should be based on such understanding of how suffering arises and how the Buddha taught methods for becoming free from such sufferings. The definition of taking refuge is that based on the intelligent fear that has arisen from contemplating the sufferings of the lower realms and/or of samsara in general and how heartfelt faith or trust in the Three Jewels can free you from those sufferings.

> *Practicing Going for Refuge to the Three Jewels*
> From the body of the guru deity seated upon the crown of your head, emanate assemblies of gurus, meditation deities, the Three Jewels, heroes and heroines, and Dharma protectors, filling space. Visualize well these objects of refuge surrounding the body of the guru deity seated upon your crown. Remembering their good qualities of body, speech, mind, and enlightened influence, think, "Please protect all mother sentient beings and me, right now, from the fear of cyclic existence in general and of the lower realms in particular." With this intention, go for refuge one hundred, one thousand, ten thousand, one hundred thousand, or however many times, saying, "I go for refuge to the gurus, meditational deities, and the Three Jewels." Properly learn the precepts of refuge from the viewpoint of understanding the temporary and final benefits of having gone for refuge to the Three Jewels.

You begin with the guru deity visualized atop your head, who emanates out the lineage masters of the practice tradition of *mahamudra*, those of the lineage of extensive deeds, those of the lineage of the profound view, and so forth coming down through Atisha and then through Lama Tsongkhapa to your own root guru. Also emanated are the buddhas, bodhisattvas, solitary realizers, arhats, heroes, dakinis, and Dharma protectors. Looking at them, contemplate as described, generating fear of the sufferings of the lower realms and then also recalling the many positive qualities of those objects of refuge. Once you've generated both fear and faith, recite the refuge prayer. Panchen Rinpoche suggests reciting the verse: "I go for refuge to the gurus, the meditational deities, and the Three Jewels." As I mentioned above in the section on the preliminaries, you can recite additional refuge verses in your daily practice if you wish.

And if you wish to count many recitations, then you can choose any one of those verses and recite it many times while familiarizing your mind with feelings of deep trust and reliance on the Three Jewels.

The measure of having developed refuge within yourself is that you then rely on the Three Jewels with total trust and confidence, as a young child relies on her mother. Such a child's reliance is totally heartfelt and intuitive. When the child falls or is hurt, she naturally and immediately cries out for her mother, trusting that help will come. When your reliance and confidence in the Three Jewels are natural and spontaneous like that, you've then succeeded in generating refuge. In the *bardo* state between death and rebirth, many frightening visions come, such as falling from cliffs and hearing terrifying sounds. If you develop the sort of confidence described here, then even during the terrifying path through the bardo, you'll recall the Three Jewels and be protected.

Generating Conviction in the Laws of Karma

Meditating on the guru deity seated upon your crown, contemplate as follows:

In the scriptures of the Conqueror it is said that in dependence upon having done virtuous deeds—the causes—only the effect of happiness arises; suffering does not arise. In dependence upon having done nonvirtuous deeds—the causes—only the effect of suffering arises; happiness does not arise. Although I have done just a small virtuous or nonvirtuous deed as a cause, if that cause does not meet with an obstruction, a very great effect will come forth. If I have not done a virtuous or nonvirtuous deed as a cause, I will not experience the effect of happiness or suffering. If a virtuous or nonvirtuous deed that I have done as a cause does not meet with an obstruction, then happiness or suffering—the effect—will certainly come forth, for actions done are not wasted.

Along with cultivating refuge, it's also important to contemplate and develop conviction in the laws of karmic cause and effect. *Karma* means action. We have to understand what sorts of effects our actions bring, adjusting our behavior accordingly.

Here we contemplate four natural qualities of karmic actions. The first is that *karma is definite*. This means that if you engage in wholesome, positive actions, that will definitely give rise to happiness, and if you engage in unwholesome, negative actions that will definitely give rise to suffering. This causal process is certain.

The second natural quality is that *karma increases*. This means that the power of both positive and negative actions continuously multiplies over time unless some other factor intervenes to obstruct this process. Anger is an example of an obstructive force that stops positive actions from multiplying. Practicing the four powers of purification is an example of an obstructive force that stops negative actions from multiplying. If such obstructive forces don't intervene, then even small actions can bring about vast effects. On a physical level, small causes can bring about huge effects. For example, one tiny seed can give rise to a huge tree that itself then produces many thousands of seeds; in this way an entire forest can develop. And a tiny spark, if unchecked, can ignite a fire that burns an entire forest to ash. Karma is similar.

A story from the Buddha's time about a monk named Golden Baby Elephant illustrates this point. It's said that when he was born, seven miraculous golden elephants were born at the same time. These miraculous elephants always followed him, and when the elephants urinated, the urine was liquid gold. When the elephants defecated, again gold came out. This miracle was the result of a karmic cause created in a previous lifetime during which this monk was reborn on a planet where there was a buddha who traveled by riding on an elephant. Out of respect to that buddha, he had made a statue of that elephant, painting the statue gold, and this small action expanded in potency until the seed of that action ripened in his later life as a monk. By understanding that karma multiplies, we develop vigilance in avoiding even small negative actions and in doing even small positive ones.

The third natural quality of karma is that if you don't commit an action, then you definitely won't experience a result. If you don't do wholesome actions, happiness won't come. If you don't do negative actions, suffering won't come. Wishing or praying for happiness or for relief from our sorrows is not sufficient. If you want certain results, you have to create the causes.

The fourth quality is that karma is infallible and indestructible. Indestructible means that if a counteractive force doesn't arise, then a karmic potential will remain until it ripens. Time itself doesn't destroy karmic potentials. They can remain, waiting to ripen, for thousands of lifetimes. So in terms of your own negative actions, if you don't want them to ripen as suffering, you must purify them.

> Furthermore, I will produce the faith of conviction in the teaching of the great strength [of karmic actions] from the viewpoint of (1) the recipient, (2) the motivation, (3) the object, (4) the basis, and so forth. Then I will make effort in the practice of adopting virtuous actions and discarding nonvirtuous ones by cultivating *all* virtues—the ten virtuous deeds and so on—and not polluting my three doors by *any* nonvirtuous action—the ten nonvirtuous deeds and so on. Please bless me, guru deity, to be able to do that.

Various factors make karmic actions more or less powerful. The first mentioned here is the *recipient* of that action. A positive or negative action done in relation to a stranger, for example, is less powerful than one done in relation to your own parents due to the power of your karmic relationship with them, for they gave you this body and raised you with kindness. Actions done in relation to those who are sick, indigent, or traveling and far from home are also more powerful due to their being more in need. Actions done toward arya beings, who've seen emptiness directly, are also particularly powerful due to the power of those beings' realizations. Your own gurus are the most powerful recipients of actions for you, due to their great kindness to you and special role of guiding you on the path.

The second factor that changes the power of karma is your *motivation* when performing the action. If you give a gift without much feeling in your heart, such giving is weak virtue. On the other hand, even if you're just giving a little food to an animal, if you do so with a heartfelt wish to attain enlightenment for the benefit of that animal and all other sentient beings, then the action becomes extremely powerful. In fact, since sentient beings are infinite in number and the benefits of enlightenment are also infinite, the karmic results of that action will be infinitely positive. Motivation also makes negative actions more or less powerful. For example, if you kill another being with intense hatred, the karma is more powerful than if you kill without such strong negative emotion.

The third basis for differentiating the power of karma is the *object* or substance involved. For an act of giving, this would be the object offered. Some objects are more powerful than others. For example, it's more powerful to give teachings than to give material goods.

The fourth basis of differentiating the power of karma is the *basis*, which here means the vows held by the person doing the action. So actions performed by fully ordained monks or nuns are more powerful than the same actions done by laypeople. And actions done by bodhisattvas are more powerful than those done by ordinary people.

Another factor that affects the power of karma is the *time frame* in which the action is done. This isn't explicitly mentioned in *Easy Path* but is implied by the phrase "and so forth." This means that observing morality now, during this degenerate time, is more powerful than observing morality when your leaders and all those around you are doing so. Similarly, practicing ethics during the golden age when the Buddha was actually present is less powerful than doing so now when the teachings are in danger of disappearing, even if you only do so for just one morning!

> With this supplication streams of five-colored nectars together with rays of light descend from the body of your guru deity seated upon the crown of your head. These streams enter the bodies and minds of all sentient beings and yourself, thereby [purifying all the misdeeds and obstructions accumulated from beginningless time. In particular these streams] purify [all the

misdeeds, obscurations, sicknesses, and spirit possessions] that prevent [the ability to practice discarding nonvirtuous actions and adopting virtuous ones. Your and all others' bodies have the nature of pristine, luminous light. All your and others' good qualities, such as long lifespan and merit, are increased and expanded. In particular,] think that these streams have produced in the minds of yourself and all others the special realization [that enables you to practice discarding nonvirtuous actions and adopting virtuous ones].

[Think:]

> Although I make such effort, the strength of the antidotes is small and the strength of the afflictive emotions is great. Therefore, if at times I am infected by nonvirtue, I will make effort to practice confession and restraint in the context of the four powers.

The four natural qualities of karma as well as these factors that make karma more powerful were taught by the Buddha himself. Just as we ordinarily trust a report about events if it comes from a friend who's always been kind to us and who we know to be very honest, our conviction in these points develops out of our trust and faith in the Buddha's compassion, wisdom, and truthfulness.

Next you supplicate the guru deity atop your crown and visualize the five-colored nectars and rays descending into your body and the bodies of all sentient beings. Your own and all others' bodies are transformed into pristine, luminous light. Think that all obstacles to realizing the teachings on karma are purified and all realizations related to those teachings such as being able to perfectly abandon all negative actions and accomplish all positive actions are actualized.

Easy Path also points out here that even though we try very hard to avoid negative actions, because the strength of our afflictive emotions is very great and because the strength of our antidotes such as wisdom is still weak, we do make mistakes. Thus we should strive in practicing the four powers of purification. I explained how to practice the four powers of purification in some detail in the section on the preliminaries. Here I want to emphasize how essential it is to generate bodhichitta and how it maximizes the effectiveness of your purification practice. The *Sutra of Antidotes* lists many practices you can do to counteract the effects of negative actions, such as reciting mantras, meditating on emptiness, reciting the names of buddhas, commissioning statues of buddhas, offering things to buddhas and bodhisattvas, making extensive offerings, and so forth. Having generated bodhichitta, engaging in prostrations while reciting the names of the Thirty-Five Buddhas is especially effective. Vajrasattva practice is also very good for purification.

Conclusion
It is the same as before.

What to Do Between Sessions
In between sessions look at the scriptures and commentaries that reveal the portion of the teaching that is shared with beings of small scope and so forth, just as described above.

The explanation of training the mind in the stages of the path shared with the being of small scope is finished.

This completes the set of teachings shared with a person of small scope. What is the measure of having achieved the realization of a person of small scope? *Easy Path* describes it as no longer having any attachment to the happiness of this life, focusing all one's thoughts on the happiness of future lives. Other texts describe it as giving more importance to the well-being of future lives than to the mundane affairs and happiness of this life.

When you've gained this realization of a person of small scope, you've begun the practice of Dharma. When you're focused on the happiness of this life, whatever positive actions you do don't yet qualify as Dharma practices. *Dharma* has the connotation of "holding" and "protecting." The three scopes of teachings protect or hold us from three different levels of suffering or problems. Small-scope Dharma practices protect us from the lower realms. Middle-scope Dharma practices protect us from the sufferings of samsara. Great-scope Dharma practices protect us from the sufferings of samsara and from individual peace, which doesn't accomplish the welfare of others. When you've realized the small-scope level of motivation, you've entered into Dharma practice but have not yet entered the path to liberation or enlightenment. It's only after you've realized the middle-scope motivation seeking liberation from samsaric existence that you enter the *path of accumulation,* the first of the five paths leading to liberation.

5. Middle-Scope Mind-Training Practices

2. Training the mind in the stages of the path shared with
   middle-scope beings
   a. Developing a desire for liberation
       (1) What to do during the actual meditative session
           (a) Preparation
           (b) Actual session
               1' Contemplating the general sufferings of samsara
               2' Contemplating the particular sufferings
           (c) Conclusion
       (2) What to do between sessions

Preparation
The preparation is the same as in the previous session, all the
way down to the supplication:

> I pray to you, unity of the objects of refuge,
> my guru supreme deity, Shakyamuni Vajradhara.

Then:

> All mother sentient beings and I have been born in sam-
> sara and then have endured a host of intense sufferings
> over a long time. This is from not having generated in
> our minds a strong thought that grasps how all of sam-
> sara has a nature of suffering and that desires liberation
> from that. Therefore, guru deity, please bless all mother
> sentient beings and me now to produce a strong thought

that grasps how all samsara has a nature of suffering and that desires liberation from that.

With this supplication streams of five-colored nectars together with rays of light descend from the body of your guru deity seated upon your crown. These streams enter the bodies and minds of all sentient beings and yourself, thereby purifying all the misdeeds and obstructions accumulated from beginningless time. In particular these streams purify all the misdeeds, obscurations, sicknesses, and spirit possessions that prevent the development of a strong thought that grasps how all of samsara has a nature of suffering and that desires liberation from that. Your and all others' bodies have the nature of pristine, luminous light. All your and others' good qualities, such as long lifespan and merit, are increased and expanded. In particular, think that these streams have produced in the minds of yourself and all others a strong thought that grasps how all samsara has a nature of suffering and that desires liberation from that.

THE PRACTICES of a person of the middle scope are covered under two headings: developing a desire for liberation and determining the nature of the actual path to liberation. As with the previous subjects, the first, how to develop a desire for liberation, is discussed in terms of both what to do during the meditation session and what to do between sessions.

The meditation session begins with the preliminaries, which are the same as before up to the supplication. For the supplication, it's good if you can do the "planting the stake" prayer. If you don't have time, you can just recite the final two lines, "I pray to you, unity of the objects of refuge, my guru supreme deity, Shakyamuni Vajradhara," which contain the essence of that longer prayer. Then pray fervently to generate renunciation. In response to this prayer, five-colored nectars and rays of light descend, filling your body and the bodies of all sentient beings. All negative actions and obscurations from beginningless time are purified, especially obstacles to realizing renunciation. Your body and all others' bodies become pristine, luminous light. You and all others realize renunciation of samsara.

THE NATURE OF SAMSARA AND THE POSSIBILITY OF LIBERATION

For you to renounce samsara, generating the desire to be liberated from it, you have to understand just what samsara is. Sometimes people think that samsara is a place—like hell, or the desire realm, or this earth. Perhaps you think that whatever city you are living in is samsara! But samsara is not a place. *Samsara* refers to a person who is trapped in a body and mind that are bound to suffer due to the forces of afflictive emotions and karma. The person—the being—who is thus bound is samsara. Liberation from samsara then entails becoming free from afflictive emotions and karma.

Once we've identified what samsara is, we can then infer that liberation is possible. In his *Commentary on Valid Cognition*, Dharmakirti uses inferential reasoning to show that liberation is possible. He explains that *samsara* refers to our own psychophysical aggregates controlled by afflictive emotions and karma. These all arise from ignorance grasping at the self. That grasping is called *ignorance* because the self that is grasped doesn't actually exist. The wisdom realizing emptiness sees this and thus acts as a direct antidote to such self-grasping. In this way the wisdom realizing emptiness destroys ignorance, the root cause of samsara, and this is liberation. By understanding what samsara is and how it arises from ignorance, you can infer that a wisdom that destroys this ignorance would lead to liberation.

To illustrate the nature of inferential reasoning, Dharmakirti gives the example of a person who wrongly believes there is no fire on a mountain in the distance. If you then show that person the thick clouds of smoke billowing from that mountain, he can infer that there is indeed a fire there. Such reasoning acts as a direct antidote to the mistaken thought that there's no fire. If you then take that person up in a helicopter and show him the flames on the mountain, he can also see the fire through direct perception.

The process is similar when overcoming the ignorance grasping at a self. Self-grasping ignorance is a wrong perception since the self grasped does not exist. If a mental perception is mistaken, then it can be removed through inferential reasoning and through direct perception. Like the person who first reasons based on seeing smoke, you can use an inference to correctly ascertain that the self grasped by self-grasping definitely does not exist. Then through continued meditation, you can eventually see this truth directly. In that way, the ignorance that is the root of samsara can be eliminated, leading you to liberation.

When you pray to be able to generate the desire for liberation from samsara, you need to understand what samsara is and how liberation from it is possible. Next, in order to generate renunciation of samsara, you contemplate first the general and then the specific sufferings of samsara.

CONTEMPLATING THE GENERAL SUFFERINGS OF SAMSARA

Meditating on the guru deity seated upon your crown, contemplate as follows:

By properly learning the ethics of abandoning the ten nonvirtuous actions, I will attain the high state of a happy rebirth, free of the suffering of the lower realms. However, if I don't obtain liberation, which abandons suffering from its root, I will not have even a moment's happiness.

I would be like a convicted criminal who is sentenced to be executed in a month and who, in the interim, must endure daily the strong suffering of such penalties as being beaten with a stick or dripped on with sealing wax. Even if an influential person were to abolish the suffering of being beaten with a stick for the present, such a criminal still would not have even the slightest mental happiness, for the suffering of execution draws closer and closer each day.

> Until I've obtained liberation, which abandons suffer-
> ing from its root, even if I attain the high position of a
> happy rebirth, when I exhaust the good karma that pro-
> pelled me there, I'll again fall into the three lower realms!
> Then I'll have to endure manifold intense sufferings for
> an extremely long time.

Contemplate how even if you refrain from the ten nonvirtuous actions and thereby attain freedom from the lower realms, this doesn't free you from samsara. Just gaining freedom from the lower realms is likened here to being a criminal slated for execution in a month. If such a prisoner were freed from the torture of being beaten and burned, he still would find no joy, for his execution would still be just days away. Similarly, when you gain a rebirth in the higher realms, after the karma that threw you there runs out, you again fall back down to lower realms. There's no security at all in that.

Since we don't recognize that this is our existential situation, con-templation on the six general sufferings of samsara is taught. So long as your birth is caused by afflictive emotions and karma, you remain in samsara. These six kinds of suffering are briefly mentioned by Asanga in his *Bodhisattva Grounds* and are taught in detail by Nagarjuna in his *Letter to a Friend*. These six kinds of suffering can also be taken as ways of meditating on impermanence, for these sufferings exist because things continually change.

> Furthermore, having taken birth in samsara by the power
> of karma and afflictive emotions, I've not gotten beyond
> a nature of suffering. As enemies can become friends and
> friends can also become enemies, I can have no confidence
> in those who offer help or harm.

The first of these six general sufferings is that there is no certainty regard-ing who will help and who will harm you. Everything is always changing. Even within one lifetime, friends can become hateful enemies and bitter enemies can become close friends. It's similar with wealth; sometimes within just one lifetime a person can go from poor to wealthy to poor again. This is a meditation on impermanence as well as on suffering. As you contemplate, check this against your own experience and what you observe in the lives of others around you. There is nothing in samsara you can truly rely upon.

> No matter how much I enjoy samsaric happiness, I'll never reach a point of satisfaction. Not only that, having increased my attachment, I'll bring forth many unbearable sufferings.

The second suffering is that your desire for happiness in samsara can never be satisfied. Instead of bringing lasting satisfaction, samsaric happiness simply leads to more and more attachment, which brings ever more suffering. You have to relate this contemplation to your own experience. This suffering of never being satisfied is the worst of sufferings. We endlessly and slavishly follow our endless, limitless desires, hoping to find satisfaction. But not only do we not find such satisfaction; the process of seeking and occasionally enjoying sensual desires only gives rise to more and more desires, endlessly, trapping us more and more in the prison of craving.

In the *Guide to the Bodhisattva's Way of Life*, Shantideva describes how we follow desire hoping for contentment but end up only increasing our desire and thereby compounding our suffering. Shantideva gives the example of wealth: if we are unable to cultivate contentment, then we strive to gain wealth. This process of trying to gain wealth causes us suffering. Then out of miserliness we cannot use it and we strive to protect it, causing us suffering. Finally, we must part with our wealth at the time of death anyway, which again causes us suffering!

Arya Nagarjuna says that the antidote to our failure to quench our desire is the practice of contentment; he calls contentment the supreme wealth. If you're content, then you're wealthy; if you're not content, then you're not wealthy. As you contemplate, relate these points to your own experiences of desire and craving.

No matter how good the bodies are that I obtain, I must relinquish them again and again. Thus I can draw no assurance from having obtained a body. I have taken conception repeatedly since beginningless time, and thus there is no perceptible limit to births. No matter how many samsaric marvels I attain, I must lose them in the end; therefore I can have no confidence in obtaining marvels. I can have no confidence in my companions, because I must go beyond this world alone and companionless.

Therefore, now that I have obtained this life of freedoms and opportunities—which is difficult to find and, once found, so valuable—I will attain in whatever way possible the precious high state of a guru buddha, in which I have abandoned all the misery of samsara. Guru deity, please bless me to be able to do that.

The third general suffering is that however many bodies you take on, you'll have to die again and again. The fourth is that there's no limit to how many births you have taken or will take. Until you're liberated from samsara, you have been and will be thrown into birth endlessly without choice. The fifth is that there's no confidence in the marvels of samsara you obtain or experience, as you always must give them up. Whatever you gather together or cherish, you'll lose it during your life or you'll lose it at death. The sixth suffering is having no one to rely on in samsara. As you cycle through birth and death, you have no one to come along with you. You are born alone, you suffer from sickness alone, and you die and go to the next life alone.

In addition to this set of six general sufferings of samsara, there are sets of three and eight sufferings. I mention these below in the next section. The eight kinds of suffering were taught as general sufferings of samsara by Nagarjuna and in detail by Arya Asanga in *Bodhisattva Grounds*. Interestingly, the Panchen Lama integrates those eight sufferings into his upcoming explanation of the sufferings specific to the human realm. The Panchen Lama's unique way of presenting those sufferings in connection with our human lives has much greater transformative power for your meditation practice.

> With this supplication streams of five-colored nectars and rays of light descend from the body of your guru deity seated upon your crown. These streams enter the bodies and minds of all sentient beings and yourself, thereby purifying all the misdeeds and obstructions accumulated from beginningless time. In particular these streams purify all the misdeeds, obscurations, sicknesses, and spirit possessions that prevent your realization of the general sufferings of samsara. Your and all others' bodies have the nature of pristine, luminous light. All your and others' good qualities, such as long lifespan and merit, are increased and expanded. In particular, think that these streams have produced in the minds of yourself and all others the special realization of the general sufferings of samsara.

After contemplating the six kinds of suffering, supplicate the guru deity atop your crown to bless you to realize the six kinds of suffering of samsara and to thereby generate a pure aspiration for liberation. Then again visualize the five-colored nectars and light rays pouring into yourself and all other beings so that you all transform into bodies of pristine, luminous light. Your lifespan and health increase, all hindrances to this realization are removed, and you perfectly gain this realization.

CONTEMPLATING THE SPECIFIC SUFFERINGS OF THE HIGHER REALMS

The Sufferings of the Human Realm

> Meditating on the guru deity seated upon your crown, contemplate as follows:

>> As long as the appropriated aggregates exist, I have not transcended the nature of suffering. What need is there to consider the sufferings of the three lower realms?

> Having appropriated the aggregates of a human, I suf-
> fer hunger and thirst, constant seeking, separation from
> agreeable friends and relatives, encounters with loath-
> some enemies, not finding what I desire, having the unde-
> sired fall upon me, birth, aging, sickness, death, and so on.

As with the previous meditations, begin by visualizing the guru deity upon your head and engaging in either an extensive or a brief version of the preliminaries. "Specific sufferings" refers to the sufferings of the three higher realms of samsara—the human, demigod, and god realms. The Panchen Lama notes that as long as you have psychophysical aggregates created by karma and afflictive emotions, you needn't resort to considering the sufferings of the lower realms to develop renunciation of samsara. This is because even the higher realms are thoroughly in the nature of suffering!

You first contemplate the sufferings of our own human realm. Since you know these sufferings firsthand, they are the most experientially powerful sufferings to focus on when meditating on *Easy Path*. There-fore, *Easy Path* gives us ten different sufferings of the human realm to contemplate! These ten correlate closely with the set of eight sufferings I mentioned above. If in your meditation you relate them to your own experiences of this life, that will be quite productive.

The first of these sufferings of the human realm is hunger and thirst, which is straightforward. The second is constant seeking, which includes the hardship and insecurity of trying to fulfill your desires, whether it be for a job, wealth, friends, comfort, or anything else. The third is given here as separation from agreeable friends and relatives. This point can also include separation from other things, too, such as your health, home, wealth, and so forth. This kind of suffering includes the grief and anguish of initial separation, the possible infliction of self-harm through grief, the mental torment of missing others, and the lost enjoyment imposed by separation. The fourth is meeting with enemies, which includes the suffering of merely seeing the enemy and then also of being criticized, upset, maimed, and possibly even killed by your enemy. The fifth is failing to find what you seek—be it wealth, relationship, popularity, or security. Failure to find what you want can induce feelings of grief similar to those described for separation from friends and loved ones. The sixth is having the undesired fall upon you, which can include meeting with illnesses, natural disasters, wars, economic hardships, and the like. No matter how much people wish to avoid what they find unpleasant, such experiences are inevitably part of our human experience.

The seventh, birth, includes all the suffering from the moment of conception up to the time when the child comes out of the mother's body. Being conceived and being born are naturally painful, frightening processes, and once you've been conceived, you are subject to all sorts of negative emotions and unpleasant experiences. The eighth, aging, begins as soon as life itself begins and includes the sufferings of degeneration of your beauty, strength, faculties, ability to enjoy sensory pleasures, and lifespan itself. The ninth is the suffering of sickness, including anything from a cold or flu to a chronic or terminal illness. The suffering of sickness includes illness-related physical changes, intense mental suffering, the inability to enjoy things you usually like such as food, having to undergo treatments such as surgery or medicinal treatments, and eventually dying. The tenth is the suffering of death itself, which of course all humans must face! At the time of death you suffer from suddenly losing all of your wealth and possessions, parting from all family and friends, leaving behind your body itself, and undergoing intense mental suffering. Death also brings the suffering of the dissolution of your physical elements, a process detailed in the teachings on highest yoga tantra.

The Sufferings of the Demigod Realm

> Having appropriated the aggregates of a demigod, one suffers
> the mental anguish of unbearable jealousy of the gods' wealth
> and the physical suffering that falls from that.

Having contemplated the sufferings of the human realm in detail, contemplate the sufferings of demigods. Demigods are tormented by acute jealousy of the wealth of the gods. They can't enjoy their own things because they continually think of the greater pleasures enjoyed by the gods. They then fight with the gods, leading to wars in which they experience much physical suffering.

The Sufferings of the God Realms

> Having appropriated the aggregates of a god of the desire realm, one suffers when fighting the demigods the loss of limbs, having one's body split open, being killed, and so forth. When confronted by the unwanted five signs of death, one suffers the dread of impending separation from the wealth of the gods and the agonies of the lower realms.
>
> Though one has appropriated the aggregates of a god of the two higher realms, one does not have the agency to remain there. Once the good action that propelled one there is used up, the inconceivable suffering of falling to a lower realm will follow.

There are three different kinds of gods corresponding to the three realms. The first realm, the desire realm, is shared with the other five types of beings—humans, animals, and so on. Among the sufferings of the gods of the desire realm is the need to constantly battle the demigods, experiencing various physical traumas in such wars. Typically, however, pleasant sensations and associates and an absence of lack mark a god's existence. But a week before the karmically propelled lifespan of a desire-realm god runs out, she sees five signs of her impending death, as her health and faculties wane.[33] At that time, she knows that her death is approaching and that she'll be separated from the wealth and pleasures of the gods. She also becomes aware that her good karma was exhausted in her enjoyment of god-realm pleasures and that she is to fall into the lower realms, where she'll experience intense suffering. Of course this awareness brings horrible anguish.

The two higher god realms are the form and formless realms. Cultivating meditative concentration causes rebirth in these realms. The gods of these two realms don't experience gross sufferings such as hunger, thirst, or war. And though these gods can live a very long time—84,000 eons for the longest-lived gods—they cannot remain there for eternity. They were thrown into those realms by karma, and when that karma runs out they inevitably fall down. The form-realm gods lose their bodies and can see through the power of their clairvoyance that their virtuous karma is used up and that they must fall down, perhaps to the lower realms. Formless realm gods don't have any form aggregate—they don't have a body—but they do have aggregates of feeling, discrimination, compositional factors, and consciousness. They also must abandon those aggregates and fall down to birth in another realm when their karma runs out. Thus there is no lasting peace or happiness in any of the higher realms.

The Three Kinds of Suffering

> In short, these appropriated aggregates act as the basis for this life's birth, aging, sickness, death, and so on and induce both the suffering of suffering and the suffering of change in this and future lives. From the mere existence of the appropriated aggregates themselves, one is established as having the nature of the aggregate of compositional factors, which is under the influence of karma and afflictive emotions.
>
> Therefore I will obtain by all means the high state of guru buddha liberated from samsara—the nature of which is these very appropriated aggregates. Bless me, guru deity, to be able to do that.

With this supplication streams of five-colored nectars together with rays of light descend from the body of your guru deity seated upon your crown. These streams enter the bodies and minds of all sentient beings and yourself, thereby purifying all the misdeeds and obstructions accumulated from beginningless time. In particular these streams purify all the misdeeds, obscurations, sicknesses, and possessions that prevent your realization of the specific sufferings of samsara. Your and all others' bodies have the nature of pristine, luminous light. All your and others' good qualities, such as long lifespan and merit, are increased and expanded. In particular, think that these streams have produced in the minds of yourself and all others the special realization of the specific sufferings of samsara.

Next the three kinds of suffering are mentioned. The first of these is the *suffering of suffering*, the manifest physical or emotional pain that even animals understand. The second of these is the *suffering of change*, which refers to moments of seeming happiness that due to their transience are seen to be a kind of suffering as well. Buddhist and Hindu meditators alike recognize this sort of seeming happiness to be in the nature of samsaric suffering.

Here I'd like to emphasize the third kind of suffering, which is having aggregates appropriated due to the force of karma. This third kind of suffering pervades all the experiences of all beings in samsara, whether they are in the lowest hell realm or the highest formless realm. So long as you have this pervasive suffering of possessing aggregates conditioned by karma and afflictive emotions, you will continue to be subject to the six, ten, and other two kinds of suffering already explained. Understanding this third kind of suffering is the basis for generating genuine renunciation of samsara. The explanation of this third kind of suffering is uniquely Buddhist.

It's important to deeply understand this all-pervasive suffering of having psychophysical aggregates controlled by karma and afflictive emotions because it is in the nature of suffering and serves as the root of all other sufferings. If you can destroy the root, then the trunk, branches, and leaves will cease with no additional effort. The point here is that your own aggregates—your body, feelings, discrimination, compositional factors, and consciousness—are in the nature of suffering. They arose propelled without choice—you have this body and mind in this life because in your past lives you craved for a mind and body. Your craving is the main factor that causes you to continue being reborn with such aggregates in future lives. Thus craving compounds your suffering, forcing you to continue taking on impure, samsaric aggregates. Only by generating the wisdom understanding how your own body and mind, your samsaric aggregates, are themselves in the nature of suffering can you genuinely begin seeking liberation.

THE FOUR NOBLE TRUTHS

Easy Path presents the general and specific sufferings of samsara including these lists of three, six, and ten kinds of suffering as a way of inducing renunciation that accords with the Buddha's teachings on the four noble truths. The first noble truth is the *truth of suffering*, and by contemplating the points here, you come to understand the nature of the first truth. As I mentioned, understanding suffering in general, the sufferings of each realm, and especially the all-pervasive suffering of possessing aggregates propelled by karma and afflictive emotions are essential for inducing renunciation of samsara itself.

After contemplating these sufferings, you contemplate how they come about through causes and conditions. This is training in the second noble truth—the *truth of the cause of suffering*. The causes of suffering are karma and afflictive emotions. Karma itself is caused by afflictive emotions. For example, when a person performs negative actions like killing or stealing, he or she does so motivated by afflicted emotional states such as anger, desire, and deluded confusion. So to understand the cause of suffering, you must deeply understand the nature of afflictive emotions. If you don't understand how these cause the sufferings of samsara, then you won't see how to eliminate samsaric sufferings from their very root.

There are three most basic afflictive emotions: desire, anger, and ignorance. In a slightly more elaborated way, you can contemplate six root afflictive emotions: anger, desire, ignorance, pride, deluded doubts, and wrong views. Then there are twenty secondary afflictive emotions, some of which are associated with desire, some with anger, and some with ignorance. All of these various afflictive emotions arise due to basic ignorance regarding the nature of the self. Basic ignorance regarding the nature of the self is the root from which all afflictive emotions, negative karma, and suffering grow.

What then is this ignorance grasping at a truly existent "I" and "mine"?

It's important that you understand that Buddhist teachers are not saying that there is no conventionally existing self at all. Even buddhas and high bodhisattvas have personal selves! A bodhisattva is a person; a buddha is a person. The problem is that you don't experience the self as it actually exists. You experience the self as if it existed independently and inherently, from its own side. In reality the self is something merely imputed by the mind, but you don't experience it in that way.

Due to your beginningless familiarity with primordial ignorance, you instinctively experience the self and other things as though they existed independently and inherently, from their own side. The buddhas and bodhisattvas don't experience themselves or other things in that manner. Take the simple example of some beautiful object. If someone else owns that object, you experience it as "his." Then, if you purchase it, you attach the label "mine" to that object, and your whole way of experiencing it changes. It appears to you as something that is inherently yours, and you become quite attached to it. Of course then if it becomes damaged or someone steals it, you will easily become upset. Bodhisattvas don't relate to objects in the way that you do!

Just as the beautiful object appears to you as inherently yours even though "mine" is just a label and is not intrinsic to the object, so also does the self appear to you in a manner that doesn't actually accord with reality. You experience the self as though it exists inherently—as though there were some truly existent entity within the body and mind that is the self. You feel as though there is some ultimate, findable referent that is the self.

Actually, this sense of an inherently existing, findable self within your aggregates is what in emptiness meditation we call the *object of negation*. It is just this that we must negate through logical analysis and reasoning! Precisely identifying this object of negation—this misconception—is the most important part of meditation on emptiness. If such a self were to exist within the aggregates, then you should be able to find it! So you meditate analytically, attempting to locate such a self within the body and the mind. As you do so, you discover that no such thing exists within your body or mind! The mind labels "self," but the mind is not the self. Through logical analysis, you discover that you cannot find any final reference point for the self. You label "self" on the body and mind, but there is nothing findable within the body or mind that is the self. "Self" and "other" are both merely labeled by the mind. All of your desire, anger, and other afflictive emotions arise as a result of clinging to the truly, inherently existing self. Once you recognize that there is no truly existing self, attachment to things as "mine" is naturally undermined, as is hatred for those who appear to be harming "me." So when you realize that the self is merely imputed, your tendency to give rise to afflictive emotions gradually diminishes, until it is eliminated all together!

I'll explain more about meditation on emptiness later in the section on special insight. But in general, it's very important to correctly identify the object to be negated, which is a misconception. And then you must use reasoned analysis. You have to use words, but there's a challenge using language to express the experience of realizing emptiness. This is illustrated by the story of a great yogi meditating in a hermitage who had realized emptiness directly. One day, some logicians who were fond of debate went to visit that yogi. They asked him to explain from his own experience what meditation on emptiness was like. The yogi pointed to a pillar and said, "When I look at this pillar, it appears to exist from its own side, but I know that this pillar doesn't exist!" The scholars felt that the yogi had fallen into nihilism by saying the pillar didn't exist, so they left without getting the point. If they'd continued questioning the yogi, he could have taught them something meaningful about how emptiness is actually experienced. This could have helped them a great deal if they could have related their philosophical training to his experiential understanding of emptiness gained through meditation. Unfortunately, they missed their opportunity!

Thus it's essential to meditate on the general and specific sufferings of samsara and then also to have some understanding of the cause of samsara in order to generate renunciation. Primordial ignorance gives rise to afflictive emotions and karma, and these in turn give rise to all the sufferings of samsara. Only the wisdom of emptiness can eliminate this primordial ignorance. Deeply contemplating these points allows you to give rise to renunciation, the thought of seeking liberation. The measure of having given rise to renunciation is being like someone caught in a burning house or someone on death row, slated for execution within about a year. A person on death row whose execution is near wishes day and night for a stay of execution and for freedom. When eating and even while sleeping, the wish to be free from his sentence is ever present. Similarly, when you've generated renunciation, the wish for freedom from the prison of samsara is with you all the time. If that death-row prisoner were given a chance to escape, he'd happily leave everything behind and run. Similarly, when you've generated renunciation, you feel happy to leave behind samsaric pleasures in order to gain liberation. Lama Tsongkhapa expressed this point clearly in a verse of his "Three Principal Aspects of the Path" by saying:

> When, by having trained in this way,
> attraction to samsaric perfections
> does not arise for even a moment
> and the wish for liberation arises day and night,
> then the thought of renunciation has been generated.

Some people have the mistaken notion that generating the wish for liberation from samsara may contradict the Mahayana aspiration to continue taking rebirth with samsaric aggregates in order to benefit others. But the Mahayana aspiration is not a craving for continued samsaric existence; rather it's a compassionate wish to continue practicing Dharma. Renunciation is actually the very foundation of all the different levels of paths and grounds taught in the Mahayana sutras and tantras. Without renunciation, you cannot progress on the Mahayana path taught in the sutras, and you also cannot progress on the paths taught in the tantras. Genuine renunciation allows you to enter the actual path of Dharma. It gives rise to powerful refuge, causes conviction in laws of karma, allows you to give up attachment to the meaningless affairs of this life, and serves as a cause for giving rise to love and compassion for other sentient beings.

THE TWELVE LINKS OF DEPENDENT ORIGINATION

The method just described for generating renunciation is based on the four noble truths. There's another way of generating renunciation of samsara, based on the Buddha's teachings on the twelve links of dependent origination. These teachings show how the twelve links function to give rise to samsara and how this process can be stopped, leading to liberation.

The image of the wheel of life illustrates both the four noble truths and the twelve links of dependent origination. Shakyamuni Buddha himself used this image to teach these two methods. He told his disciples that they should draw this wheel and hang it on the doorway or wall of monasteries because it so profoundly illustrates these teachings on how samsara arises and how to be liberated from samsara.

The entire wheel of life is depicted in the clutches of the Lord of Death, indicating that everything within samsara is subject to impermanence and death. The wheel of life consists of a central hub with a number of rings around it. The central hub and the inner rings illustrate the teachings based on the four noble truths that have just been explained. Inside the central circle, there is a pig with a rooster and a snake coming out of its mouth. This central hub illustrates the three root afflictive emotions that cause samsara: the pig represents ignorance, the rooster desire, and the snake anger. That the rooster and the snake are coming out of the pig's mouth illustrates how desire and anger arise from ignorance. A small ring around the central hub depicts the white and black karmic processes—how those who've created positive karmic actions rise to upper realms and those who've created negative karmic actions fall down to lower realms. The next ring out is divided into five sections, each of which depicts the sufferings of one of the types of rebirth—hell beings, hungry ghosts, animals, humans, and gods. All of this is a graphic depiction of the sufferings of samsara discussed above.[34]

The outermost ring depicts the twelve links of dependent origination. These twelve links describe how we circle within samsara, from life to life, propelled by ignorance clinging to an intrinsically existing self. *Ignorance* is the first link. Actually, there are two varieties of ignorance—ignorance grasping at a truly existent self and ignorance of karmic causality. Ignorance about karma gives rise only to negative actions. An example is someone performing animal sacrifices hoping to attain happiness; one gains only a suffering result from that! The other kind of ignorance, which misunderstands the nature of reality and grasps at a truly existent self, can give rise to positive, negative, or neutral actions. Nagarjuna quite correctly points out: "Those who entertain the view of eternalism go to higher rebirths, those who entertain the view of nihilism go to lower realms." One who embraces nihilism engages in many negative actions due to not believing in karmic causality. One who embraces eternalism, on the other hand, grasps at a truly, inherently existent self, and up to a certain point, such ignorance can be useful. How can that be?

As beginners, we engage in positive actions out of a wish for good rebirths in the future. Wishing to benefit the truly existent self we are grasping at, we strive to create good karma. Even the initial wish to understand selflessness arises from a sense of having a truly existent self! Actually, until we've reached quite a high level of spiritual realization, even our good actions are necessarily grounded in this ignorance grasping at a truly existent self. Until you've seen emptiness directly and attained the path of seeing, you necessarily continue creating karma for future rebirths within samsara. Once someone has attained the path of seeing, they no longer create karma for further samsaric rebirths. They can still experience suffering due to karma created prior to seeing emptiness directly, but they no longer create karmic actions for new samsaric rebirths. Wherever you're born in samsara—even within the higher realms—that birth is necessarily propelled by karma created under the influence of ignorance about the nature of reality.

Thus you can do positive actions and attain higher rebirths based on such ignorance, but you can never attain liberation without abandoning it. Basic ignorance about the nature of reality is like a farmer who plants seeds in a field. The seeds would then be the second link, *karmic formations*. When these karmic actions are planted—or imprinted—on the third link, *consciousness*, then they can connect to a future life. They can ripen into results in future lives. Karmic formations can be positive, giving rise to good rebirths, or negative, giving rise to suffering rebirths in the lower realms.

Once the first link of basic ignorance has led you to engage in the second link of karmic formations, and these are imprinted on the third link, consciousness, this naturally gives rise to the fourth link, *name and/or form*. These are the name and form of a lifetime subsequent to the one in which the karmic formations were created. Here *form* refers to the physical aggregate—the body of that lifetime. And *name* refers to the four mental aggregates of that life. We include the word "or" here because beings in the formless realms don't have bodies. In the first moment of being conceived, too, humans have mental aggregates but have not yet appropriated a body.

So once name and form exist, one naturally gives rise to *sense faculties*, the fifth link. For a human fetus, of course the sense faculties don't exist initially, and they develop gradually as the body grows through five distinct phases of development in the womb. The sense faculties include the sense organs—the eyes, ears, nose, tongue, body, and mind—as well as their respective sense powers.

Once the sense faculties have developed, one is compelled to experience the sixth link, *contact*. Contact is when the sense organs engage with their respective objects. When contact occurs, there is bound to be *feeling*, the seventh link. Feeling is of three types: pleasant, unpleasant, and neutral. Feeling is an omnipresent mental factor. Whenever there is contact, one of these three feelings is present.

Once feelings are present, *craving*, the eighth link, is bound to arise. If the feeling that gave rise to it was pleasant, then craving will be for more, while if the experience was unpleasant, then craving will be for release from that experience. Craving can also include attachment to the aggregates themselves—the thirst for existence.

Craving naturally gives rise to the ninth link, *grasping*. Grasping is an intensified form of craving. During our lives, grasping gives rise to other afflictive emotions. And at the time of death, grasping at the body provides the necessary condition for past karma to give rise to the tenth link, *becoming*. The second link was karma at the time of the causal action, likened to planting a seed. The tenth link of becoming is karma at the time of the result and can be likened to the crop produced from that seed.

The ripening of becoming naturally gives rise to the eleventh link, *birth*, and birth itself inevitably leads to the twelfth link, *aging and death*. From the moment of birth, we begin aging, and whoever is born will die.

Of course, of those who are born, some will and some won't make it to old age, but all will die.

Of these twelve links of dependent origination, two are karma, three are afflictive emotions, and the rest are suffering results of those. I mentioned that the second and tenth links are karma. This is karma that can propel further rebirths in samsara. Craving and grasping are like water and sunlight that cause that karmic seed planted in the second link to ripen into a resultant samsaric rebirth, which is the karmic result of the tenth link. Ignorance, craving, and grasping are together the three links that are afflictive emotions. These are essential afflictive emotions involved in giving rise to karma and to all the sufferings of samsara. The other seven links are samsaric suffering that results from the karma and afflictive emotions just mentioned.

As you contemplate these twelve links, understanding the cause-and-effect relationships they illustrate helps you to generate renunciation. Right now you are experiencing the results of causes you set created in a past life. You see, in some past life under the influence of ignorance, you performed actions that were imprinted on your consciousness. These gave rise to your current human body and mind—your name and form—along with your sense faculties, which are experiencing contact with their respective objects and feelings.

You were born, you are now aging, and eventually you will die. Now, while you are alive, under the power of ignorance misconceiving the nature of reality, you are creating new karma that is being imprinted on your consciousness. At the end of this life or in some future life, those karmic causes will be activated by craving and grasping, leading again to becoming, giving rise to more and more cycles of birth and aging and death within samsara. Karma created in one lifetime can ripen in the very next lifetime or can remain as an imprint for many lifetimes until it ripens.

Once you create karma under the power of ignorance, craving and grasping at the time of death can cause that karma to ripen into the result of further samsaric rebirths. Craving and grasping are like the water and sunlight that cause the karmic seeds to bring forth their bitter fruits of further lifetimes of suffering.

In this very lifetime, under the influence of ignorance, you can create many causes for future rebirths in the lower realms. Within samsara, as you experience the results of some chains, other chains are being created. And it's also clear that by breaking this cycle at the point of ignorance itself, the twelve links can be reversed and brought to an end.

Conclusion
It is the same as before.

What to Do Between Sessions
Furthermore, in between sessions, look at the scriptures and commentaries that show how all samsara has the nature of suffering, and so on, just as described above.

The conclusion of the session is the same as described earlier. Between sessions, it's good to study teachings on the four noble truths and the twelve links of dependent origination. The other activities between sessions are the same as already explained.

DETERMINING THE NATURE OF THE PATH TO LIBERATION

Having generated the wish for liberation by contemplating in accord with the four noble truths and/or the twelve links of dependent origination, next you must determine the actual nature of the path leading to liberation. All the practices required to gain liberation are included within the *three higher trainings*. These are the trainings in ethics, concentration, and wisdom. Ordinarily, ignorance gives rise to manifest afflictive emotions such as desire and anger, and then based on these emotions you engage in all sorts of negative actions. By training in ethics, you restrain from engaging in those external, negative behaviors. Such external discipline keeps you from getting distracted by chasing after what you desire, fighting against enemies, and so forth. This creates a lifestyle that allows you to begin developing meditative concentration. Such concentration subdues your manifest negative emotions such as anger and desire as well as mental sinking and excitement. Such a concentrated mind creates the foundation for being able to use wisdom to destroy the very root of samsara—ignorance itself. You begin your meditative session on the nature of the path to liberation very much as you begin sessions on the previous topics.

b. Determining the nature of the path to liberation
    (1) What to do during the actual meditative session
      (a) Preparation
      (b) Actual session
      (c) Conclusion
    (2) What to do between sessions

Preparation
The preparation is the same as in the previous session, all the way down to the supplication:

> I pray to you, unity of the objects of refuge,
> my guru supreme deity, Shakyamuni Vajradhara.

Then:

> All mother sentient beings and I have been born in sam-
> sara and have endured a host of intense sufferings over a
> long time. This is due to not learning properly the path
> of the three higher trainings after developing a desire for
> liberation. Therefore, guru deity, please bless all mother
> sentient beings and me now to be able to learn properly
> the path of the three higher trainings after developing a
> desire for liberation.

With this supplication streams of five-colored nectars together with rays of light descend from the body of your guru deity seated upon your crown. These streams enter the bodies and minds of all sentient beings and yourself, thereby puri-fying all the misdeeds and obstructions accumulated from beginningless time. In particular these streams purify all the misdeeds, obscurations, sicknesses, and spirit possessions that prevent learning properly the path of the three higher trainings after developing a desire for liberation. Your and all others' bodies have the nature of pristine, luminous light. All your and others' good qualities, such as long lifespan and merit, are increased and expanded. In particular, think that these streams have produced in the minds of yourself and all others the special realization of learning properly the path of the three higher trainings after developing a desire for liberation.

Actual Session
Meditating on the guru deity seated upon your crown, contemplate as follows:

> Consciousness itself is neutral. First, with "I" and "mine" as objects, it produces the thought grasping at inherent existence. Because of self-grasping, it produces wrong views such as attachment to whatever is associated with "self," aversion to what is associated with "other," and pride that conceives myself as superior to others. Depending on those, doubt and wrong views are produced, which conceive the nonexistence of a teacher who indicates selflessness and of the Three Jewels, the four truths, and the karmic cause and effect that are taught by that teacher. Depending on that, the other afflictive emotions spread. Through the influence of these, karma is accumulated, giving rise to experiences of the various unwanted sufferings of samsara.
>
> Therefore the root of all suffering is finally ignorance. Thus I will attain by all means the high state of guru buddha who has abandoned from the root all samsaric sufferings. In order to do that, I will learn properly the path of the three higher trainings.

Visualizing the guru deity atop your head, begin by thinking about how ignorance gives rise to the sufferings of samsara. Consciousness itself is neutral; it is neither inherently virtuous nor nonvirtuous. But when it gives rise to a sense of an inherently existent self, then attachment to me and mine, aversion to others, and pride arise. Depending on those, all sorts of other wrong views arise. Depending on those wrong views, other afflictive emotions spread, leading to the creation of karmic actions. In this way, primordial ignorance gives rise to samsara. Recognizing this, aspire to attain the state of a guru deity by practicing the three higher trainings beginning with the training in ethics.

> In particular, since there's great benefit in observing eth-
> ics and great disadvantage in not doing so, I will observe
> ethics properly, just as I have promised, without giving
> this up even at the cost of my life.

Ethics are the foundation of all other spiritual qualities, bringing great benefit. Ethics are like the earth itself. All living and non-living things stand and depend on the earth. Similarly, all spiritual qualities and practices rest on and develop from your being ethical. Attaining good future rebirths depends on your being ethical. Success in developing concentration and wisdom requires ethics.

Training in ethics entails practicing morality in general and then can also include taking specific commitments such as individual-liberation vows, bodhisattva vows, and tantric vows. The beginning point for ethical training is restraint from the ten negative actions—killing, stealing, sexual misconduct, lying, harsh speech, gossip, divisive speech, covetousness, wrong views, and ill will. You should train yourself to restrain from these behaviors by relating empathically to the pain you cause others when you commit them. If you empathically contemplate how you'd feel to be killed, robbed, cheated on, and so forth, you'll see that the pain is totally intolerable. Thinking like this again and again, you will naturally want to refrain from causing others such suffering.

The Buddha said that if one person were to make offerings to countless buddhas for countless eons with precious objects equaling the number of grains of sand in the Ganges River, and if someone else were to observe even one ethical training for just one day at this time when the continued existence of the Dharma is in danger, the virtue accrued by the second person would be far greater. The reason for this is that ethical restraint is so rare now! During times of famine, even a small amount of food becomes especially precious and beneficial for preserving life. Similarly, in this degenerate time, whatever efforts you make to train in ethics are especially precious and powerful.

In the morning, if you were to go in front of a statue or holy image in your home and commit strongly to avoiding killing, stealing, or otherwise harming others that day, then you yourself create such virtues on that day. If you do that each day, then you will protect others from a lot of harm while also creating vast merit!

Even if you cannot yet uproot your afflictive emotions with wisdom or subdue them with meditative concentration, you can stop yourself from expressing them outwardly by training in ethics. You don't need to be a highly advanced practitioner to do so; anyone can practice ethics in daily life. Doing so immediately gives you and those around you more peace of mind and insures good future rebirths, giving you the opportunity to continue practicing Dharma so you can eventually attain liberation.

> Furthermore, as lack of knowledge is a door through which a transgression occurs, I'll listen and understand the precepts as antidotes to that. As lack of respect is a door through which a transgression occurs, I'll respect teachers, the precepts they explain, and my companions of pure conduct who also properly study the precepts as antidotes to that. As lack of conscientiousness is a door through which a transgression occurs, I'll be conscientious by developing mindfulness, vigilance, self-respect, and moral shame as antidotes to that. As having many afflictive emotions is a door through which a transgression occurs, I'll meditate on foulness as an antidote to

desire, love as an antidote to hatred, dependent arising
as an antidote to ignorance, and so forth. I will properly
learn pure ethics, unsullied by faults. Guru deity, bless me
to be able to do that.

With this supplication streams of five-colored nectars together
with rays of light descend from the body of your guru deity
seated upon your crown. These streams enter the bodies and
minds of all sentient beings and yourself, thereby purifying all
the misdeeds and obstructions accumulated from beginningless time. In particular these streams purify all the misdeeds,
obscurations, sicknesses, and spirit possessions that prevent
learning properly the path of the three higher trainings after
developing a desire for liberation. Your and all others' bodies
have the nature of pristine, luminous light. All your and others'
good qualities, such as long lifespan and merit, are increased
and expanded. In particular, think that these streams have
produced in the minds of yourself and all others the special
realization of learning properly the path of the three higher
trainings after developing a desire for liberation.

There are four occasions when people are likely to engage in negative
actions. To effectively practice ethics, you must guard these four doors
to bad ethics. The first door is not knowing what to take up and what to
avoid doing. The antidote to that is learning the teachings.

The second door is disrespecting or disregarding your teachers and the
Three Jewels. If you don't maintain respect, then it's easy for bad ethics
to increase. The antidote to this is cultivating respect for your teacher
and the Three Jewels by thinking of their many good qualities and great
kindness to you.

The third door is lack of conscientiousness. Even if you understand
what's ethical, if you aren't conscientious, you'll do harmful actions
mindlessly. The first antidote to this is mindfulness, which entails being
aware of what you're thinking and doing. You also need vigilance, which
entails occasionally taking time to check up on yourself, analyzing

whether what you've been doing is genuinely ethical or not. Another antidote to lack of conscience is self-respect, feeling that you value and care enough about yourself that you will not do unethical things. Self-respect stops you from doing negative things even when you believe that no one else will know you've done them. And finally, a healthy sense of moral shame is helpful here; this means feeling that you will avoid doing negative actions because you'd be embarrassed for those who care about you, including your teachers and the buddhas, to know you've done them.

The fourth door to bad ethics is having many intense afflictive emotions. Even if you're trying to be conscientious, intense hatred or desire can overwhelm you, leading you to do hurtful, unethical things. The antidote to this is training yourself in the antidotes to your afflictive emotions. If you have intense desire, meditate on the foulness and impermanence of the things you crave. If you have intense hatred, meditate on loving-kindness. If you have intense ignorance, meditate on dependent arising. If you meditate on these antidotes as soon as afflictive emotions arise, this will help a great deal. And if you guard all four of these doors as described, you will gradually become purer and purer in your ethics.

The Buddha said there are two types of noble beings who are as rare to find as the *udumvara* flower, which only blooms at the time of a buddha. One of these is someone who simply doesn't commit negative actions and the other is someone who, when he or she does make ethical mistakes, admits the faults by engaging in the four powers of purification. So if you do make ethical mistakes, then purify with the four powers. Both the Buddha and Arya Nagarjuna said that any negative actions can be purified.

I mentioned some examples of this earlier. Another illustration is the story of Jungawo, who lived during the Buddha's time. Jungawo suffered from intense, extreme desire, which led him to engage in many negative actions. His desire was so extreme that he couldn't focus on Dharma practice. So, as a skillful means, the Buddha sent his disciple Maudgalyayana, who had great miraculous powers, telling him to take Jungawo to the hell realms to see people being boiled and tormented there. Maudgalyayana did so, explaining to Jungawo that he'd be reborn there if he continued engaging in negative actions. He then took Jungawo to the Heaven of the Thirty-Three and showed him many beautiful goddesses there, explaining that he'd be reborn there if he engaged in virtue. Jungawo entered into Dharma practice with a small-scope motivation of attaining such a higher rebirth, but then he gradually developed genuine renunciation of samsara and went on to become an arhat in that life. By engaging in purification and making sincere efforts in your training in ethics, you can definitely progress!

Although all of the three higher trainings are mentioned, *Easy Path* mainly focuses on the training in ethics here. This is because the trainings in concentration and wisdom will be covered in detail in the context of the practice of the six perfections for a person of great scope.

Conclusion
It is the same as before.

What to Do Between Sessions
Furthermore, in between sessions, look at the precepts given in terms of individual liberation and so on according to how it was presented previously. [Everything else is] just as described above.

This concludes the explanation of the mind training in the stages of the path shared with the being of middle scope.

Between sessions of meditation on this topic, you should study commentaries on how to restrain from the ten nonvirtuous actions and also on any vows or commitments you've taken.

As we conclude this discussion of the trainings in common with a person of the middle scope, you should understand that gaining the actual realization of renunciation, the continuous and single-pointed wish for freedom from the prison of samsara, is extremely important if you wish to practice the great scope. Master Shantideva pointed out that if the wish for your own freedom from samsara has not yet even arisen in a dream, then it's totally impossible for you to generate such a wish for others! If you haven't yet faced your own sufferings, then you will not be able to genuinely empathize with and generate compassion for the sufferings of others. Great compassion and bodhichitta entail understanding the general and specific sufferings of all the infinite mother sentient beings. So you must first understand suffering explained in the middle-scope trainings as they apply to yourself in order to then empathically apply that understanding to the sufferings of others.

6. The Seven-Point Cause-and-Effect Method for Generating Bodhichitta

NOW WE TURN to the teachings for persons of great scope. Generating bodhichitta is the gateway to great-scope practice. The altruistic mind of bodhichitta is extremely precious. If you put all your efforts into generating bodhichitta, you'll be truly safe. Bodhichitta itself protects you and guides you to enlightenment. Bodhichitta purifies your negativities and leads you to accumulate infinite merit. It causes happiness in this life, happiness in future lives, and the ultimate bliss of full enlightenment. With bodhichitta you'll be happy both when things go well and when things go poorly. Bodhichitta secures your own welfare and also the welfare of others.

There are two main sections here: how to give rise to bodhichitta and, after giving rise to bodhichitta, how to train in the path of the bodhisattvas. There are two methods for giving rise to bodhichitta: the seven-point cause-and-effect method and the method of equalizing and exchanging self with others.

The seven-point cause-and-effect method was taught by the Buddha in the short, middling, and extensive Perfection of Wisdom sutras, by Master Kamalashila in the middle version of his *Stages of Meditation*, and also by Master Atisha. Equalizing and exchanging self for others was taught by the Buddha in the *Array of Trees Sutra*, by Nagarjuna in his *Compendium of Sutras* and in his *Precious Garland*, by Shantideva in his *Guide to the Bodhisattva's Way of Life*, and by Atisha.

The Seven-Point Cause-and-Effect Method

3. Mind training in the stages of the path of a person of great
scope
  a. How to generate bodhichitta
    (1) The actual generation of bodhichitta
      (a) How to develop bodhichitta through the seven-
point cause-and-effect instructions
        1' What to do during the actual meditation session
        a' Preparation
        b' Actual session
        c' Conclusion
        2' What to do between meditation sessions

Having previously practiced equanimity toward all sentient beings, we cultivate [the seven-point cause-and-effect instructions], from recognizing all beings as our mothers up to the generation of bodhichitta.

Preparation
It is the same as in the previous session, all the way down to the supplication:

> I pray to you, unity of the objects of refuge,
> my guru supreme deity, Shakyamuni Vajradhara.

Then pray:

> Guru deity, please bless the minds of myself and all mother sentient beings to produce the special realization of equanimity for all sentient beings that is free from attachment holding some close and aversion keeping some distant, as well as of the recognition of all beings as our mothers, the recollection of their kindness, the wish to repay their kindness, love, compassion, [the exceptional attitude of universal responsibility,] and bodhichitta.

Thereby streams of five-colored nectars together with rays of light descend from the body of your guru deity seated upon your crown. These streams enter the bodies and minds of all sentient beings and yourself, thereby purifying all the misdeeds and obstructions accumulated from beginningless time. In particular these streams purify all the misdeeds, obscurations, sicknesses, and spirit possessions that prevent producing the equanimity for all sentient beings that is free from attachment holding some close, aversion keeping some distant, and so on. Your and all others' bodies have the nature of pristine, luminous light. All your and others' good qualities, such as long lifespan and merit, are increased and expanded. In particular, think that these streams have produced in the minds of yourself and all others the special realization of the even-mindedness that is free from attachment and aversion, holding close and keeping distant all sentient beings.

As mentioned in this prayer, you meditate on equanimity prior to beginning the seven-point cause-and-effect method for generating bodhichitta. That is, you begin with the general preliminaries up through this prayer, and then you meditate on equanimity itself.

Equanimity Meditation

Meditation on equanimity is not one of the seven points; it's a preliminary. The tradition of meditating on equanimity prior to the seven points was taught by Kamalashila. The Kadampa master Chengawa differed from Kamalashila, advising that one start right in with meditation on compassion. His view was that one should begin meditating on compassion and then extend that compassion equally to all beings. He felt that equanimity would arise naturally as a result of such compassion practice. The Buddha himself encouraged meditation on equanimity prior to meditating on compassion, however, and Lama Tsongkhapa followed Kamalashila's approach. *Easy Path* follows this tradition.

In the sutras, the Buddha mentions three kinds of equanimity practice. One is like what Kamalashila taught, focusing on how all beings are equal in wanting happiness and not wanting suffering. A second kind of equanimity practice is cultivating intimacy and fondness for all beings, seeing everyone as precious; this induces an even-minded love free from discrimination that craves some people and rejects others. The third kind of equanimity practice is seeing all beings as one's own family, one's mothers and fathers, which also induces equanimity free from craving and aversion. Sometimes when meditating on equanimity one prays that others may achieve even-mindedness free from attachment to some and aversion to others. Here, though, you are cultivating such even-mindedness on the level of the subject—in your own mind.

Actual Session
While meditating on the guru deity on your crown, visualize before you a sentient being toward whom you have indifferent feelings who has neither helped nor harmed you. Then think:

> This being does not desire suffering and desires happiness. Therefore I will neither hold this being close and help him at times nor keep him distant and harm him at other times, and I will instead be equanimous, free of attachment and aversion that hold some close and keep others distant. Please bless me, guru deity, to be able to do that, and so on.[35]

Visualizing your guru atop your head and making requests, you then visualize a person toward whom you feel neutral, or indifferent. You'll be progressing from developing equanimity for someone toward whom you feel indifferent, attached, and then averse. Begin with the person you feel neutral toward because it's easier to develop equanimity with that person than with the others.

Having brought this person to mind, contemplate how he or she desires happiness and does not want to suffer. There is absolutely no difference at all between this person and you in terms of how sincerely or deeply that other person wishes to have happiness and to avoid suffering. The Panchen Lama put this point very nicely in the *Guru Puja* where he wrote:

There is no difference between myself and others:
none of us wishes even the slightest of sufferings
nor is ever satisfied with the happiness we have.
Realizing this, I seek your blessings to enhance the bliss and joy
    of others.

There are two ways of understanding what it means to have gained equanimity. One is genuinely seeing this other person as totally equal to yourself in wanting happiness and not wanting suffering. The other is seeing the other person without any sense of attachment or aversion. When you've generated such a state of mind, you move on to the next contemplation.

> When you have equanimity toward that being, visualize before you a sentient being that you know and find appealing, and cultivate equanimity. Your lack of equanimity with him or her is due to attachment. Thinking "In the past I produced my beginningless samsara as well through attachment to what is attractive," stop your attachment and cultivate equanimity.

Next you visualize a friend or relative you find appealing—someone you feel fondly toward. Your attachment to this person may initially make it difficult to feel even-minded toward him or her. Thus you should contemplate how it's due to your attachment to what you find attractive that you've been compelled to continue in samsara since beginningless time. Understanding how such attachment prolongs your suffering helps to stop your attachment for that person.

> When you feel equanimity toward that being, visualize before you a sentient being you know and find unappealing and cultivate equanimity toward him or her. Your lack of equanimity is due to the anger that arises from conceiving that being to be completely disagreeable. Thinking "There is no way I can develop bodhichitta if I don't have equanimity toward that being," stop your anger and cultivate equanimity.

Then change the object of our visualization to an enemy—someone you find disagreeable. Think of how your difficulty feeling even-minded toward this person is your own aversion, which totally blocks you from developing bodhichitta. So use this awareness to stop your aversion and anger toward this person.

> When you have equanimity toward that being, visualize before you both a sentient being of attractive qualities, like your mother, and a sentient being of unattractive qualities, like your enemy. Then think:
>
>> From their own perspectives, these two are similar in wanting happiness and not wanting suffering. And from my viewpoint there's no counting from beginningless time the number of times that even this being I now conceive as a close friend has been my principal enemy. There is no counting from beginningless time the number of times that even this being I now conceive as an enemy has been my mother and cared for me with mercy. Therefore, to whom should I be attached and to whom should I be averse? I will be equanimous, free from attachment holding some close and aversion keeping others distant. Please bless me, guru deity, to be able to do that.

Next visualize two people, one who is attractive to you and another you find disagreeable. Contemplate how these two people are totally the same in wanting happiness and not wanting suffering. By recognizing from your heart that there's not the slightest difference between them in that sense, you'll come to recognize that your own craving for one and aversion for the other is unreasonable. Therefore, resolve to abandon such craving and aversion. You can also reason that the individual you're fond of has been your enemy numberless times in previous lives. And your enemy has been your mother, child, and dear friend countless times in previous lives. Thinking like that, pray to your guru deity to bless you to realize equanimity.

When you have equanimity toward those two, cultivate equanimity toward all sentient beings. The way to do that is as follows:

> All sentient beings, from their own perspectives, are similar in wanting happiness and not wanting suffering. From my perspective, all sentient beings are my relatives. Therefore I will neither hold some close and privilege them nor keep some distant and harm them but will be even-minded, free of attachment and aversion. Please bless me, guru deity, to be able to do that.

Next cultivate equanimity toward all sentient beings using the same lines of reasoning already discussed. Think about how all beings everywhere are totally equal in wanting happiness and not wanting suffering. Also recognize how all sentient beings have been your mother, father, child, and dearest loved ones countless times as you've wandered in samsara since beginningless time! Contemplate like that again and again until you begin to become even-minded toward all. Strive to let go of your habit of discriminating others into categories of friend, enemy, and stranger. This bad habit causes you much suffering, leads you to harm others, and blocks your development of bodhichitta. Replace it with a sense of intimacy and even-mindedness toward all beings. The measure of having realized equanimity is that when you think of or come across others, you no longer give rise to such discriminations. You no longer feel the agitation and discomfort in your heart of being attached to some and averse to others.

Recognizing Others as Mothers

After developing equanimity, you begin meditating on the seven-point cause-and-effect method for realizing bodhichitta. The first point is seeing all sentient beings as having been your mothers.

> Next is the method of cultivating the recognition of all beings as our mothers up to the generation of bodhichitta. Meditating on the guru deity on your crown, think as follows:

Someone may ask, "Well, by what reasoning are all sentient beings my relatives?" As there is no beginning to samsara, there's no beginning to my births. And within that continuum of passing from life to life, since those births are countless, I cannot point out a single place or direction into which I've not been born. I cannot point out a single type of sentient being's body I have not assumed, and I cannot count the times I have assumed such a body. I cannot point out even one sentient being who has not been my mother, and I cannot count the number of times that anyone has been my mother. No sentient being has not been my mother in a human form, and I cannot count the number of times that anyone has been and still will be my mother in human form. Therefore I should think that all sentient beings are by all means my mothers who have kindly cared for me.

Recall that all the meditations begin with visualizing your guru atop your head, because *Easy Path* is grounded in tantric practice, which takes guru yoga as the very heart of your Dharma practice. This integration of guru yoga with each contemplation is a profound means of enhancing your practice of the path.

The first of the seven points of this method for generating bodhichitta is recognizing all sentient beings as your mothers of previous lives. You have taken infinite samsaric rebirths since time without beginning. Over the course of your immeasurable wandering, you've been infinitely interconnected with others, and every being has been your mother countless times.

Since you don't ordinarily think of all beings as your mothers, it's natural for questions and doubts to arise, and such doubts are given here along with lines of reasoning and contemplations to address those doubts.

You may think, "Well, as there are innumerable sentient beings, then not quite *all* sentient beings have been my mother." It does not follow that because sentient beings are numberless, all cannot have been my mother. For just as sentient beings are without number, so too are my births. Therefore I should recognize that all sentient beings have been my mother.

Since sentient beings are countless, you may doubt that each of them could have been your mother. The line of reasoning here is to recall that your previous births are also countless! You have been reborn infinitely to those countless mothers.

You may think, "As I and all sentient beings do not recognize each other, they are not my mother." It does not follow that because I and all sentient beings do not recognize each other, they must not be my mother. Recall instead how, even within this lifetime, there are many instances where a mother and child do not recognize each other.

You may doubt that they are your mothers because you don't recognize them as such, but that proves nothing. Even within this lifetime, there are cases where children separated from their parents at birth cannot recognize each other. Those with impaired memories also sometimes cannot recognize even their own parents or other family members. That the process of taking rebirth under the power of karma and delusions impairs our memories of our past lives in no way disproves that all other sentient beings have been our kind mothers.

Furthermore, you may think, "Although all sentient beings were my mother in former lives, it is not correct to say that they are my mother now, because that has already passed." Well then, it would follow that yesterday's mother is not my mother because she is already in the past today.

There is no difference between yesterday's and today's mother, both in the quality of being a mother and in caring for me with kindness. Likewise, with respect to being my mother and caring for me with kindness, there is no difference between my mothers of former lives and my mother of this life. Therefore I should think that all sentient beings are by all means my mother.

You may think that even if others were your kind mothers in previous lives, that is the past and it's irrelevant now. We debate that thought by noting that according to that line of reasoning, you would also wind up dismissing the kindness your mother showed you yesterday because now it's today! Yesterday is past, but the kindness someone showed you yesterday is still worthy of respect and gratitude. In the same way there's no difference between the kindness showed to us by a mother of a previous life and the kindness of the mother of this life. Both are equally worthy of respect and gratitude.

By contemplating these things repeatedly over time, you will come to a point when you intuitively and spontaneously experience all beings as your mothers. At that point, you've realized the first of these seven points. When that happens, you will naturally feel a strong sense of intimacy, love, and concern for everyone you meet. You will spontaneously feel like everyone is your dear family and will be filled with openhearted warmth.

Remembering the Kindness of Others

Remembering the kindness of other sentient beings is utterly essential to realizing bodhichitta. Both the seven-point cause-and-effect method and the method of equalizing and exchanging self with others include meditations on others' kindness. In the seven-point method, you focus on others' kindness to you in past lives. In equalizing and exchanging self with others, you focus on others' kindness not only in the past but also in the present and future, as will be discussed in detail later.

> When you have experience [of recognizing all beings as your mothers], contemplate their kindness. Meditating on the guru deity on your crown, bring to mind a clear appearance of this life's mother in front of you—not when she is young but when she is old. Then think as follows:

My mother has been so not only in this life but innu-
merably from beginningless time. In particular, in this
lifetime, she sustained me at first with tenderness in her
womb. At birth she placed me on a soft cushion. She
lifted me toward her on the tips of her ten fingers, held
me to the warmth of her flesh, welcomed me with a loving
smile, looked at me with joy-filled eyes, wiped snot from
my nose with her tongue, and cleaned my excrement with
her hand. [During childbirth] she suffered [far more than
me], just as if she were losing her life. At my slightest
illness she suffered greatly. She provided me with mea-
sureless happiness and benefit in accordance with her
own resources. She gave me lovingly all her wealth, which
she obtained by working her fingers to the bone without
considering her propriety, hardship, reputation, or even
her own life.

Think: "Because she protects me from immeasurable misery
and harm, she is extremely kind."

Having made requests to your guru deity atop the crown of your head,
visualize your mother in her old age. Even if she's not yet old, you can
imagine her that way. Doing so makes it easier to remember and emo-
tionally connect with her kindness to you. Think and imagine in detail
the specific examples of her kindness described here. You can also recall
additional, specific things she's done for you. Of course, you should
continue with this until you feel a deep emotional connection to her
kindness. Then contemplate that she has been similarly kind to you over
the course of countless previous lives as well!

When you have experience of that, meditate on other close
ones, such as your father. The way of doing that is as follows.
After visualizing the form of someone close such as your father,
think:

> This person has been my mother countless times through-
> out my beginningless lifetimes. When he or she was my
> mother, this person cared for me with kindness just like
> my mother of this lifetime did. Therefore this person is
> extremely kind.

After you've generated some genuine experience from meditation on the kindness of your mother of this life, think of someone else close to you, such as your father. Think of how he was also your mother and showed you all the same sorts of kindness described above. You can also include other relatives and friends at this point. Again contemplate the kindness you received until you can generate an emotional experience of having received infinite kindness over countless lifetimes from each person.

> Once you've had experience of that, meditate on all sentient
> beings toward whom you have neutral feelings. The way you
> do that is as follows. After visualizing neutral sentient beings
> in front of you, think:

>> Right now it seems that there is no connection at all
>> between me and these beings. However, these beings have
>> been my mothers countless times throughout my begin-
>> ningless lifetimes. When they were my mothers, they
>> cared for me with kindness just like my mother of this
>> lifetime did. Therefore they are extremely kind.

Next you engage in precisely the same contemplations but toward some-one you typically feel neutral or indifferent about.

> Once you've had experience of that, meditate on your enemies.
> The way you do that is as follows. After visualizing your ene-
> mies in front of you, think:

>> What use is holding these now as enemies? These beings
>> have been my mother countless times throughout my

beginningless lifetimes. When they were my mother, they provided me with immeasureable benefit and happiness. They protected me from immeasureable harm and suffering. In particular, when they were not around, I could not stand even slightly still. Moreover, when I was not around, they could not stand even slightly still. We were intimate in that way countless times. This present situation [of being enemies] is due to our bad actions. Otherwise they are only my mothers who cared for me with kindness.

Once you've had experience of that, think of the kindness of all sentient beings.

Having gained some experience meditating in this way on a neutral person, visualize your enemies in front of you. They've harmed you just once in this life, but they've benefited you infinitely in previous lives. Contemplate their vast, past kindnesses to you until the present brief harm is seen as insignificant. Recognize how the current, temporary relationship of being enemies is just a result of your own negative actions. The seeming enemy is seen to be in reality your own kind mother. Having meditated like that, expand your meditation outward, contemplating the infinite kindness you've received from more and more beings, until you experience a sense of having received a mother's love and kindness from all sentient beings as vast as the vastness of space.

Wishing to Repay Others' Kindness
The third of these seven points is meditation on wishing to repay the infinite kindness of all mother sentient beings.

Having thought about kindness in that way, meditate on repaying kindness. Recalling the guru deity on your crown, think as follows:

My mothers, who've cared for me with kindness from beginningless time, are disturbed by the spirits of the afflictive emotions. They are thereby crazed, without self-control. They have neither eyes to see the path of high status and definite goodness nor a spiritual teacher to guide to the blind. As they are disturbed by committing wrong actions every moment, they are overwhelmed. If I neglect those who are walking on the edge of the frightful abyss of samsara in general and the lower realms in particular, it would be very shameful. Therefore, in order to return their kindness, I will liberate them from the suffering of samsara and then establish them in the bliss of liberation. Please bless me, guru deity, to be able to do that.

With your guru deity atop your head, meditate on repaying the kindness of all mother sentient beings. Negative emotions are here likened to spirit possessions that are making your former mothers insane. That they have no eyes to see the "path to high status" means that they lack the wisdom understanding the laws of karmic causality and the nature of the training in ethics in order to gain rebirths in the three higher realms. That they have no eyes to see the "path to definite goodness" means that they lack the wisdom understanding emptiness, which would grant them the state of liberation from samsara. They are, in other words, blind both to the perfect conventional view understanding the nature of causality and to the perfect transcendental view of ultimate truth. Not only are they blind within samsara, they also have no spiritual teacher to guide them safely on the path. They are bereft. These instructions on seeing your former mothers as tormented by the demons of afflictive emotions and as out of control comes from Master Shantideva's *Compendium of Trainings*. Thinking of your former mothers' terrible state inspires the wish to repay their past kindness. The ultimate way to repay their kindness is to engage in spiritual practice so that you can liberate them from the sufferings of samsara.

An additional, slightly different pith instruction is to imagine your own mother being carried away on turbulent rapids, calling out for your help. Imagine that you're standing on the shore and that you have the capacity to save her. Once you've heard her cries, it would be utterly unbearable to let her drown. To stand on the shore singing, playing, or picnicking would not only be horribly shameful and immoral, it would be impossible. So, after visualizing like that with your mother of this life, visualize that all sentient beings are drowning in the ocean of samsaric suffering and crying out for your help. You do have the capacity to save them because you have a precious human rebirth that allows you to attain enlightenment and thereby free them. Think that failing to use your precious human rebirth to attain enlightenment in order to liberate all mother sentient beings would be like someone who sang and played beside the river as his drowning mother cried out to him for help.

Cultivating Love

Next, wishing to repay the kindness of mother sentient beings, cultivate love for them.

Here is how you cultivate love. Having visualized one who is intimate, such as your own mother, think:

How can this person have uncontaminated happiness? She does not have even mere contaminated happiness. What she now exaggerates as being happiness will become suffering. Desiring some happiness, she makes an all-out effort physically and mentally, but she is creating the cause of the suffering of bad rebirths in her next life. In this life as well, she is tired and troubled. Therefore she never has real happiness and creates only misery.

How wonderful it would be, therefore, if this person had happiness and the causes of happiness. May she have happiness and the causes of happiness. I will provide her with happiness and its causes. Please bless me, guru deity, to be able to do that.

When you have experience of that, take as your object first other close persons such as your father, then neutral beings, your enemies, and finally all sentient beings, and meditate as before.

You begin the cultivation of love by focusing on someone you're already intimate with, because doing so is easier than focusing on a stranger or an enemy. This is because a feeling of intimacy and warmth is an essential part of love. When, grounded in such feelings, you wish for that other person to have the happiness that he or she currently lacks, that's love. You can only cultivate love for those who lack happiness. You cannot cultivate love toward buddhas because they lack no happiness, but all other sentient beings are deprived of ultimate, uncontaminated happiness, so you can cultivate a sense of intimacy along with the wish for them to gain every sort of happiness they lack.

Of course ordinary beings do occasionally experience contaminated, temporary happiness. Contaminated happiness is not happiness from its own side but rather is the elimination of a specific kind of suffering. For example, if you're hungry and then you eat, you've temporarily eliminated the suffering of hunger. Such contaminated happiness is not authentic happiness but is rather an elimination of suffering that we then call happiness. Such happiness can bring other sufferings as side effects. For example, if you're hungry and eat, your contaminated happiness can easily give way to indigestion, high cholesterol, weight gain, and so forth. Contaminated happiness is therefore the elimination of a specific suffering that itself can lead to further suffering. Such happiness is not at all sufficient, and our former mothers often don't even have this contaminated happiness! On top of that, they often create negative karma while seeking such fleeting pleasures. Cultivate love wishing them the highest, most sublime, unending happiness. Wish them uncontaminated happiness, a permanent happiness totally unmixed with afflictive emotions.

As expressed in the prayer above, love has four infinite aspects as it develops. The first is infinite wish, which arises with thoughts of how nice it would be if everyone could enjoy genuine happiness and its causes. The second is infinite prayer, which arises with your heartfelt prayers that all sentient beings might actually have the highest happiness and its causes. The third is infinite determination, which arises with a sense of personal responsibility to ensure that all sentient beings enjoy happiness and its causes. The fourth is infinite supplication, which arises with requests to the guru deity to bless you to be able to succeed in leading all sentient beings to happiness and its causes. So first you cultivate those four states of love toward close people, then people you usually feel neutral toward, then enemies, and then all sentient beings.

When training in love and compassion, it's very helpful to memorize verses that powerfully express these qualities and then to recite verses all the time. You can bring them to mind or recite them aloud whether you're walking, driving, working, eating, spending time with your family, or whatever. Shantideva's *Guide to the Bodhistava's Way of Life* contains many excellent verses for this purpose, including:

> Whatever the miseries of sentient beings may be,
> may they ripen upon me alone.

The *Guru Puja* also has many excellent verses such as:

> And thus, perfect, pure, compassionate gurus,
> I seek your blessings that all karmic debts, obstacles, and suf-
>   ferings of mother sentient beings
> may without exception ripen on me right now
> and that I may give my happiness and virtue to others
> and thereby install all beings in bliss.

There's also a powerful verse by Kashmiri Pandita that says:

> If I experience happiness,
> I give it as collected offerings to the gathering—all sentient
>   beings;
> by virtue of this, may happiness fill the extent of space.
> If I experience suffering,
> may I be able to bear the sufferings of all sentient beings
> and dry out the ocean of sorrows.

Meditating as described above during your formal sessions and then reciting verses like these while engaged in other daily activities is an effective means for continuously developing love and compassion.

When there comes a time that, whether you see friends, relatives, enemies, or strangers, you naturally cherish them all as intimate and precious and you quite spontaneously wish for all of them to have every happiness, that's the sign of having succeeded in realizing immeasurable love.

Cultivating Compassion

> Here is how you cultivate compassion. Meditating on the guru deity on your crown, first bring to mind some beings who are tormented by misery, such as sheep who are being slaughtered by a butcher. The way you do that is as follows: Visualize the sheep in front of you, and think about how they are being tormented by misery. Their limbs are bound, and the skin on their chest is split open. As the butcher's hand reaches inside, they understand directly that they are about to die. They look at the butcher's face with eyes rolling in terror. Then think:
>
> > Therefore, how wonderful if they were free from suffering and all the causes of suffering. May they be free from suffering and all the causes of suffering. I will free them from suffering and all its causes. Please bless me, guru deity, to be able to do that.

The fifth of the seven points is meditation on compassion. There are two sequences of contemplations for giving rise to great compassion. One goes from cultivating compassion for friends to neutral persons to enemies to all sentient beings. The other method is to begin with those with more intense suffering and then gradually move to those who are experiencing less suffering. *Easy Path* follows this second approach. Compassion differs from love in that compassion focuses on sentient beings' suffering, wishing from one's heart to free them from that suffering. Focusing on especially intense suffering can be particularly powerful in evoking compassion.

You again begin with your guru deity atop your head. Then you imagine sentient beings who are experiencing great misery. Bring them to mind and empathize with their suffering, thereby giving rise to compassion. Think of sentient beings in general as being like sheep being slaughtered. This method described is how sheep are slaughtered in Tibet. You can also think of how they kill sheep and cows on industrial farms in the West. The point is to engage in a creative visualization of beings being slaughtered, suffering terribly. Based on heartfelt empathy for their suffering, cultivate the four infinite aspects of compassion described in the text, which correspond with the four aspects of love described earlier.

> When you've had experience of that, take as your object of observation beings who harm other beings by eagerly engaging in a variety of nonvirtuous actions and wrongdoing, who hold wrong views, who abandon the teachings, who practice corrupt ethics, or who heedlessly misuse the wealth of the Sangha. Then meditate. The way you do that is as follows. Visualize their forms in front of you and think:
>
>> If these beings do such things now, they will not have happiness even in this life. Immediately after death, without doubt they will be reborn in the lower realms. When they're born there, they will necessarily experience a host of intense miseries for a long time. Therefore, how wonderful if they were free from suffering and all the causes of suffering. May they be free from suffering and all the causes of suffering. I will free them from suffering and all its causes. Please bless me, guru deity, to be able to do that.

Then focus on sentient beings who are doing especially heavy negative actions. Imagine and empathize with the sufferings they experience now and the horrible sufferings they will experience in the future. As you empathize with this suffering again and again, cultivate the four infinite aspects of compassion.

> When you have experience of that, visualize before you persons close to you, such as your mother, and think:
>
>> These persons have been making an all-out effort physically and mentally in this life to aid their friends and guard against their enemies. Tormented by both the suffering of change and the suffering of suffering, they have not had even the slightest occasion of happiness. In this life they are also busy doing wrong actions and have not produced a virtuous mind. Immediately after death they will be reborn in lower realms and will have to experience a host of intense miseries for a long time. Therefore, how wonderful if they were free from suffering and all the causes of suffering. May they be free from suffering and all the causes of suffering. I will free them from suffering and all its causes. Please bless me, guru deity, to be able to do that.
>>
>> When you have experience of that, meditate as above toward neutral beings, then enemies, and finally all sentient beings.

Next focus on people close to you, such as your own mother, thinking about their present and future suffering. Again you cultivate those four infinite aspects of compassion. Then do the same with neutral persons, enemies, and all sentient beings.

If you find it difficult to generate compassion for all sentient beings, go back to meditating on how all beings have been your mother in countless previous lives and have been so kind to you. Think about their great kindness. You can also think about how your attaining all the realizations of the path up to full enlightenment is totally dependent on those other sentient beings. If you repeatedly practice viewing others as kind and then think about the various sufferings they experience and continue creating further causes to experience, despite their desperately wanting happiness, such reflections will help you generate compassion.

The benefits of love and compassion are really remarkable. Recall that when the Buddha was meditating under the Bodhi Tree and was attacked by hosts of demonic forces, he didn't respond with magic or weapons. Instead he entered into single-pointed meditation on loving-kindness and thereby subdued them all. In the *Sutra Perfecting the Gathering of Dharma*, the Buddha taught, "There is one Dharma that when realized is like gathering all the Dharma in the palm of your hand. That Dharma is great compassion." If you succeed in giving rise to great love and compassion, you'll naturally be able to realize all other Dharma teachings. Kadam Master Chengawa said that whether you wish to gain influence over many people or subdue your enemies, the best method is loving-kindness. Sakya Pandita said that love subdues those who are gentle and love subdues those who are violent. In the *Precious Garland*, Arya Nagarjuna said:

> The merit of feeding others
> three hundred kinds of food three times each day
> cannot compare with the merit gained
> from a moment's meditation on love.

Even hearing the word *love* has the power to bring calm, peace, and tranquility. Meditating on love for all the beings on one planet has the power to bring a rebirth as the king of that whole planet. Meditating on love for all beings in the three realms creates the cause to take rebirth as Brahma, lord of the three realms. And meditating on love for all mother sentient beings has the power to cause you to become a buddha!

The Exceptional Attitude of Universal Responsibility

> When in that way you have transformed your mind with love and compassion, cultivate the exceptional attitude. Here is how you do that. Meditating on the guru deity on your crown, think as follows:

> I will free from suffering and the causes of suffering all sentient beings, who are bereft of happiness and tortured by misery. I will join them with happiness and the causes of happiness. In particular, I will help all mother sentient beings to attain the high state of a completely perfect buddha, which is the abandonment of the two obscurations together with their predisposing latencies. Please bless me, guru deity, to be able to do that.

Having meditated on seeing all beings as your mothers, remembering their kindness, wishing to repay their kindness, cultivating love, and cultivating compassion, next comes meditation on the exceptional attitude of universal responsibility. This very special kind of altruistic mind combines love and compassion together in one meditation, but here they are no longer left at just the level of immeasurable intention. At this point you intensify that intention so that you generate the exceptional attitude of shouldering the responsibility yourself to free all beings from suffering and lead them to happiness. You voluntarily take that responsibility on yourself. It's called "exceptional" because it's superior to the minds of hearers and solitary realizers. Arhats do have great, universal compassion, but they don't have this exceptional mind accepting personal responsibility to effect the welfare of all sentient beings.

Bodhichitta

> After that is the way to meditate on bodhichitta. Meditating on the guru deity on your crown, think as follows:

> "Well," someone may ask, "Do you have the ability to establish all sentient beings in the high state of a completely perfect buddha?" At present, I cannot establish even a single sentient being in the high state of a completely perfect buddha. Furthermore, although I attain the high state of either of the two arhats, I could provide only for the welfare of a few sentient beings, but I

would not have the ability to establish *all* sentient beings
in the high state of a completely perfect buddha. Who
has such ability? A completely perfect buddha has it. The
good qualities of a buddha's body include being adorned
by the bright, complete marks and signs. Their speech
has good qualities such that in each instant their voice,
which has sixty qualities, gives teachings effortlessly to
all sentient beings, each in their own language. The good
qualities of their mind is their direct realization of all
conventional and ultimate phenomena as well as their
great compassion for all sentient beings, which is like a
mother's loving-kindness for her only child. Because they
bestow their compassion without discrimination, they do
not begrudge for even a moment the time spent taming
[disciples]. Their enlightened influence is effortless and
spontaneous. Even by a single emanation of light from
their body, speech, and mind, they're able to establish in
the high state of omniscience an immeasurable number
of sentient beings.

In brief, only completely perfect buddhas have separated from all kinds of faults and possess all kinds of
good qualities. Therefore, if I am going to accomplish the
welfare of both myself and others, I must attain the high
state of a buddha. Thus I will attain by all means the high
state of a completely perfect buddha as soon as possible
for the sake of all sentient beings. Please bless me, guru
deity, to be able to do that.

By making that prayer, a second body emerges from the guru
deity on your crown, like passing of the flame of one candle to
another, and merges with you. Imagine yourself as Conqueror
Shakyamuni seated on a cushion of lotus, moon, and sun on a
high and wide jeweled throne supported by eight great lions,
and so on. [Your body is the color of refined gold. Your head
has a crown protrusion. You have one face and two arms. Your

right hand presses the earth. In your left hand, which is in the gesture of meditative equipoise, you carry an alms bowl filled with nectar. You wear elegantly the three saffron-colored robes of a monk. Your body has a nature of pristine, luminous light and is adorned by the marks and signs.] Imagine that you sit in the cross-legged position [amid an aura of light radiating from your body].

Clearly picturing yourself as Shakyamuni Buddha, imagine that you are emanating your body, resources, and roots of virtue in the form of the five-colored nectars together with rays of light. These reach all sentient beings. Then imagine that all sentient beings thereby attain the perfect happiness of high status and definite goodness.

The seventh practice is the result: the generation of bodhichitta itself. For this you meditate on the guru deity atop your crown. Recognize that you cannot lead all sentient beings to enlightenment in your current state and that, even if you attain the state of an arhat or solitary realizer, you could only benefit a few sentient beings. Contemplate the buddhas' qualities of body, speech, and mind as described. The buddhas' great compassion for all sentient beings without discrimination is a very important quality. The buddhas' skill in taming and liberating sentient beings is effortless and spontaneous. When the time is right for a sentient being, then a buddha effortlessly benefits that one. So you resolve to attain buddhahood in order to be able to benefit all sentient beings.

The section above concludes with the practice of taking resultant bodhichitta as the path, which was described in detail in the chapter on the preliminaries.

Conclusion
It is the same as before.

What to Do Between Meditation Sessions
Furthermore, in between sessions look at the scriptures and commentaries that show the presentation of love, compassion,

and the altruistic intention to attain enlightenment for the sake of all sentient beings, and so on, according to how it was presented above.

Between meditative sessions read and contemplate teachings about loving-kindness, compassion, and bodhichitta. The rest is the same as before.

7. Unique Instructions for Realizing Bodhichitta

NEXT, *Easy Path* teaches the second method for generating bodhichitta: equalizing and exchanging self with others. However, the Panchen Lama teaches this method in a unique manner that had been passed down in an oral tradition from Lama Tsongkhapa. If you look in Lama Tsongkhapa's *Great Treatise on the Stages of the Path* or his *Middle-Length Stages of the Path*, you'll see that he first teaches the seven-point cause-and-effect instructions and then teaches equalizing and exchanging self with others separately after that. In general, equalizing and exchanging self with others is only recommended for beings of higher mental capacity. These instructions require such high mental capacity because they rely on the conventional method of taking the sufferings of others upon yourself and giving your own happiness and well-being to others and the ultimate method of seeing the emptiness of self and others. Each of these requires high mental capacity. Lama Tsongkhapa himself innovated a unique method for making these powerful instructions more accessible for beginners by combining them with the seven-point cause-and-effect instructions, like two rivers flowing into one powerful current. Lama Tsongkhapa did not write these unique instructions down. They were passed orally from teacher to student until Panchen Lama Losang Chokyi Gyaltsen put them in writing for the first time in *Easy Path* as well as in the *Guru Puja*.

In this approach, which is very effective for beginners, you begin by meditating on the first three points from the seven-point cause-and-effect instructions: seeing all beings as your mothers, recalling their kindness, and wishing to repay their kindness. The purpose of those three meditations is to give rise to great love. Practitioners of very high capacity who can realize great love solely through equalizing and exchanging self with others don't have to engage in these initial steps, but most of us will find this instruction very useful. In this unique approach, great love is generated in two ways. First you generate it as a result of those first three contemplations. Then you intensify that love by meditating on equalizing self with others, on the faults of self-cherishing, and on the advantages of cherishing others. All of this gives rise to very intense, universal love. Having given rise to such love, you meditate on actually exchanging self with others as well as taking and giving, which is an enhancement practice for love and compassion. This naturally leads to the realizations of the extraordinary attitude of universal responsibility and to bodhichitta itself. So you can see that everything from the seven-point cause-and-effect method is included in this special approach to equalizing and exchanging self with others. A key point in these instructions is the skillful means they provide for realizing universal love, from which all the subsequent realizations arise.

Shakyamuni Buddha himself generated bodhichitta through equalizing and exchanging himself with others. Once when he'd been reborn in hell as a horse pulling a chariot, the horse beside him was suffering terribly. Feeling unbearable compassion for his companion, he asked the Lord of Death to allow him to take on that other horse's burden. Totally exchanging self-cherishing for cherishing others, he gave rise to bodhichitta![36] In another lifetime he'd been reborn as a prince who saw a hungry tigress and her cubs starving to death and, motivated by powerful compassion, he gave his body to the starving tigress. It's said that Maitreya, the future Buddha, realized bodhichitta long before Shakyamuni Buddha, but that due to the great force of Shakyamuni Buddha's love, compassion, and bodhichitta motivation, he gained buddhahood before Maitreya. This is the power of equalizing and exchanging self with others.

GENERATING LOVE FOR MOTHER BEINGS

First meditate on equanimity—even-mindedness toward all sentient beings— recognition of all beings as having been your mother, remembrance of their kindness, and the wish to repay that kindness.

Following this oral tradition coming from Lama Tsongkhapa, prior to formally engaging in the specific meditations for equalizing and exchanging self with others, you meditate on equanimity, on recognizing all beings as having been your mothers, on recalling their past kindness, and on wishing to repay that kindness. These result in the experience of great love.

You begin with equanimity meditation from the tradition of Kamalashila as described earlier. When meditating on the kindness of others in the tradition of equalizing and exchanging self with others, you reflect not only on their past acts of kindness to you when they were your mothers but on all of their past, present, and future acts of kindness! Both methods include contemplating others' infinite kindness, but the timeframe and vastness of the contemplation differs in this way. Here, though, begin as described in the last chapter by contemplating their kindness to you when they were your mothers.

I described in the last chapter how to meditate on the immeasurable kindness of mother beings, but because this point is extremely important, I want to emphasize that you should take your time and go into detail. Think of your mother in this life and recall the hardships she went through carrying you in her womb for nine months. She had to be so careful what she ate or drank, she endured morning sickness, and she had to modify how she slept and moved. She went through intense pain giving birth to you. When you were a newborn, she gazed at you with loving eyes, cleaned you with her own hands and even her own mouth, fed you, protected you from harm, woke up in the middle of the night to care for you, and endured all sorts of suffering to look after you. Mothers sacrifice rest, sleep, and even their own health or lives to care for their babies. She taught you to speak and then to read. Even after you'd grown up, she did her best to provide you with resources, education, and guidance. And she's done this not just once but in lifetime after lifetime. After meditating like that again and again, next focus on your father of this life, thinking of how he's been your mother in countless lifetimes showing you immeasurable kindness. Then contemplate the same way regarding your relatives, friends, and enemies. Finally, extend this meditation to all sentient beings, meditating on how they've all been equally and heartbreakingly kind to you across beginningless oceans of time.

Once you've gained an experience of that, meditate on wishing to repay that limitless loving-kindness. This will naturally give rise to warmth, intimate affection, and love for all beings. You will naturally begin to see everyone as precious, and just meeting with beings will bring you joy like a mother seeing her cherished child. Having realized great love in that way, by then going on to meditate on equalizing and exchanging self with others, mixing the two great rivers of bodhichitta meditation into one very powerful current, you'll be able to rise to a very special, inner realization of great love.

Equalizing Self with Others

> Then visualize all sentient beings surrounding you. Analyze, thinking, "Of the two, self and other, which do I cherish in my mind, which do I neglect?" Then produce with its natural intensity the mind that cherishes yourself and neglects others. At that time think as follows:

> It is not correct to cherish myself and then neglect others, because we are the same in wanting happiness and not wanting suffering. Therefore I must cherish others just as I cherish myself; for if someone cherishes me, I am pleased, and so, if I too cherish others, they will be pleased.

Before exchanging self with others, you meditate on equalizing self with others as described here. Visualizing all sentient beings around you, first observe how you ordinarily tend to cherish yourself and neglect others. Notice how you're almost constantly thinking about your own comfort, status, and happiness, while the well-being of others rarely occurs to you unless it impinges on your own. The contemplation taught here corresponds to the verse in the *Guru Puja* that says:

There is no difference between myself and others:
none of us wishes even the slightest of sufferings
nor is ever satisfied with the happiness we have.
Realizing this, I seek your blessings to enhance the bliss and joy
    of others.

Thus, one reason presented for equalizing the sense of importance you give to your own welfare and to the welfare of others is that we're all exactly the same in wanting happiness and not wanting suffering. A second reason mentioned in *Easy Path* is grounded in empathy: you recognize that when others cherish you and treat you kindly this pleases you, so then you can see that cherishing others will please them as well!

Since you already meditated on equanimity prior to meditating on the kindness of mother beings, you may wonder why a kind of equanimity practice appears again here. The earlier meditation is called "common equanimity practice," as it is common to both Hinayana and Mahayana practitioners. It focuses on overcoming the tendency to discriminate others into categories of friends, enemies, and strangers. Here you're developing a higher, uncommon sort of equanimity that is unique to Mahayana practitioners. This second kind of equanimity is more difficult to generate. It's a mind that embraces all beings with equal love and compassion. With this sort of equanimity, you mentally and physically strive to benefit all beings equally. You no longer put your own welfare ahead of that of others.

One can approach the development of this sort of equanimity from the perspective of conventional truth and from the perspective of ulti-mate truth. Trijang Rinpoche, a former tutor of the present Dalai Lama, taught a set of nine methods for accomplishing such equanimity. Of these nine, the first six approach it from the perspective of conventional truth, with three practices relying on reasons related to others and three relying on reasons related to yourself. The final three methods approach the subject from the perspective of ultimate truth. These nine provide an elaborate means of developing this special sort of Mahayana equanimity.

The first of these nine lines of reasoning is that just as you cherish your own happiness all the time, even in your dreams, so also do all other beings, including even tiny insects. As there's not the slightest difference between their wish for happiness and your own, there's no basis for disregarding the welfare of even one sentient being or for discriminating between others and yourself. The second line of reasoning is that if ten hungry beggars were to come to your door looking for food, since they're all equally in need, there's no basis for discriminating among them. Similarly, as all sentient beings are equally deprived of even contaminated happiness, which is as rare as stars in the daytime, and certainly of uncontaminated happiness, there's no reason to discriminate among them. The third contemplation is that if you were to come across a group of sick people, there would be no good reason to discriminate, providing medicine to some and not to others. Similarly, all sentient beings are equal in being sick with the illness of afflictive emotions, so there's no reason to be kind to some and not to others. These first three contemplations rely on reasons related to others—realistically empathizing with their condition.

The next three contemplations rely on reasons related to yourself—understanding your own condition in relationship with others. The first is that in order to achieve liberation or full enlightenment yourself, you totally have to depend on other sentient beings. Your development of love and compassion, your practices of ethics and patience, and so forth totally depend on training in relation to others. All your future happiness and realizations depend on others. You've received immeasurable kindness from others in countless lifetimes when they were your mother, father, husband, wife, relative, friend, and so forth. And you'll continue receiving limitless benefit from them in the future. So there's no reason from your own side to discriminate among them now, cherishing some and not others.

The second of these contemplations addresses the qualm that might arise that, even if others have been kind to you in the past, they've also harmed you. For this, contemplate how their harms are quite small when compared with their vast kindness. It's easy to make the mistake of focusing more on harm than on help. But even in this life, if you think about the many ways others have helped you from the moment of your birth until now, providing sustenance, education, opportunities for work, friendship, and so forth, then you'll see that others' help certainly outweighs their harm to you. By focusing on your receiving so much kindness from all others, develop equanimity.

The third of these contemplations is that there's no reason to discriminate between yourself and others because we're all utterly alike in our mortality. We're all going to die, our lives are short, and when we'll die is uncertain. In samsaric existence, we're like a group of criminals all slated for execution tomorrow, so petty discriminations are really pointless.

The first of the three contemplations from the ultimate perspective is that there are no inherently existent friends or enemies. When others temporarily help us, we develop craving. When they harm us, we develop aversion. Our view of others becomes distorted so that some appear as friends and others as enemies as though such qualities were present inherently within those others, whereas these are just distorted projections from our side. "Friends" and "enemies" don't ultimately exist! From the ultimate perspective there are no true friends or enemies. Therefore, buddhas don't perceive truly existent friends or enemies. Dharmakirti's *Commentary on Valid Cognition* says that if one person were to apply sandalwood perfume to the Buddha's right side and another person were to cut the Buddha's left side with a knife, the Buddha wouldn't discriminate, seeing one as a friend and the other as an enemy. Such categories don't exist in an ultimate analysis.

The second contemplation from an ultimate perspective is recognizing how the idea that there are truly lasting friends or enemies is something imputed by your own mind and doesn't correspond at all to reality. This was taught in the meditations in common with a person of middle scope in terms of the uncertainty of samsaric relationships. Even within this life, friends become enemies and enemies become friends. This is quite true between individuals and between nations as well! Even within a single day, relationships can change dramatically due to changes in circumstances. And over the course of many lifetimes, your son may take rebirth as your mother or your enemy may become your cherished daughter. Therefore, clinging to ideas of real, permanent friends or enemies is unrealistic and pointless. There are no truly existent, lasting friends or enemies; such concepts are actually delusions. Relationships are uncertain and always changing.

The third contemplation is that clinging steadfastly to truly existent, permanent friends and enemies is like clinging to the idea that "this side" of a mountain is inherently "this side." In reality, "this side" is only "this side" while you're over here. If you travel over to "that side" of the mountain, then "that side" will become "this side" to you! Everything in the universe is relational. There are no fixed, independently existing things. "Friends" and "enemies" only exist relationally, from a certain perspective. The very person you consider a friend is, at the same time, considered an enemy by others. And your enemies are others' friends. This proves that they are not actually either from their own side, inherently. They only appear that way in dependence upon labels imputed from the perspective of the person labeling. All three of these reasons show why belief in inherently existent, permanent friends or enemies is totally unrealistic.

If you engage in these nine contemplations in conjunction with the meditations described in *Easy Path*, that will be an effective means of developing the unique Mahayana equanimity that equalizes self with others.

The Faults of Self-Cherishing

> Furthermore, wanting to make everything marvelous for myself, I have cherished myself from beginingless time. Not only did this not accomplish my own or others' welfare, it caused me a host of suffering. Therefore self-cherishing is the source of all troubles, such as the miseries of the lower realms and of samsara in general. Thus I will not produce the self-cherishing that has not been produced, and I will abandon that which has been produced.

Next contemplate the faults of self-cherishing. Ordinarily it appears as though self-cherishing helps you. You engage in cherishing yourself seeking happiness, but doing so only leads to suffering. You must meditate extensively on how and why self-cherishing is the source of all your troubles and sorrows. Self-cherishing is based on ignorance and wrong views. Based on ignorance grasping at an independent, truly existent self, you narcissistically over-focus on your own comfort, pleasure, status, and so forth. Based on self-cherishing, you give rise to craving, aversion, and the whole range of afflictive emotions. Thus you engage in negative actions, giving rise to so much misery. Self-cherishing causes you to harm others and also to harm yourself. A verse from the *Guru Puja* that summarizes the faults of self-cherishing is:

> This chronic disease of self-cherishing
> is the cause creating my unsought suffering.
> Perceiving this, I seek your blessings to blame, begrudge,
> and destroy this monstrous demon of selfishness.

Self-cherishing drags us to the lower realms. It causes all the problems between nations, in families, and in relationships. It's the source of all your worries and sorrows in this life and also in future lives, and it blocks your attainment of the high levels of the bodhisattvas and of enlightenment itself.

The Benefits of Cherishing Others

> Cherishing others is the source of all good qualities. Therefore I'll develop newly the cherishing of others that I've not yet produced, and I'll increase from high to higher that which I have already produced. Please bless me, guru deity, to be able to do that.

Next comes reflecting on the benefits of cherishing others. In *Eight Verses of Mind Training*, Geshe Langri Tangpa compares sentient beings to wish-fulfilling jewels, gems that can bestow anything you request. When you cherish others, you see them as extremely precious like that. You treasure them. Arya Nagarjuna expresses something similar in his *Discourse on Wish-Fulfilling Jewels* when he says that there's no difference between sentient beings and wish-granting cows, buddhas, deities, and gurus. When you love others, you see them as precious, as sources of good. Master Atisha regularly taught that for him the Three Jewels of refuge, his special deity, his guru, and the sentient beings of the three realms were all equally important. In his *Compendium of Trainings*, Shantideva similarly wrote that one should venerate and please sentient beings, poetically likening them to wish-granting jewels, wish-granting cows, precious vases, and also to gurus and deities. He explained that for someone traveling the path to enlightenment, cherishing other sentient beings is utterly essential.

There are two merit fields in relation to which we create the causes of enlightenment. One is the field of enlightened beings, such as the visualized merit field described earlier. The other equally important one is the field of sentient beings. Without others, you cannot practice compassion, generosity, ethics, patience, and so forth. All the good qualities of the stages and paths come from cherishing others!

Earlier you contemplated the kindness of others in past lives when they were your mother. Here you contemplate on others' kindness in the past, present, and future. In terms of mother sentient beings' kindness in the present, you think about how everything good in your life depends on others. The food you eat was mainly grown by others. Eggs, milk, and cheese came from others' bodies. If you're not vegetarian, then the meat you eat was others' bodies! The materials for your home, your clothing, and so forth came from others. Any knowledge or wisdom you may have arose in dependence on the kindness of others who educated you. And of course the meaning and joy you find in being loving, generous, or ethical totally depend on the other sentient beings in relation to whom you engage in those feelings and behaviors.

Regarding the kindness of mother sentient beings in the future, you can think about how all the spiritual practices leading to higher rebirth, liberation, and enlightenment necessitate relying on other sentient beings. The practices of ethics, generosity, patience, love, compassion, and bodhichitta all totally depend on others. Giving rise to any positive spiritual realizations and qualities is utterly dependent on others. So contemplate the infinite kindness of all mother sentient beings toward you in the past, present, and future, developing a deep sense of appreciation, treasuring them from your heart.

You can also recall that if you wish to please the buddhas, you must cherish and please other sentient beings. When the Buddha was a bodhisattva who first generated bodhichitta, his sole purpose was to benefit all other sentient beings. As he practiced the path, all along he strove to benefit others. And once he attained buddhahood, his whole being was completely dedicated to the welfare of others. So of course it's your loving and helping others that most pleases the buddhas!

A verse from the *Guru Puja* that's helpful for reflecting on the advantages of cherishing others is:

> The mind that cherishes mothers and would secure them in
>   bliss
> is the door leading to infinite qualities.
> Seeing this, I seek your blessings to cherish wandering beings
> more than my life, even should they rise up as my enemies.

The mind that cherishes others is grounded in reality. It is characterized by warmth, affection, and loving-kindness for others. It naturally gives rise to other positive emotions and leads you to wisdom. It grants happiness in this life and happiness in future lives. It leads you to the high realizations of a bodhisattva and to the non-abiding nirvana of buddhahood itself! Cherishing others is the source of all good qualities.

ACTUALLY EXCHANGING SELF WITH OTHERS

> In brief, Shakyamuni Buddha abandoned self-cherishing and cherished others. He is a perfect, manifest buddha because he worked only for the welfare of others. If I also had done that, I would have become a buddha a long time ago, but I did not do it, and therefore I have wandered in samsara up until now. Currently, with self-cherishing dwelling in my heart, I cannot newly produce the cherishing of others. Even that cherishing of others that I have produced I cannot sustain continually.

> Therefore, not generating for even a moment the mind that
> cherishes myself and neglects others, I will abandon self-
> cherishing and cherish others.

Having engaged in the contemplations already described, next comes
the actual exchange of self for others. Of course, you cannot literally
change places with others, but you can replace the addiction to narcissis-
tic self-cherishing with a heart that sincerely cherishes others. Recalling
that the Buddha did just that and thereby became enlightened while
you've not yet done so and thus have continued suffering in samsara,
resolve to abandon self-cherishing and to dedicate yourself to cherishing
others. Two verses from the *Guru Puja* that you can use to enhance your
meditation at this point are:

> In brief, infantile beings labor only in self-interest,
> while buddhas work solely for the welfare of others.
> Understanding the distinction between the failings of one and
>   advantages of the other,
> bless me to equalize and exchange myself for others.
>
> Self-cherishing is the door to all torment,
> mother-cherishing the foundation of all excellence.
> Bless me to make my core practice
> the yoga of exchanging myself for others.

With these verses, you strongly resolve to abandon self-cherishing while
cultivating the cherishing of others. You also request your guru's blessings for success to make this the essence of your practice.

TAKING AND GIVING MEDITATION

> Then I will have taken upon my own mind all sufferings and
> misdeeds of others. By giving others all my happiness and vir-
> tue, I will free all sentient beings from suffering and provide
> them with perfect happiness.

Having generated unique, Mahayana equanimity and then having meditated on the faults of self-cherishing, the advantages of cherishing others,
and the exchange of self for others, next engage in taking and giving
meditation to intensify your love and compassion. This naturally leads
to the generation of bodhichitta itself.

One practices taking and giving based on cherishing others, seeing
them as precious and as the source of all that is good. Arya Nagarjuna,
in his *Tales Pleasing a Child*, quotes a set of "verses to venerate sentient
beings" by the Buddha in which he says:

> When I was training as a bodhisattva I gave up my spouses,
> children, flesh, blood, as well as my eyes and so forth in order to
> serve and please sentient beings. Therefore, if someone harms
> sentient beings, that also amounts to harming me. If someone
> venerates sentient beings, that amounts to venerating me. How
> can someone who harms sentient beings claim to have devo-
> tion to me?

If it's possible for you to actually benefit sentient beings, eliminating
their suffering and bringing them happiness, that's fantastic. When you
cannot actually do so, then you should train your mind for benefiting
others through taking and giving. Such mind training will enhance your
love and compassion.

Chenga Lodro Gyaltsen taught that one begins by practicing giving
and then practices taking. However, the First Dalai Lama Gendun Drup
and Gyaltsap Je teach the opposite order, saying that taking comes first
followed by giving. The First Panchen Lama clearly agrees with them,
teaching taking and then giving in *Easy Path* and also in the *Guru
Puja*. This sequence is more reasonable. If you give people food or gifts
when they're in terrible pain, then they can't enjoy them much. So first
engage in taking away the others' suffering, strengthening compassion.
Then engage in giving others happiness, which enhances love. Nagarjuna expressed this clearly in his *Precious Garland* when he wrote,
"May sentient beings' karma ripen on me, and may my happiness ripen
for them."

In an actual meditation session, if you're practicing both taking and giving in one session, then do so in the order just described. The practice is ordinarily done that way. However, it's also acceptable to do one full meditation session on compassion, taking on the suffering and afflictive emotions of others in a deep and extensive way. Then you can do another full session meditating on love, imagining you are giving away your body, wealth, and good karma to others in the form of whatever will bring them the greatest possible well-being and joy. This can be done to deepen your practice of these two positive emotions.

Taking

The practice of taking is a training in compassion. You empathize with the sufferings of others and develop compassion, wishing to free them from their miseries. For this, it can be quite effective to think of others who are suffering in particularly intense ways, as we saw above with the example of the sheep at slaughter. Here you can think of people who are enduring acute illness, loss, or other painful experiences. You can also think of beings in hell, whose sufferings are horrific and uninterrupted. Visualize those beings and then vividly and empathically imagine their sufferings, developing strong compassion wishing to relieve their pains. Imagine taking their suffering and the causes of their sufferings away from them by taking them upon yourself instead. After first thinking of those going through very intense sufferings to develop your compassion, you then apply the same visualizations of taking on suffering and its causes from your mother, your father, a neutral person, an enemy, and finally all sentient beings.

As you practice taking, you can visualize your self-cherishing in the very center of your heart, either in the form of a black seed or like a small light there. When you take away others' sufferings and its causes, you can visualize those coming away from them toward yourself in the form of darkness, like black smoke. Imagine this darkness imploding into the self-cherishing in your heart, destroying it completely. Alternately, you can visualize others' suffering striking your self-cherishing like a lightening bolt, obliterating it.

Giving

The practice of giving is a training in loving-kindness. You can begin by thinking of your mother or others who you naturally cherish, focusing on how they are deprived of the uncontaminated bliss of liberation or enlightenment. Not only that, they are even deprived of contaminated, samsaric happiness, which they find only rarely by undergoing many hardships. Contaminated happiness arises only from good karma, but people often create bad karma in pursuit of their own happiness, and so they suffer more and more. Generate the thought that wishes them happiness and the causes of happiness. Imagining their gaining both contaminated and uncontaminated happiness, progress through the four levels of great love: thinking how wonderful it would be if they had happiness, wishing that they have such happiness, committing yourself to causing them to have such happiness, and requesting blessings to be able to lead them to such happiness. Based on such loving feelings, practice giving—visualizing transforming your own body, wealth, and collection of virtuous karma into whatever is needed for those beings to gain both contaminated and uncontaminated happiness. Visualize love radiating from the center of your heart, granting others everything. Again, gradually expand the scope of your practice to include relatives, friends, strangers, enemies, and finally all sentient beings.

Taking and Giving in Daily Life

The practice of taking and giving is not just for when you're sitting on your meditation cushion. It should pervade your daily life. This means you integrate love and compassion into all aspects of your life! When you see others suffering or when you yourself suffer, use this as a basis for cultivating empathy and compassion, and then practice taking. When you see others experiencing happiness or you meet with some joy, use this to practice love through imagining giving such happiness to all sentient beings.

Master Atisha integrated such practice into all aspects of his life. It's said that wherever Atisha went, he kept his head tilted slightly to the right symbolizing his blocking the subtle energy channel on his right side through which the energy of aversion and anger flow. Even his posture symbolized love.

When Kashmiri Pandita met the Tibetan translator Trukpo Lotsawa, he asked him, "How have you been? Have you been happy, have you been suffering?" Trukpo Lotsawa answered, "I've been happy, I've not suffered." Kashmiri Pandita responded with the verse mentioned earlier:

> If I experience happiness,
> I give it as collected offerings to the gathering—all sentient
>   beings;
> by virtue of this, may happiness fill the extent of space.
> If I experience suffering,
> may I be able to bear the sufferings of all sentient beings
> and dry up the ocean of sorrows.

Taking and giving practice is very effective when you meet with difficulties. When you suffer from physical sickness, loss, or mental anguish, losing hope or becoming depressed doesn't help at all. But if you can practice taking at such times, then your suffering becomes a causal factor for progressing on the path and creating vast merit. While you are suffering, empathize with similar sufferings undergone by others. Pray that by your suffering you can take away the sufferings of all those others, totally freeing them from suffering and its causes. In this way your undergoing suffering becomes meaningful, helping you to practice the path to enlightenment.

Even when you are tormented by intense negative emotions like desire, hatred, ignorance, jealousy, and pride, transform the experience through the practice of taking. For example, if you see something very beautiful and then are tormented by desire, you can practice compassion by thinking of the limitless other beings who suffer from craving, addictions, and attachments. Visualize taking their suffering and the causes of those suffering upon yourself. In this way, even your negative emotions can become causes for virtue and compassion! As Kashmiri Pandita said, when you suffer, visualize taking on others' sufferings as well and pray to "dry up the ocean of sorrows."

When you meet with positive conditions and happiness, you can also visualize giving your happiness and its causes to others. When you eat delicious food, instead of generating more craving, you can reflect on how this enjoyment has arisen due to the kindness of enlightened beings and sentient beings. Visualize sharing the pleasurable experience with all sentient beings. You can also pray that all beings may experience the taste of the uncontaminated nectar of liberating wisdom.

You can also integrate the practice of taking and giving with your breath. With each in-breath, you take on the sufferings of all sentient beings, and with each out-breath you give happiness and its causes to all others. A verse from the *Guru Puja* summarizes this integration with the breath:

> Bless me to cultivate bodhichitta
> through love, compassion, and the exceptional attitude
> conjoined with the wondrous method of mounting taking and
>   giving upon the breath
> in order to rescue all wanderers from the vast ocean of
>   samsara.

It's also very good to memorize and recite verses in your daily life to inspire you in taking and giving practice. You can memorize the lines above from *Easy Path* or other verses quoted above for this purpose. The following verse from the *Guru Puja* is very powerful:

> And thus, perfect, pure, compassionate gurus,
> I seek your blessings that all karmic debts, obstacles, and
>   sufferings of mother sentient beings
> may without exception ripen on me right now
> and that I may give my happiness and virtue to others
> and thereby install all beings in bliss.

BODHICHITTA

> Furthermore, I do not presently have the ability to do this. Who has the ability? A completely perfect buddha does. Therefore I will attain the high state of a completely perfect buddha for

the sake of all mother sentient beings. Please bless me, guru deity, to be able to do that.

By meditating on taking and giving to enhance your love and compassion, you eventually give rise to the exceptional attitude of universal responsibility, which encompasses both love and compassion. With this exceptional attitude, you take personal responsibility for others' well-being.

You generate a very powerful feeling that you will not leave the welfare of all mother sentient beings to others—you will not leave the responsibility to the buddhas and bodhisattvas. Rather you happily take it upon yourself alone. Having recognized all others as infinitely kind to you, you feel you can't leave repaying that kindness to others! You lovingly, compassionately commit to freeing all beings from their sufferings and the causes of those sufferings.

Having made such a commitment, you recognize that you don't currently have the ability to engineer the welfare of others. Recognizing that only a buddha, who is omniscient and has perfect love, compassion, and skill at benefiting others, can accomplish this, you generate aspirational bodhichitta, wishing to attain buddhahood in order to be able to accomplish the welfare of all sentient beings. Having generated aspirational bodhichitta, which is a wish, you next give rise to engaged bodhichitta. Here, bodhichitta goes beyond the level of an aspiration to become actual training in the factors that give rise to enlightenment. The commitment of engaged bodhichitta entails training in the six perfections that ripen your own continuum and in the four ways of gathering disciples to directly benefit other sentient beings.

8. The Bodhisattva Vow

HAVING GIVEN RISE to bodhichitta, you next take and keep the bod-hisattva vows. In the stages-of-the-path tradition, you ordinarily first take the aspirational vows and then later take the vows of engaged bodhichitta. This is how it's done in six-session guru yoga. Shantideva presents another system of taking these two vows simultaneously. *Easy Path* follows Shantideva's system.

> (2) The way of adopting the mind generation through a reli-
> gious ceremony
> (a) The necessity to obtain the vow not obtained
> (b) The way to guard the vow obtained and not ruin it

The Necessity to Obtain the Vow Not Obtained
In the stages-of-the-path literature, it's explained how aspira-tional bodhichitta and engaged bodhichitta are taken in suc-cession. However, according to Santideva's system it is easy to practice them simultaneously. The way to do that is as follows.

Do the stages of the preparatory practices in general, and in particular practice to the point of experiencing the objects of observation of the actual sessions, from the way of relying on the spiritual teacher up to generating bodhichitta. Then meditating on the guru deity on your crown, think as follows:

> For the sake of all mother sentient beings, I will quickly attain the high state of a completely perfect buddha. In order to do that, I will keep the bodhisattva vow from now

until I reach the essence of enlightenment, learn the great
waves of the bodhisattva's deeds, and until buddhahood
sustain the thought, "I must attain buddhahood for the
welfare of all sentient beings."

Then imagine yourself repeating after your guru, Shakyamuni
Buddha:

All buddhas and bodhisattvas,
please pay attention to me.

Just as the previous tathagatas generated the altruistic
    aspiration
and gradually abided in the bodhisattva trainings,
so also will I generate the altruistic aspiration for the
    welfare of all beings
and learn gradually the bodhisattva trainings.

Through reciting this three times, believe that you have obtained the bodhisattva vow. Then develop enthusiasm, saying:

Now my life is fruitful—I have fulfilled this human
    life.
Today I have been born in Buddha's family; I have
    become Buddha's offspring.
Now all that I do will accord with Buddha's family;
I will not defile its purity and excellence.

Having meditated on bodhichitta as described in the last chapter, to
take the vows simultaneously you visualize your guru deity atop your
head and imagine repeating the verses in the text after your guru deity
does so, going through them three times. The verses in *Easy Path* are the
same verses that the Panchen Lama used in the *Six-Session Guru Yoga*
text that he composed, but here we think we are taking the two sets of
vows simultaneously rather than in succession. At the end of the third

repetition, develop conviction that you've given rise to the aspirational and engaged bodhisattva vows.

Then, to stabilize your bodhisattva vows, recite the verse of joy that appears here and also in the *Six-Session Guru Yoga* about being reborn in Buddha's family. Rejoicing in having taken bodhisattva vows stabilizes them.

PROPERLY KEEPING THE BODHISATTVA VOWS

The Way to Guard the Vow Obtained and Not Ruin It
Meditating on the guru deity on the crown of your head think as follows:

> For the sake of all mother sentient beings, I will quickly attain the high state of a completely perfect buddha. In order to do that, I will think about the benefits of bodhichitta and then adopt it three times during the day and three times during the night. Then, whatever sentient beings do, I will not give up on even a single one. In order to increase bodhichitta, I will make effort to gather the two accumulations [of merit and wisdom], make offerings to the Three Jewels, and so forth.

Having taken the bodhisattva vows, you must keep them well. So here you visualize your guru deity atop your head and request blessings to be able to do so. Part of doing so is reflecting on the vast benefits of bodhichitta and generating it three times each day and three times each night. You commit to never give up on even one sentient being, whatever any of them may do from their side. You commit to engage in the practice of gathering the two accumulations of merit and wisdom, which give rise to buddhahood, and also to make offerings to the Three Jewels.

> Furthermore, I will abandon the causes that ruin the altruistic aspiration, such as the four black practices—deceiving with false actions even for the purpose of joking around; creating

regret in others who are doing virtuous actions; saying unpleasant words out of anger to bodhisattvas, those who have entered the Great Vehicle; and misleading others without having the exceptional attitude. I will train properly in the causes that increase the altruistic aspiration—relying on the four white practices and so forth.

In brief, I will keep until I reach the essence of enlightenment—though it cost my life—a pure bodhisattva vow not sullied by the faults of the eighteen root transgressions and forty-six wrong deeds. Please bless me, guru deity, to be able to do that.

You also commit to abandon the four black practices listed here. The meaning of the first three is straightforward. The fourth means not misleading others unless you're doing so motivated by the exceptional attitude of universal responsibility. A classic example of how one might mislead others with such an attitude is lying to a hunter to protect a deer he's trying to kill. In his *Guide to the Bodhisattva's Way of Life*, Master Shantideva says that lying is sometimes permitted when motivated by compassion.

You also commit to adopting the four pure, white practices that are antidotes to those four black practices. These are not intentionally lying; being sincere and honest with all sentient beings; regarding bodhisattvas as your teachers, venerating, and praising them; and guiding those with whom you are karmically connected by encouraging them to cultivate bodhichitta. Engaging in these four actions will block you from doing the four black actions and will help enhance your bodhichitta.

Meditate in this way on the resolve to keep your bodhisattva vows without degeneration until you achieve full enlightenment. Avoiding the four black actions and engaging in the four white actions is a commitment that comes with taking the aspiring bodhisattva vows. The eighteen root and forty-six secondary bodhisattva vows are commitments that come with taking the engaged bodhisattva vows. You conclude this meditation by requesting blessings from your guru deity and inviting nectars and light rays, which descend into you, as described earlier.

9. Engaging in the Bodhisattva's Deeds

NEXT COMES how to train in the enlightening conduct of a bodhi-sattva. The first set of trainings is the six perfections, which ripen your own mind. The second set is the four ways of gathering disciples, which ripen the minds of others. You have to ripen your own mental continuum before you can ripen others', so the six perfections are presented first.

B. How to train in the deeds of a bodhisattva after generating
 that altruistic intention
 (1) How to learn the bodhisattva deeds in general
 (a) What to do during the actual meditation session
 1' Preparation
 2' Actual session
 a' The six perfections, which mature your own mind
 b' The four ways of gathering disciples, which
 mature the minds of others
 3' Conclusion
 (b) What to do between meditation sessions

Preparation
It is the same as in the previous session, all the way down to the supplication:

> I pray to you, unity of the objects of refuge,
> my guru supreme deity, Shakyamuni Vajradhara.

Then pray: "Guru deity, please bless me and all mother sentient beings to train properly in the great waves of the profound and vast bodhisattva deeds," and so on.

THE SIX PERFECTIONS, WHICH MATURE YOUR OWN MIND

The six perfections—the perfections of generosity, ethics, patience, joyous effort, concentration, and wisdom—were introduced briefly in the introduction. Before looking at each perfection in more detail here, I'll share some general points that apply to all six. When bodhisattvas engage in the perfections, six noble factors characterize their practices. The first of the six is *noble reliance* on bodhichitta—they engage in those practices motivated by bodhichitta. The second is *noble entity*. For this, one who has taken the bodhisattva vows makes three prostrations to the buddhas and bodhisattvas each morning and prays:

> All buddhas and bodhisattvas in the
> ten directions, please pay attention to me.
> I, the bodhisattva named [add your name here],
> having given my body and wealth together
> with my roots of virtue to all sentient beings,
> will strive to use today's situation to benefit beings,
> enjoying food, clothes, home,
> bed, and so forth only to benefit sentient beings.[37]

As a bodhisattva training in the path, you offer everything including your positive karma to all sentient beings. Here you also specifically dedicate certain things for today, deciding to focus on offering a particular object, service, ethical training, or practice for the benefit of others as part of your training on the path. In this way you revitalize your bodhisattva commitments daily.

The third is *noble purpose*, remembering that your purpose in doing positive actions such as giving or being patient is to gain enlightenment so as to give temporary and ultimate happiness to all sentient beings.

Fourth is *noble skillful means*, which means to engage in the perfections with an understanding of the lack of true existence—of emptiness. Fifth is *noble dedication*, dedicating the merits you create from your practices to gaining enlightenment for the benefit of others. Sixth is *noble purity*, purifying self-cherishing by means of bodhichitta and purifying self-grasping by means of the wisdom understanding emptiness in all your practices, thereby keeping your practices free of afflictive emotions and obscurations.

There is another list of four factors to apply to your practice of all six perfections. The first of these is *giving*, which here means giving things without any miserliness or attachment. The second is *protection*, which entails protecting the virtuous karma you create from being harmed by anger or wrong views. The third is *purity*, which refers to engaging in your practice of the perfections with an understanding of the pure view of emptiness. And fourth is *multiplication*, which refers to multiplying the virtues accrued by rejoicing in your own virtuous actions and then dedicating them.

The Perfection of Generosity

Meditating on the guru deity on your crown, think as follows:

> For the sake of all mother sentient beings, I will quickly attain the high state of a completely perfect buddha. In order to do that, I will train properly in the practice of the three types of giving:
> 1. *Giving teachings.* Teaching the excellent Dharma to the best of my ability and without looking for gain, respect, fame, and so on to sentient beings who are bereft of teachings

The *Ornament of Mahayana Sutras* defines the bodhisattva's practice of the first perfection, generosity, as having four features: it is an antidote to miserliness, it can fulfill the aspirations of beings, it is enacted from the perspective of nonconceptual wisdom, and it is able to ripen the minds of sentient beings. That same text describes three types of giving: the giving of Dharma, fearlessness, and material things. *Easy Path* discusses these same three. *Giving Dharma* is defined as teaching others to the best of your ability without worldly aims—for fame, reputation, wealth, and so forth. Informally answering people's questions about Dharma or giving them advice when they're in need can also be considered giving Dharma. Reciting mantras or the names of buddhas in the ears of animals can also be the giving of Dharma. When you read scriptures or recite your own daily sadhanas, if you think of the humans, animals, gods, and spirits around you and recite for their benefit, this can also be a practice of giving teachings. You can practice such generosity to others by reciting verses about impermanence or the verse from the *Vajra Cutter Sutra* that says:

> A star, a visual aberration, a flame of a lamp,
> an illusion, a drop of dew, or a bubble,
> a dream, a flash of lightning, and a cloud:
> see conditioned things as such.

When you give away your own stock of virtuous karma during taking and giving practice, this is also considered giving Dharma. It's important to understand that generosity is not the physical action of giving. In Buddhist psychology, generosity is defined as a mind that is able to give away material goods, Dharma, and so forth. Generosity is a state of mind.

> 2. *Giving fearlessness.* Protecting sentient beings who are
> being harmed by humans, nonhumans, and the elements
> from the fear of those

Giving fearlessness is defined as protecting sentient beings who are being harmed by humans, nonhumans, or the elements. "The elements" here includes fires, earthquakes, floods, tornadoes, and the like. Simple acts of giving fearlessness can include saving an insect that's being carried away by water or about to be burned. If you find worms or insects in the heat of the scorching sun, moving them to the shade is giving fearlessness.

Your own cultivation of equanimity, love, and compassion can also be considered a form of giving fearlessness because this protects seeming "enemies" from being harmed by you in this and future lifetimes!

> 3. *Giving material things.* Giving away necessities to sentient beings who are poor and bereft, according to their needs, having abandoned stinginess and not anticipating reward or fruition

Giving material things can include giving away your wealth and possessions, your spouse and children, as well as your body and life. These are described as small, middling, and big giving when categorized by degree. During taking and giving practice, when you give away your body and wealth, this is considered giving material things. When you offer flowers, fruits, and the like to the Three Jewels, that's also a practice of giving material goods. In terms of giving your body, while this would include donating organs or giving your life for others, it also includes offering physical service to others. For example, helping sick people is such an offering. Some bodhisattvas intentionally take rebirth as servants to help others, and that's also a form of giving one's body.

Easy Path mentions just these three types of giving. The *Six-Session Guru Yoga* includes a fourth kind of giving in connection with the commitments of the Ratnasambhava Buddha family. That is giving love. When you meditate on love for all sentient beings, wishing to give them all happiness and its causes, this is giving love.

> In brief, for the sake of all mother sentient beings, I will quickly attain the high state of a completely perfect buddha. In order to do that, I will give to all sentient beings, without any sense of loss, my body, all my roots of virtue, as well as my pleasures. Please bless me, guru deity, to be able to do that.

Increasing generosity is practicing giving.

Having meditated on these types of generosity, you pray to the guru deity, and then nectars and light rays descend as before. Cultivate the conviction that you've actualized the realization of the practice of generosity. The physical act of giving is not the measure of one's generosity. The elimination of all poverty in the world is also not the measure of one's generosity; if it were, then the past buddhas would not have perfected their generosity as there's still poverty. The bodhisattva All Liberated sequentially gave away his chariot, his son, his wife, and his body; his mental ability to do so without attachment was his practice of the perfection of generosity. The true measure of the perfection of generosity is a mental state of dedicating everything to other sentient beings. This is the inner, mental perfection of generosity—being able to give everything without any attachment.

The Perfection of Ethics

Next is the practice of ethics. Meditating on the guru deity on your crown, think as follows:

For the sake of all mother sentient beings, I will quickly attain the high state of a completely perfect buddha. In order to do that, I will abandon the negative actions that transgress the vows I have taken—to forsake the ten nonvirtuous deeds and so forth. Then I'll produce those pure ethical virtues that were not produced in my mental continuum—the six perfections and so forth. Those that have been produced, I'll increase higher and higher. Then I'll lead all sentient beings as well into the pure, ethical virtues and so forth, establishing them in the paths of maturation and liberation. Please bless me, guru deity, to be able to do that.

Next, visualizing your guru deity atop your head, meditate on the perfection of ethics. Three types of ethics are described here: the ethics of refraining from negative actions, the ethics of engaging in virtuous actions, and the ethics of benefiting sentient beings. I mentioned earlier that higher rebirths are characterized by having better bodies, wealth, and associates than rebirths in the lower realms. Generosity causes wealth, ethics causes a better body, and patience causes better associates. Thus these first three perfections play an important role in causing good future rebirths.

The ethics of refraining from negative actions mainly refers to restraining from the ten nonvirtuous deeds. Compassion is the root of the Buddha's teachings, and such restraint from nonvirtue is referred to as the essence of the Buddha's teachings. These practices block the door to the lower realms, and thus refraining from the ten nonvirtuous actions is sufficient karmic cause for gaining future human rebirths. To attain rebirth in the form and formless god realms, you must also engage in the levels of meditative concentration that propel you from the desire realm into those realms.

The ethics of engaging in virtuous actions refers to practicing the six perfections. All the trainings of bodhisattvas can be encompassed within those. These trainings accomplish your own purposes, leading you to enlightenment.

The third kind of ethics is benefiting other sentient beings, leading them on the path to liberation and full enlightenment. This includes the four ways of gathering disciples.

Ethics, again, is primarily a mental training. Ethics is defined as protecting the mind, training it to completely abandon any thoughts of harming others. To refrain from killing, you train your mind to not wish to harm others. To refrain from sexual misconduct, you train your mind away from desire. Learning to spontaneously want to do virtue and to avoid nonvirtue, which harms yourself and others, is training in ethics.

The Perfection of Patience

Next is the practice of patience. Meditating on the guru deity on your crown, think as follows:

> For the sake of all mother sentient beings, I will quickly
> attain the high state of a completely perfect buddha. In
> order to do that, though all sentient beings may rise up
> as my enemies, I will offer help in return for their harm
> without producing anger even for a moment. Then,
> within my own and others' mental continua, I will com-
> pletely accomplish the Buddha's teachings—the perfec-
> tion of patience—and so on.

For the perfection of patience you again begin with the guru deity atop
your head, praying for blessings prior to meditation. The first type of
patience described here is avoiding anger and instead striving to benefit
those who harm you. Such patience does not come easily, so you need
lots of methods for training your mind. Meditate on the infinite kindness
of others, seeing them as incredibly precious, as described above in the
quotes from Nagarjuna, Shantideva, and Atisha. You can also recall how
serving sentient beings is serving the buddhas.

It also helps to reflect on the karma of your situation. Your being
harmed depends not only on the other person but also on your own
karmic imprints. Chenga Lodro Gyaltsen said that you yourself set up a
target for the archer to hit by doing negative actions in the past, so when
the arrow of suffering strikes, think of it as purifying your past karma and
be content. You contributed to the situation. Even so, it may still be hard
to generate compassion for those who torment you. If you recall that
being harmed by them depends on your own negative karmic imprints,
you can see that their harming you is purifying your past karma while
setting up causes for them to suffer in the future. You've made yourself
into a causal factor for them to suffer in the lower realms in the future.
By contemplating like that you generate compassion.

> Furthermore, when I receive unwanted sufferings—such as
> being bereft of food, wealth, home, or bedding, being sick, and
> so on—the experience of such suffering is the effect of previ-
> ously accumulated bad karma. Dependent on this experience of
> suffering, much bad karma will be purified. Therefore I should

not dislike it, and especially I should forbear and be patient with suffering that arises for the sake of practicing Dharma. Dependent on that I will approach the path of omniscience. Therefore I will willingly accept these sufferings and halt my own and others' streams of misery in the lower realms and in samsara in general.

The second kind of patience is accepting or embracing suffering. There are many kinds of suffering we can embrace! For monks and nuns, there are difficulties finding food and clothing. During the Buddha's time, the ordained Sangha went begging daily for alms and so had to bear harsh speech, not finding food, or being given very bad food out of disrespect. Patience was required to overcome anger or discouragement. Of course, laypeople also often meet with suffering related to their jobs! And we can't entirely avoid the sufferings of heat, cold, rain, droughts, floods, and other difficulties that come from the environment. Whatever we try to do, sufferings will naturally come our way. Even if we're just sitting, walking, or trying to sleep, sufferings arise. We all sometimes receive criticism. The sufferings of aging, sickness, and death are unavoidable. Even when you're trying to help others, you'll sometimes meet with difficulties. Suffering will also arise as you engage in spiritual practices such as worshiping the Three Jewels, serving your teachers, studying, meditating, and the like. Sufferings arising in the context of spiritual practices are also to be embraced.

Actually, suffering has many beneficial qualities. *Easy Path* mentions that suffering purifies bad karma created in the past. We sometimes say, "Suffering is the broom, sweeping away negative karma." The *Guru Puja* makes this same point:

> Even if the environment and beings are filled with the fruits
>   of negativity
> and unwished for sufferings pour down like rain,
> I seek your blessings to take these miserable conditions as a path
> by seeing them as causes to exhaust the results of my negative
>   karma.

In addition to seeing suffering as a means of purification, you can also use suffering to develop empathy and compassion for others. As mentioned above, if you practice taking and giving meditation when you suffer from illness or other difficulties, this is an excellent way of embracing suffering and taking it as a path to love, compassion, and enlightenment itself. If you only get upset by your suffering, this makes things worse.

To embrace suffering, you have to see its good qualities. Not only does suffering purify your negative karma and serve as an excellent basis for increasing empathy, love, and compassion, understanding suffering is also essential for generating the sincere wish to practice Dharma. Shantideva has pointed out that remaining firm in the face of suffering, looking honestly at your painful experiences, allows you to generate renunciation of samsara. Shantideva expressed additional good qualities of suffering, such as how it eliminates pride. When everything is going well, it's easy to develop an inflated ego! Suffering destroys such arrogance. Shantideva also notes how suffering induces empathy for others in samsara, thus giving rise to compassion. Next he says that for one who understands how karma works, suffering inspires restraint from negative behavior and enthusiasm for wholesome actions.

Actually, it's easier to remember Dharma practice when suffering than it is when you're happy. As expressed in the verse from Kashmiri Pandita cited above, both happiness and suffering provide opportunities to train in the spiritual path. When you're joyful, recall how happiness comes about due to the kindness of buddhas and sentient beings. Your good karma arose through accepting guidance from enlightened beings and from relating positively to other sentient beings. So when happy, pay homage to the enlightened beings and dedicate your happiness to others. And when you suffer from physical or emotional problems, if possible, practice taking and giving meditation. If you can't manage to take on the sufferings of others, then at least pray that others be free from experiencing the sufferings you're facing. Also think of how this suffering is purifying your past karma and be content.

If you transform your daily experiences into Dharma practice in these ways, you'll be happy and all the while accomplish massive accumulations of merit regardless of what is happening in your life.

Furthermore, I will develop belief in the subjects that bodhisattvas must train in [the five paths, the ten grounds, the six perfections, the four ways of gathering disciples]; the twelve branches of scripture; unsurpassed enlightenment; the inconceivable powers of great beings, buddhas, and bodhisattvas; the blessings of the Three Jewels; and the fruition of virtuous and nonvirtuous actions. If I do that, the effect will be very great.

Having come to believe in those, I will therefore train properly in the subjects of the bodhisattva trainings—the topics that are expressed in the twelve branches of scripture—in order to attain unsurpassed enlightenment. Please bless me, guru deity, to be able to do that.

The third type of patience in *Easy Path* is the forbearance required for sustaining Dharma practice. This does not refer to being patient with physical sufferings that come with study or meditation. It rather refers to the inner forbearance required for developing new understanding of spiritual truths. This sort of patience is very important. Often it's not easy to face and challenge your own doubts and wrong understandings. With this sort of patience, you're willing to challenge yourself by studying the teachings, analyzing, contemplating, and so forth, until you come to new, and clear conviction. Until you gain such conviction, there are times when you cannot yet bear certain truths. When you study deeply, reason, face all your doubts honestly while continuing to contemplate, and eventually generate a reasoned conviction about karma, impermanence, or emptiness, then you've gained the patience of being able to accept or bear a new truth. Bodhisattvas on the patience level of the path of preparation gain a particularly powerful version of this sort of patience, but all of us can cultivate such patience through study and reasoned analysis.[38] Without it, you won't really have stability or conviction in the Dharma. If you accept things out of faith too easily, then later those beliefs can be easily blown over by changing circumstances. But if you study the scriptures and analyze them through reason and experience, then you can come to a firm, stable conviction that will bring strength to your practice.

Eight types of such patience are mentioned. One is engaging in spiritual practices regarding the qualities of the three objects of refuge, studying and dwelling on those qualities to increase your faith and conviction. Second is forbearance as you train to actualize the realizations of the selflessness of persons and of phenomena. Third is the patience of engaging in contemplations of the mental qualities of buddhas and bodhisattvas that you also want to attain, such as innate wisdom, the six types of clairvoyance, and the six perfections. Fourth is the patience of correctly discerning what actions you should take up and what you should abandon. Fifth is patience of meditating on the qualities of the goal itself, full enlightenment. Sixth is patience regarding all the methods that encompass the trainings and paths of bodhisattvas required to achieve that enlightened state. Seventh is patience in studying and contemplating suffering, impermanence, and other difficult topics to be understood on the path. Eighth is patience when studying the twelve branches of scripture, which refer to categories of teaching by the Buddha himself.[39]

After meditating on these aspects of patience, again invite nectars and rays of light, cultivating the conviction of having actualized the realizations of these topics.

The Perfection of Joyous Effort

> Next is the practice of joyous effort. Meditating on the guru deity on your crown, think as follows:

>> For the sake of all mother sentient beings, I will quickly attain the high state of a completely perfect buddha. In order to do that I will never give up my joyous effort and will produce enthusiasm even if it is necessary to attain the high state of a buddha by staying in the Unrelenting hell for a hundred thousand eons for the sake of achieving a single quality of a buddha—the marks, signs, and so on—and achieving a single quality of a bodhisattva, such as generosity. Then, gathering in my mind all the virtu-

ous qualities of the profound and vast teachings, I will establish others as well on the path of virtue and attain unsurpassed enlightenment. Please bless me, guru deity, to be able to do that.

Begin meditating on joyous effort by praying to the guru deity atop your head. Like the *Guru Puja*, *Easy Path* discusses joyous effort from a negative perspective, emphasizing how it overcomes the laziness of being discouraged, even if one must remain in hell for a hundred thousand eons to progress on the Mahayana path. The major marks or minor signs mentioned are physical characteristics of a fully enlightened buddha attained as results of vast merit. Thus, even if one must remain in hell for that long to attain one such mark or sign or to complete just the first perfection—generosity—joyous effort will prevent discouragement.

A positive description of joyous effort comes with understanding how it's produced through four powers. The first is the *power of conviction*—developing clear conviction that the result of your effort exists and is achievable. This includes conviction that you can achieve the resultant state of full enlightenment. Such conviction is powerful in giving rise to joyous effort! Second is the *power of firmness*, which is induced by three types of healthy pride. The pride of action is firmly feeling "I alone can do this without depending on others." Pride of power is thinking "even if others aren't skillful in achieving their own and others' purposes, I can accomplish them!" Power over afflictive emotions is feeling that "I will not be discouraged or overwhelmed by afflictive emotions; I will overcome them!" These three kinds of positive pride generate the power of firmness. Third is the *power of joy*, which refers to rejoicing in the positive actions you've done. For example, if you had a good meditation session yesterday, recall that, rejoice, and think to do similarly today! Rejoicing in your past positive actions helps you to continue doing them. Fourth is the *power of elimination*, which refers to eliminating the tendency to do practices incompletely, leaving some parts out. For your practice of the stages of the path, this entails doing all the preparatory practices well and then including all the parts of the particular practice you're focusing on. In the context of meditation, the power of elimination for beginners entails engaging in many short sessions rather than long sessions of meditation. A third advice that's part of the power of elimination is that if you're doing a meditation session and you begin feeling foggy, or you're having imbalanced energy, or your meditation lacks vibrancy, then you should pause your meditation, revitalize your winds, and then return to meditation. If you continue pushing when you feel foggy, this will decrease your joy in practicing.

Next we'll look at kinds of joyous effort. The *Ornament of Mahayana Sutras* lists four types of joyous effort, while the *Treasury of Knowledge* lists five, adding irreversible joyous effort to the shorter list. *Armor-like joyous effort* occurs prior to beginning a virtuous action and refers to donning the inner armor of strong-minded resolve to endure whatever challenges or obstacles may arise on the way to completing that positive action. *Joyous effort of application* occurs while actually engaging in a virtuous project or practice. It entails doing so with a great sense of joy. *Joyous effort of fearlessness* also occurs while you're engaging in a virtuous practice or project and refers to remaining courageous, not becoming discouraged or giving up on the task even when difficulties arise. *Irreversible joyous effort* is a resolute mind that ensures that no obstacles along the way can shake your initial resolve; this irreversible firmness brings the task or project excellently through to completion. *Joyous effort of not being content* entails not being content with your past realizations and accomplishments and rather striving for higher realizations and accomplishments for the welfare of others.

The various sorts of laziness are the obstacles to joyous effort. Procrastination, thinking to put off virtuous actions until tomorrow, the next day, or even your next liftetime is one sort of laziness. To eliminate such procrastination, remember that this precious human body you've obtained will soon come to an end, that without Dharma practice you may take rebirth in the lower realms after death, and that once you fall there it'll be very difficult to again obtain a higher rebirth like this again! Being attached to negative activities—having bad habits—is another form of laziness. The antidote to this is contemplating the suffering of the lower realms, recognizing that if you don't break your bad habits, then you'll certainly be reborn there.

Having low self-esteem, losing hope or courage, is another form of laziness. Thinking things like "I can't ever achieve the state of perfect enlightenment with qualities like omniscience!" is laziness of low self-esteem in relation to the goal. There are two contemplations to eliminate this. One is to recall that even insects have buddha-nature—the potential to attain enlightenment. If all sentient beings have such potential, then certainly you who are a human being with human intellect who have access to the Dharma can do so! Thinking like this gives rise to joy and confidence. You can also think of how even the buddhas were once ordinary beings like yourself; they practiced the path and thereby achieved the goal, so you can do likewise.

Another version of the laziness of low self-esteem can arise in relation to the path to be practiced. Reading of how bodhisattvas give away their limbs and bodies for the welfare of others and then thinking that such a path is too difficult for you to practice is an example of such laziness. To counteract this form of laziness, think about how it's totally impossible to count how many times you've lost your head, limbs, and body due to being eaten by others in past lives! If you tried to pile up all the bodies, limbs, and heads from times you've been killed in the hell realms, murdered, eaten alive as an animal, and so forth, the pile couldn't even be fit within the billionfold realms. Entire galaxies couldn't hold the corpses! The sufferings you endure on the path are much shorter than those you'd have to go through in the future if you continue cycling in samsara endlessly. Also the sufferings that come on the path are less intense because you face them with the benefit of Dharma wisdom in general and the view of emptiness in particular! In terms of those seemingly difficult practices like giving away limbs and so forth, it's also important to understand that they're not recommended for beginners. You must begin training in generosity by giving vegetables and other food to others. This is not difficult. Eventually you overcome any attachment to giving food. You continue training gradually, and eventually there will come a time when there's no attachment even to your own body and you can give it joyfully.

Another sort of laziness of low self-esteem is losing hope of ever accumulating the very extensive merits required to attain full enlightenment.

To overcome such feelings, dwell on the recognition that once you've generated bodhichitta, which has infinite qualities, embracing infinite sentient beings, aiming toward the infinite goal of leading them all to full enlightenment, then the extensive accumulation of merit becomes easy. Once you generate bodhichitta and take the bodhisattva vows, it becomes easy to accumulate extensive merits even in one moment. Dwelling on such thoughts gives rise to joyous effort in eliminating hindrances and developing the factors conducive to progressing on the path.

Thus, to cultivate the practice of joyous effort, you must first eliminate these types of laziness and then cultivate the four powers mentioned earlier. Through such training, joyous effort will develop more and more.

The Perfections of Concentration and Wisdom

Next is the practice of concentration. Meditating on the guru deity on your crown, think as follows:

For the sake of all sentient beings, I will quickly attain the high state of a completely perfect buddha. In order to do that I will master the concentrations that are worldly and transcendent from the viewpoint of their entity. I will master the concentrations from the viewpoint of their divisions: calm abiding, special insight, and the unification of the two. I will master the concentrations from the viewpoint of their function: abiding in mental and physical happiness in this life. I will master the concentration that acts as the basis for good qualities [of body, speech, and mind] and the concentration that provides for the welfare of sentient beings. That is, I will master all types of bodhisattva concentration. Please bless me, guru deity, to be able to do that.

Next is the practice of wisdom. Meditating on the guru deity on your crown, think as follows:

For the sake of all sentient beings, I will attain the high
state of a completely perfect buddha. In order to do that
I will train in all the forms of bodhisattva wisdom: the
wisdom that realizes the ultimate—an awareness of their
mode of abiding; the wisdom that realizes the conventional—an awareness of the five sciences;⁴⁰ and the wisdom that realizes how to provide for the welfare of others.
Please bless me, guru deity, to be able to do that.

Easy Path discusses the perfections of concentration and wisdom mainly
in terms of developing calm abiding and special insight. These will be
covered in detail in the next two chapters.

THE FOUR WAYS OF GATHERING DISCIPLES, WHICH MATURE THE MINDS OF OTHERS

Meditating on the guru deity on your crown, think as follows:

For the sake of all mother sentient beings I will quickly
attain the high state of a completely perfect buddha. In
order to do that, I will establish all sentient beings in the
paths of maturation and liberation, having relied on the
following good methods of providing for others' welfare
[i.e., the four ways of gathering disciples]:
1. Giving what is necessary
2. [Having assembled them,] speaking pleasantly—giving
   the teachings by means of subduing [those followers
   who are difficult to tame] and guiding [those who are
   more agreeable]
3. Providing guidance to benefit disciples—showing how to
   practice the meaning of what has been taught
4. Being in harmony with the meaning—practicing ourselves in accord with what we have taught to others
Please bless me, guru deity, to be able to do that.

Conclusion
It is the same as before.

Between Sessions
Furthermore, in between sessions look at the scriptures and commentaries that show the great waves of bodhisattva deeds, which are both profound and vast, and so on as described previously.

The six perfections are taught primarily to ripen your own mental continuum. After ripening your own mind through practicing the six perfections, you engage in the four practices to ripen the minds of other sentient beings—the four ways of gathering disciples. Here you begin with your guru atop your head, praying and inviting nectar and light rays to descend as before. The first of these four is *giving what is needed*, being generous with material goods and so forth to gather disciples. The nature of this giving is the same in the perfection of generosity, but the intention is different. With the perfections of generosity, the main intention is to alleviate others' poverty, while here the main intention is to gather them to give them teachings. Whenever you give something with the wish to teach the other person Dharma, it becomes this sort of practice. These two kinds of generosity are not mutually exclusive. Second is *speaking pleasantly*, which means giving the teachings in a way that is pleasant to hear and is suited to the mental state of the disciples. The third is *providing guidance to benefit disciples* to practice what has been taught. The fourth is *being in harmony with the meaning*, which means putting what you are teaching into practice yourself.

In general, you must ripen your own mind first in order to be able to ripen others' minds. That is why the six perfections come before the four ways of gathering disciples. But you don't have to wait until you've totally completed the earlier practices to begin the later ones. It's primarily a matter of knowing which you should emphasize at any given point in your practice.

10. Calm Abiding

Gungtang Rinpoche praised the approach to calm abiding taken in *Easy Path* as very beneficial and skillful for beginners. *Easy Path* takes a practical approach by introducing an object of meditation and then, in the experiential context of concentrating on that object, shows what sinking and excitement are, revealing how to eliminate them as they are about to arise. Rather than initially presenting the framework of the nine stages, six powers, four mental engagements, and so forth, it shows quite simply how to identify and counteract the main obstacles to stable meditation—sinking and excitation. If you follow the approach taught in *Easy Path*, then you'll begin to experience some bliss through your practice, and understanding of these other points will come experientially.

In the context of *Easy Path* you do study those nine stages, six powers, and so forth, but you don't think about those things when practicing concentration. You don't analyze which power you're applying and the like. Instead, you simply begin focusing on the object of meditation and applying antidotes to obstacles as they arise. In this way, you gradually give rise to the experiences of the various levels of meditative concentration and see for yourself which antidotes need to be applied when.

The fifth of the six perfections is called the *perfection of concentration*. "Concentration," or "meditative concentration," is a translation of the Sanskrit *dhyana* and is a general term for focusing the mind. It's closely related to the Sanskrit *samadhi*, which means "single-pointed concentration." And these are also very close in meaning to *calm abiding*, which is *shamatha* in Sanskrit. Calm abiding is by nature a form of concentration, but not all forms of concentration qualify as calm abiding. As these three states are so closely related, I'll teach them together in this chapter.

PREPARING FOR CONCENTRATION MEDITATION

(2) In particular, the way of learning the last two perfections
   (a) The way to train in calm abiding—the entity of concentration
      1' What to do during the actual meditation session
        a' Preparation
        b' Actual session
        c' Conclusion
      2' What to do between meditation sessions

Preparation
In general prepare by doing the stages of the preliminary practices [as explained before]. In particular prepare by relying on the assemblage of causes for attaining calm abiding. Train in the contemplations of the beings of small and middle scopes.

You can see here that calm abiding is described as the very entity of concentration and is presented as a means of training in the perfection of concentration. Then the preparations for calm abiding practice are taught. You must set up the factors required for success in calm abiding practice. First, the six preliminary practices are mentioned; these are the same as described earlier and apply to all meditation topics. Then there are specific factors needed for calm abiding. One such factor is to train in the contemplations common to beings of small and middle scopes taught earlier.

In an isolated place that you find agreeable and that has good companions and a good environment, abide in pure ethics. Then give up extreme socializing, interacting with many people, as well as gross thoughts of longing for desired objects.

Having few desires and being content, sit upright upon a comfortable cushion in the lotus posture with your hands in the gesture of meditative equipoise, pacify your winds, and so on.

For additional causal factors, Arya Asanga mentions thirteen in *Hearer Grounds*. *Easy Path* mentions just six factors, following the tradition of Kamalashila. The first of these is to abide in an agreeable, isolated place conducive to meditation. Such a place would ideally have four qualities: be blessed in the past by the Buddha himself or by bodhisattvas or other great beings, have good friends with similar views and practices to yourself, be a healthy place where the elements are in harmony and that's free from diseases or pollutants, and have readily available food and water. The second of these six causal factors is to abide in pure ethics, which entails restraining from the ten nonvirtuous actions and also keeping any vows and commitments you've taken. Third is to give up extreme socializing, getting distracted by mingling with many people. Fourth is to abandon gross thoughts of longing for desired people or things. Fifth is having few desires, and sixth is being content.

To sit upright on a comfortable cushion includes adopting the seven-point Vairochana posture described in chapter 1, which is conducive to the practice of calm abiding. Sitting in such a posture, you engage in the final preliminary of pacifying your winds. When you are stressed or upset, your breathing pattern becomes uneven, forceful, or agitated. If your mind is disturbed, then your breathing pattern is disturbed; if your breathing is disturbed, then your mind is not at peace. You pacify or subdue your winds in order to bring the breath to a natural, peaceful pattern. This is done through the nine-round breathing practice.

In the nine-round practice, with each in-breath you imagine inhaling the enlightened energy of all the buddhas and bodhisattvas in the form of light, and with each out-breath, you imagine exhaling one of the three poisonous afflictions. The nine rounds are made up of three sets of three breaths. For the first three breaths, breathe in through the left nostril and out through the right. With these first three out-breaths, visualize exhaling all energy of anger or hatred through the right nostril. For the next three breaths, breathe in through the right nostril and out through the left. With each out-breath visualize that all desire energy is exhaled through the left nostril. For the final three breaths, breathe in and out through both nostrils, visualizing expelling all ignorance energy through both nostrils. If you repeat this cycle of nine breaths twenty-one times, you will indeed find that your winds become subdued.

If you wish to do the nine-round breathing in accordance with the tantric tradition, then the actual pattern of breaths is the same, but you add the visualization of inner energy channels of your subtle body. You visualize the central channel, very straight, running through the core of your body, understanding the subtle winds associated with ignorance primarily flow through it. Just to its right is the "channel of anger," so called because the subtle winds associated with anger primarily reside in this right channel. Just to the left of the central channel is the "channel of desire," so called because the subtle winds associated with desire primarily reside in this left channel. With each exhale you visualize the winds associated with those afflictive emotions being expelled.

THE OBJECT OF CONCENTRATION

Many different objects of concentration are used in the Buddhist and Hindu meditative traditions. Some focus on the breath. Even pebbles or roots can serve as focal objects. From a Buddhist perspective, the two most important objects of concentration are one's own mind and the form of a buddha or enlightened deity. The mind is particularly taken as the focal object in the practice called *mahamudra*. Meditation on the mind itself is important because it helps you to learn about the nature of the mind and how to subdue it. A mind that's not subdued is the root of samsara, while subduing the mind gives rise to all the realizations up to buddhahood itself. Thus, taking the mind as the object of your concentration meditation is a skillful way to progress on the path. Taking the Buddha's or a deity's body as the object of concentration is also very skillful. Four benefits of doing so are that it naturally becomes a means of remembering the Buddha, it prepares the mind to more easily engage in the deity yoga of tantric practice, such visualizations bless your mental continuum, and they thereby make it easier for you to give rise to spiritual realizations. *Easy Path* emphasizes this approach.

Actual Session

Although many objects of observation are taught, it is best to focus on the deity's [i.e., Buddha's] body because it serves many purposes: principally it will be the best way to recollect Buddha, one will become a suitable vessel to meditate on the deity yoga of the tantras, and so forth.

The way to do that is as follows: Imagine a ray of light, like a spider's thread, emanating from the heart of the guru deity on your crown. At the tip of that ray, upon a cushion of lotus and moon, is seated the Conqueror, Shakyamuni Buddha, appearing the mere size of an Indian bean seed. His body is the color of refined gold. His head has a crown protrusion. He has one face and two arms. His right hand presses the earth. In his left hand, which is in the gesture of meditative equipoise, he carries an alms bowl filled with nectar. He wears elegantly the three saffron-colored robes of a monk. His body has a nature of pristine, luminous light and is adorned by the marks and signs. Amid an aura of light produced from his body, he sits in the cross-legged position.

Then observe one-pointedly this [appearance of Buddha] seated in the space directly in front of your navel, and meditate.

From the heart of your guru visualized in the form of Shakyamuni Buddha atop the crown of your head, imagine a thin ray of light like a spider's thread radiating to the space in front of you at the height of your navel. Visualizing it too low will tend to induce a dull, sinking mind, while visualizing it too high will tend to make the mind too excited. There, visualize a lotus and moon cushion with another Shakyamuni Buddha atop it, gold in color and the size of a bean. He should be about the distance of one full-length prostration in front of you. In terms of the size of the meditation object, there are two traditions. One says to visualize it as large as possible to create extensive merit. The other says that focusing on a small object—for example, bean-sized as described here—is more skillful as it helps you to merge or fuse your mind with the object of concentration. This tradition of focusing on a small object is more commonly followed.

> Or otherwise imagine that from the guru deity on the crown of your head there emerges, like the flame of one candle passing to another, a duplicate guru deity, which then merges with you. Therefore meditate, focusing your mind one-pointedly on the lack of inherent existence of the rainbow-like appearance of yourself as the Conqueror Shakyamuni seated in the full-lotus posture on a mandala cushion of multicolored lotus, moon, and sun, which is upon a high and wide precious throne, held up by eight great lions, and so forth.

Next an alternative way of focusing on the image of Shakyamuni Buddha's form is given. Like one candle lighting another, you imagine a duplicate of your guru buddha atop your crown dissolving into you, transforming you into Shakyamuni Buddha. Your own body visualized that way then becomes your object of concentration.

Whether you're visualizing Shakyamuni Buddha as yourself or in front of you, if you find it difficult to get a clear sense of his form, then at the beginning it's recommended to place a very good painting or statue in front of you. Meditate by staring with great concentration at the statue or painting, studying the details of color, shape, eyes, robes, begging bowl, and so forth. Concentration is developed by the mental consciousness, not the eye consciousness, so you can't progress very far using this method of gazing. But at the beginning such gazing can be very helpful for developing your mental image of the deity. Once you've developed a clearer mental image, stop using your eye consciousness and focus on the mental image. Although it's a mental image, you do imagine it spatially oriented as yourself or in the space in front of you. Visualize the Buddha's body as made of light, translucent like a rainbow, but with all the detailed features of a physical body, such as the eyes, hands, and so forth.

At that time if you want to meditate on gold and it appears red and so on, or you want to meditate on the object in a sitting posture but it appears standing up, or you want to meditate on a single object but it appears as many, then meditate, focusing your mind one-pointedly on the basic object of observation, without paying attention to those [extraneous appearances].

At first there does not quite arise a clarity that has a nature of clear, bright light, but you should meditate, focusing the mind one-pointedly on a mental image of the body that is half focused. Furthermore, you should make a strong aspiration, thinking, "During this session, I will never let sinking and excitement arise. And if they do arise, I will recognize them immediately and abandon them." Then focus the mind one-pointedly on the object of observation.

Once you have a clear mental image of Shakyamuni Buddha, you shouldn't change that image in terms of its size, color, or posture. If the Buddha in your concentration changes color from gold to red, then you've lost your object of meditation. Similarly, if the Buddha stands up or changes his posture, then that's not good meditation. It means you've lost your object of concentration. So bring the mind back to the original image and focus on that.

Visualize Shakyamuni Buddha in the nature of rainbow light while still having all the detailed features of his form. If your mental image is clear then that's good. But if your image is rough without many details, then don't strive to fill them in yet. If you push for details, you'll lose your stability. Once you get a rough picture, focus on that to gain stability. As stability develops, clarity and details will come more easily later on. At the beginning, stability is more important than clarity. So focus on developing stability using a rough image at the beginning and let the details come later.

FIVE FAULTS AND EIGHT ANTIDOTES

That very focusing is merely being mindful of the mind's object without forgetting it and then maintaining that state of mind continually. This is the excellent method for a beginner to achieve the mental abidings.

Prior to beginning a meditation session, it's very beneficial to motivate by setting a clear aspiration to meditate for a certain length of time. In the beginning, shorter sessions are best. You might decide to focus for ten, fifteen, or thirty minutes, resolving strongly that if sinking or excitement arise in your mind during that time, then you'll apply the antidotes to them. Frequent, short sessions and a strong resolution are important in the beginning. If you begin with long sessions, then you may fall into mental sinking or even doze off, thinking that you're engaging in meditation! Alternately, you may spend a long session with your mind quite distracted. In either case, you'll then develop a bad habit. Such bad habits are very difficult to undo and so become obstacles to gaining authentic calm abiding. So do short sessions and stop while your meditation is still good. Between sessions, introspect to see how well your concentration is coming along. If you do many short, good-quality meditation sessions, then as you gradually lengthen them, you'll develop exemplary meditation.

Laziness

In short, when we cultivate a complete meditative stabilization, we must practice from the viewpoint of relying on the eight applications of the antidotes that abandon the five faults. As it is said:

It arises from the cause of relying
on the eight applications that abandon the five faults.

Furthermore, when we apply ourselves to meditative stabilization, there is the fault of laziness. Therefore, there are the four antidotes to that:
1. *Faith*, which sees the good qualities of meditative stabilization

2. *Aspiration* that is intent on attaining meditative
   stabilization
3. *Joyous effort*, which strives for meditative stabilization
4. *Pliancy*, the effect of that striving

The five faults and eight antidotes to those faults were taught by Maitreya in *Discerning the Middle and Extremes*. The first of the five faults is laziness, the dissipation and procrastination that come from an inability to focus. The four antidotes to laziness are faith, aspiration, joyous effort, and mental and physical pliancy. The four antidotes to eliminate laziness are related; each induces the next. Faith in the advantages of calm abiding gives rise to the aspiration to accomplish it. Such aspiration induces joyous effort, which allows you to attain mental and physical pliancy. Mental and physical pliancy eliminate laziness entirely.

Faith here means that you see the good qualities or advantages of concentration. It's similar to when you see advertising for an item and so wish to have it. *Aspiration* is like generating the desire to actually buy the item. Going out to the store to purchase the item is like *joyous effort*. Joyous effort actually allows you to attain calm abiding. Then, *mental and physical pliancy* are like the pleasure of actually having bought it.

To generate faith, you have to see the good qualities of concentration, so four benefits are taught. The first is that once you've attained calm abiding, even if you engage in spiritual practices continuously, day and night, you won't experience any physical or mental fatigue or tension. You'll also be able to completely immerse yourself in any spiritual practices you do, whether reciting sadhanas or cultivating compassion. A third benefit is that it's much easier to gain special insight into emptiness once you've gained calm abiding. And with calm abiding it also becomes very easy to engage in the completion-stage practices of highest yoga tantra. By focusing single-pointedly on the channels, winds, and drops of your subtle body, you can very easily gather the winds into the central channel. In particular, with calm abiding you will easily cause the winds to enter, abide, and dissolve into the indestructible drop in the center of the heart chakra, giving rise to simultaneously born great bliss. These are all benefits that arise from developing calm abiding. If you understand such benefits well, then your faith will give rise to aspiration, which itself will give rise to joyful effort, leading you to attain physical and mental pliancy, totally overcoming laziness.

Forgetting the Instructions

When striving for meditative stabilization, there is the fault of forgetting the instructions. The antidote to that is mindfulness. Moreover, mindfulness is not just not forgetting of the object of observation; it is having an incisive ascertaining consciousness that has made the mind strong from focusing it one-pointedly on the object of observation.

The second fault is called *forgetting the instructions*, which actually means losing track of the object you've set out to meditate upon. If you're intending to meditate on the form of the Buddha and you lose that object, this fault has occurred. The antidote to such forgetting is mindfulness. Here we must recall or remain mindful of the object of our meditation. Such mindfulness has three features: it necessarily focuses on the mental image of something with which you are familiar, it focuses on that image single-pointedly, and it eliminates distraction.

Sinking and Excitement

When engaged in meditative stabilization, there are the faults of both sinking and excitement. The antidote to those is introspection. Introspection examines well whether sinking and excitement are arising or not. Therefore those of sharp minds are able to recognize when both sinking and excitement are starting to arise and abandon them right then. Those of middling abilities abandon them immediately upon arising. And those of lowest mental abilities recognize sinking and excitement shortly after they arise and abandon them.

The third fault is sinking and excitement. Introspection, vigilantly checking on whether either of these has arisen, is their antidote. While your main focus is on your meditation object, another small part of the mind introspects, checking up to see if either sinking or excitement is occurring. *Sinking* occurs when the mind becomes dull, losing the intensity or vitality with which it holds the object of meditation. The strength or vivid clarity of the mind is lost, and so it's like the mind sinks down somewhat. In *Melody of Laughter of Losang's Teachings: Responses to Questions*, Panchen Losang Chokyi Gyaltsen describes three levels of sinking. First is subtle sinking, during which your mind holds the image in meditation with clarity and vitality but the vitality has diminished a little bit. With middling sinking, even though you hold the object with clarity, there's no vitality at all. With gross sinking, you continue holding the object but there's neither clarity nor intensity.

Excitement occurs when the mind becomes distracted outwardly to a desired object. The technical definition is "a secondary mind that is in the nature of the mental factor of desire, which disrupts calm abiding." Excitement also has three levels. With subtle excitement, you've not lost the object of meditation and desire has not yet arisen, but the object of desire is about to arise to your mind. With middling excitement you're still focused on the object of concentration but part of your mind is already distracted to desire. When you've totally lost the object of meditation, having become distracted by desire, that's gross excitement.

Since distractions in meditation can be caused by anger, worry, or even by the wish to do other wholesome actions, you may wonder why excitement is defined solely as distraction caused by desire. Desire is the most important factor that distracts our meditation. Of the three realms—desire, form, and formless realms—those newly achieving calm abiding are necessarily in the desire realm. Those in the other two realms have already achieved calm abiding, which is how they got to those realms. We live in the desire realm, so distractions caused by desire are the predominant factors that must be overcome for us to achieve calm abiding.

To counteract sinking and excitement, you must introspect, vigilantly checking on whether either of these has arisen. Those of highest capacity detect sinking or excitement just before they occur, thereby preventing them. Middling practitioners detect them just after they happen. Least capable meditators detect them not long after they've arisen.

Question: What is the difference between sinking, excitement, and lethargy?

Answer: Lethargy has the subjective aspect of heaviness of mind and body, and the object of observation is unclear. Gross sinking is as if the mind has come under darkness; although the mind does not scatter to another object of observation, the strength of mindfulness has weakened, and the factors of clarity and subjective clarity are not present.[41] In subtle sinking the factors of clarity and subjective clarity are present, but the ascertaining consciousness that holds the object of observation has loosened a little.

There's a difference between sinking and lethargy. *Lethargy* is a state in which the mind has become foggy. The mind and body become heavy and are no longer useful for meditation. At such times it's often necessary to take a break from meditation. With gross sinking, you lose both clarity and intensity but are still holding the object of meditation. At such times, it's good to attempt to apply antidotes to sinking. If those don't work, then again it's wise to take a break from meditation to refresh yourself.

When there is both clarity and stability but the intensity of the clarity diminishes a little bit, this is subtle sinking. Due to repeated problems with subtle sinking, gross sinking arises, so it's best to apply antidotes as quickly as possible. Also, since you don't lose the object of meditation during subtle sinking, some meditators mistake this for calm abiding. If you make that mistake and fail to apply the antidotes to subtle sinking, then your meditation doesn't progress, and you don't achieve the mental and physical bliss and pliancy of calm abiding.

The antidotes [to sinking, excitement, and lethargy] are:
1. Reflection on the good qualities of the Three Jewels
2. Contemplation of the signs of appearances
3. Practice of the instructions on mixing the mind, winds, and space

When your introspection reveals sinking, excitement, or lethargy, then you must apply their respective antidotes for your meditation to progress. Since sinking is a low state of mind, to counteract it you must elevate your mind, filling it with joy. Sadness, dullness, and depression are related to sinking. One means of bringing joy to the mind is to think about the good qualities of buddhas and bodhisattvas. Another is to visualize the entire environment filled with brilliant light rays. If that doesn't work then a forceful method for eliminating sinking can be used. This method was taught by Master Padampa Sangye and also by Khedrup Rinpoche in his *Twenty-One-Verse Booklet*. For this, visualize yourself in a rainbow body with the central channel running straight up through its center. Place your mind inside the center of your heart chakra, imagining it as the size of the egg of a small bird. Utter *Phat!* and imagine that egg going from your heart to your throat. Utter *Phat!* again and imagine it going from your throat to your crown. Utter *Phat!* a third time as the egg exits through your crown and utterly merges with limitless space.[42] Stay for a few minutes in that state of union with the limitless expanse of space itself. This is the forceful means of counteracting sinking.

> Subtle excitement is when the mind does not stay without moving on the object of observation and scatters a little. As an antidote to this you should meditate relying on mindfulness and introspection. Coarse excitement is when the mind does not stay on the object and scatters to desirable objects, though one relies on mindfulness and introspection. The antidote is to meditate on impermanence and the sufferings of both the three lower realms and samsara in general. You can also practice the instructions on cutting excitement forcefully.

With subtle excitement, you've not lost your object of concentration, but there's a slight distraction to an object of desire. You eliminate this through mindfulness and introspection. In this context, *mindfulness* refers to remembering the object of your meditation, holding it in your awareness, while *introspection* entails monitoring the quality of your concentration to determine if this focus has caused your distraction to fade away. If that doesn't work and desire continues, then as taught in *Essence of the Middle Way*, meditate on impermanence, the sufferings of lower realms, and the sufferings of samsara in general. These counteract or calm the agitation of excitement. If these don't work, you can employ the instruction for forcefully eliminating mental excitement. This forceful method involves vase breathing—breathing in slowly and deeply, pressing the upper winds down to your navel.[43] At the same time, you tighten the muscles of your pelvic floor, bringing the lower winds up. In this way, your upper and lower winds meet together in a "kiss" at your navel. You then hold your breath, also holding the upper and lower winds, concentrating on the navel. Hold the vase breath for however long is comfortable, count five breaths, and then do another vase breath. When you release that one, count seven breaths and then do another vase breath. You can continue this process, counting more breaths between each vase breath until you get to fifteen or twenty-one breaths, by which time the mental agitation and excitement will have ceased.

Not Applying the Antidotes or Over-Applying the Antidotes

> When both sinking and excitement arise, there is the fault of not applying [the antidote]. The antidote to that is to recognize immediately that sinking and excitement have arisen and rely on application [of the antidotes], which abandon them. Moreover, when a consciousness engages the object of observation very tightly, it has intensity and clarity, but excitement predominates, and it is difficult to obtain stability. If the consciousness is not very tight and becomes loose, it has stability, but sinking predominates, and it's difficult to obtain clarity. Therefore, measuring your own experience, think, "If I just heighten my mind, it will produce excitement," and loosen it a little. Think, "If I just let my mind go, it will produce sinking," and heighten your mind slightly; then it will be just right.
>
> Therefore, at the juncture of both [sinking and excitement], turn the mind away from scattering and excitement and seek

the factor of stability. When this factor of stability arises, watch for sinking and then bring forth a consciousness that has clarity and intensity. By alternating [stability and clarity] and then sustaining them, you will achieve a faultless meditative stabilization. But you cannot have confidence just in subjective clarity, which is without [intensity of] clarity—an intense mode of apprehension of the ascertaining consciousness.

Even when you have stopped subtle sinking and subtle excitement in that way, and the mind has entered a continuous meditative stabilization, there is the fault of over-applying [the antidote]. As an antidote to that, do not apply the antidote to sinking and excitement but loosen the mind and set it in equanimity.

The final two faults in meditation are not applying antidotes when necessary and over-applying the antidotes when there's no need to do so. Here the Panchen Lama is describing how to experientially discover when to apply them and when not to.

To thoroughly discern just how and when to apply or not apply the antidotes, the Kadampa Geshe Laksorwa advised relying on the explanations in Maitreya's *Discerning the Middle and Extremes* (which we've been following), integrated with those in Asanga's *Hearer Grounds*. Those texts explain the nine stages of mental abiding, the six mental powers, and the four mental engagements. By understanding those topics in an integrated way, you'll really see when you should or should not apply antidotes. Geshe Laksorwa didn't fully explicate how to integrate an understanding of the six mental powers and the four mental engagements with the nine stages of meditation, but Geshe Sharawa did. These instructions will help you to understand meditation very well, and they can be applied to your process of studying and contemplating as well.

Nine Stages of Mental Abiding

By practicing well in that way, we will attain the nine stages of mental abiding and then will achieve calm abiding, which has mental and physical pliancy.

The first of the nine stages of mental abiding is called *setting the mind*. In *Hearer Grounds*, Asanga describes this stage as placing the mind internally on your mental object of meditation that has been previously indicated to you by your teacher. Now Buddhist psychology teaches that all virtuous states of mind are accompanied by five determining mental factors—aspiration, faith, mindfulness, stabilization, and wisdom. Vaibashikas believe that all mental states, including negative ones, have an aspect of stabilization to them, but all higher Buddhist schools agree that only wholesome states of mind have this stabilization aspect. So if some degree of the secondary mental factor of stabilization is present in all wholesome mental states, one may wonder how the concentration at this first level of mental abiding is unique. The difference is in the degree of intensity with which the mind withdraws into the object of concentration. At this first stage of mental abiding, the mind withdraws into the object more intensely. The sort of concentration present ordinarily with virtuous actions is not as strong as this. Here, there's an absorption into the object and also a higher quality of concentration. With this initial level of deeper concentration, the danger arises of the mind's sinking or even of your falling asleep! This state is also like when you're absorbed in watching a movie and become oblivious to what's going on around you.

This first level of mental abiding is accomplished through the wisdom of studying. By repeatedly hearing about the object of your meditation, this first level is achieved. In terms of meditative experience at this stage, the inner experience is of discursive thoughts coming very frequently, like a waterfall. It feels like your discursive thoughts have increased, but that's not so. It's just that you've now become aware of their constant flow! At the beginning of this first level, you can remain concentrated on the object for the length of three or four full breaths. When, through repeated training, you're able to remain concentrated single-pointedly for the duration of twenty-one full breaths, you've achieved the measure of having accomplished this level.

The second mental abiding is called *continuous setting*. Earlier your meditation was frequently interrupted, but at this level you have some experiences of sustained focus. The first level came through hearing or study, and this level arises through the wisdom of contemplation. The rest of the nine stages arise from the power of meditation. The inner experience at this level is that discursive thoughts arise sometimes, and sometimes there are periods of peace or rest when they don't arise. Sinking and excitement are quite prevalent at both of these first two levels; they both involve less concentration than they do sinking and excitement. Pabongka Rinpoche says that the measure of having accomplished this second level is that you can sustain the continuity of your mind's placement on an object of meditation for about the length of time it takes to recite one mala of *mani* mantras.

Some scholar yogis, such as Ven. Losang Norbu, say that one attains a small degree of mental and physical pliancy at this second level. Actual mental and physical pliancy come at the ninth level, but a very small or subtle pliancy comes from this second level on. Pemang Pandita agrees with this view, noting that one experiences some joy at this phase, which brings a little bit of physical and mental pliancy. From this point on, you begin experiencing the pleasure of meditation.

The third level is called *patch-like placement*. Here you concentrate, and then when you get distracted, you catch it right away and bring your mind back. You don't lose the stream of concentration. At the second level, it was like discursive thoughts sometimes took a rest. From the third to the seventh levels, the inner experience is as if discursive thoughts are tired. It's like they are exhausted and cannot plague you anymore. Of the six powers, this third level is accomplished by the power of mindfulness.

The fourth level of mental abiding is called *close placement*. Here you're able to make the object of your meditation smaller and more refined, and your mind absorbs into the object of meditation more and more deeply. The mind withdraws into the object more and more fully. From this fourth level onward, you never get so distracted that you fully lose your object of meditation. You can still suffer here from intense dullness and agitation but without actually losing the object. This level is also achieved through the power of mindfulness, which matures and is perfected here.

The fifth level is called *disciplining*. Here, through the experience of single-pointed concentration, your mind is so filled with joy that it becomes naturally subdued or disciplined. On the fourth level, the mind withdrew deeply into the object, so now the danger of subtle sinking is the primary obstacle. At this level you rely on the power of vigilant introspection to detect subtle sinking arising or about to arise. Detecting it, you recall the great benefits of calm abiding in order to elevate the mind and thus counteract subtle sinking. One difference between fourth and fifth levels is that on the fourth there's still the danger of middling sinking and excitement, while on the fifth only their subtle versions arise.

The sixth level is called *pacifying*. At this level, subtle sinking can still occur, but it's no longer the main obstacle. At the fifth level, you practiced introspection to counteract the main obstacle of subtle sinking and uplifted your mind to counteract that. At this sixth level the main obstacle is subtle excitement caused by elevating the mind a bit too much. Again the power primarily relied upon at this level is introspection, which is brought to perfection on this level of mental abiding. Through introspection, you now understand well the qualities of meditative stabilization and also all the various obstacles to concentration.

The seventh level is called *thoroughly pacifying*, because at this level you thoroughly pacify all craving, aversion, mental uneasiness, displeasure, fogginess, sleepiness, and so on. Because both mindfulness and introspection have been fully perfected, it's very difficult for you to experience subtle sinking or excitement at this level, but you do still have to engage in effort to sustain your meditative concentration. The power relied upon here is joyful effort, which is still used to counteract subtle sinking or excitement. The mental engagement required from the third to the seventh levels is called "interrupted and engaged mental engagement" because on those levels, as you developed increasing concentration and decreasing distraction, there have still been some interruptions by dullness or agitation but you've continued engaging.

The eighth level is called *making single-pointed*. Here your single-pointed concentration is no longer interrupted by even the subtlest sinking or excitement. Actually, scholars differ slightly on the point of whether some subtle sinking and excitement can occur at the early part of this eighth level. Ngulchu Dharmabhadra says that at the first phase of this level, you can suffer from subtle sinking and excitement but at the later phase you cannot. Jamyang Shepai Dorje, the well-known Geluk textbook author, agrees with that view. On the other hand, Gyaltsap Darma Rinchen says that at this stage there is no subtle sinking or excitement, and Pabongka Rinpoche agrees with this position. From the perspective of the four types of mental engagement, the third through the seventh levels are described as having interrupted engagement, while the eighth is described as having uninterrupted engagement, so that tradition assumes that there is no subtle sinking or excitement on the eighth level. From an experiential perspective, some conceptual thoughts may arise on this level, but they naturally subside into the practitioner's single-pointed concentration. It's like a great, still ocean with small waves on the surface. Within one's deep state of peace, subtle discursive thoughts may arise, but they are naturally pacified into single-pointed concentration itself. At the first level, conceptual thoughts seemed to increase, and at the second level they seemed to sometimes rest. From the third to the seventh level, it was like conceptual thoughts were tired or exhausted. At this eighth level, it's like all conceptual thoughts are absorbed into meditation itself. At this level, you make a slight effort at the beginning of a meditation session, and then the mental engagement is uninterrupted.

The ninth level is called *setting in equipoise*. At this level, you can single-pointedly and uninterruptedly absorb within the object of meditation without any effort at all. Your concentration is no longer interrupted by any factors whatsoever. You no longer experience the absorption of discursive thoughts into meditative concentration itself because they don't arise. This level of mental abiding—a single-pointed absorption without any interruptions from sinking or excitement—is called "approximate calm abiding" or "the single-pointed mind of the desire realm." It is not yet actual calm abiding.

Genuine calm abiding comes through continuing to practice single-pointed concentration until exceptional experiences of mental and physical bliss and pliancy arise. At the end of the ninth level, mental pliancy arises prior to physical pliancy. Physical bliss arises prior to mental bliss. This process begins when, through the power of your meditative concentration, all the winds of your subtle body that are unserviceable—

that are destructive or don't flow helpfully—are expelled through the crown of your head. The sensation is like a person with a shaven head outdoors on a cold winter day having someone touch his head with a warm hand. There's a sense of warmth and bliss. This expelling of unserviceable winds gives rise to the experience of mental pliancy. With mental pliancy, you're able to pacify all aspects of your mind and mental factors that previously prevented you from engaging in wholesome actions continuously. All negative states of mind and negative mental factors that give rise to resistance to positive states of mind are totally pacified, inducing mental pliancy. Your mind becomes serviceable to continually engage in wholesome states without any resistance whatsoever.

That mental pliancy triggers a serviceable, subtle wind that now totally pervades the body. This very smooth, gentle wind pervading your body causes the body to also become serviceable, so that it too can engage continuously in virtue without any resistance or difficulty. Mental pliancy is a mental experience, and physical pliancy is a physical experience. As the movement of the mind and the movement of the subtle wind are one and the same thing, these changes occur interdependently. Due to that gentle, serviceable wind pervading the body, a physical feeling of bliss or joy arises. When the physical bliss is achieved, one's body feels very light, like cotton. After achieving this, you continue engaging in single-pointed concentration. As you continue practicing single-pointed concentration, it seems experientially as though your body itself gets absorbed into the object of your meditation, so that you no longer even experience your own body. Some practitioners say it's as though every single thing in the universe—your body, your thoughts, and the whole universe—have absorbed into your own meditative mind. At that point you experience mental bliss. This mental bliss is so strong that you feel as though the bliss itself might become a distraction from your meditation, but if you continue practicing, then the intensity of the bliss decreases. When that bliss vanishes, you have attained genuine, perfect calm abiding!

In the post-meditative state, the subjective experience is like having attained a new body. Your negative emotions naturally subside or diminish. Your sleep naturally gets mixed with concentration, so that you cannot tell the difference between them, and you experience exceptional dreams. In terms of your mental clarity, you feel as though you could mentally count the subtlest particles one by one. In terms of purity and radiance, you feel as though you can see all the objects on a distant mountain. If you used mind as your object of meditation, then the mind's clarity, awareness, and emptiness are experienced here, giving rise to an exceptional bliss.[44] Pemang Pandita notes that at the ninth level of mental abiding, you can mix activities such as walking or sitting with single-pointed concentration effortlessly.

Calm abiding is defined as a state of single-pointed concentration characterized by exceptional mental and physical bliss and pliancy attained as a result of single-pointedly focusing on one's object of meditation. It's important to say "exceptional" here because lesser levels of bliss and pliancy are experienced on the seventh through the ninth levels of mental abiding, and minor levels of bliss and pliancy are experienced from the third level on. *Exceptional* bliss and pliancy only come with calm abiding.

The exceptional bliss that arises with calm abiding is not the same as the simultaneously born wisdom of great bliss that comes in the completion stage of highest yoga tantra. When someone progresses in calm-abiding practice through highest yoga tantra practice, they achieve the eighth and ninth levels of mental abiding through practicing the generation stage. They then use their single-pointed concentration to engage in completion-stage practices, focusing on vital points of the subtle, vajra body to achieve calm abiding and special insight simultaneously.

Conclusion
It is the same as before.

What to Do Between Meditation Sessions
Look at the scriptures and commentaries that present calm abiding and so forth as described previously.

With this we've finished the chapter on calm abiding.

11. Special Insight:
The Perfection of Wisdom

BEFORE ADDRESSING the instructions on special insight, I'd like to share a few quotes about the benefits of meditation on emptiness. In the *Sutra Bestowed to Kumara Ratnadatta*, the Buddha said, "Manjushri, if someone listens to this teaching even with doubt, that one accumulates more merit than bodhisattvas practicing the six perfections for hundreds of thousands of eons without skillful means. What need is there to mention if someone listens to it without doubt?" In the *Sutra of the Tathagata's Treasury*, the Buddha said that if someone who has committed the ten negative actions enters intensively into the teachings on selflessness and has conviction and faith in the primordial purity of all phenomena, that sentient being will not go to the lower realms. In the *Sutra of Ajatashatru*, the Buddha said, "[If] someone who has committed the five uninterrupted negative actions later hears, enters into, and generates faith in this Dharma, then I do not call that person's karma a karmic obscuration." In his *Four Hundred Stanzas*, Aryadeva mentions in verse 180:

> Those of little merit
> have no doubts about this Dharma.
> Even by merely generating doubt,
> samsara is torn to tatters.

These passages make clear how even merely studying emptiness, much less deeply contemplating and meditating upon it, is extremely powerful for counteracting negative karma and putting an end to samsara. Even the mere suspicion that things do not exist inherently as they appear to is more powerful than the vastest positive actions performed without that insight.

PREPARATION

> (b) The way to train in special insight—the entity of wisdom
>   1' What to do during the actual meditation session
>   a' Preparation
>   b' Actual session
>   c' Conclusion
>   2' What to do between meditation sessions

> *Preparation*
> It is like the explanation on calm abiding, but there are differences:
> 1. Relying properly on a skilled spiritual teacher, one listens to his or her precepts on special insight.
> 2. Having made the guru inseparable from the special deity, one makes fervent supplication.
> 3. One makes effort to assemble [the two accumulations], purify, and so on.

> One should intertwine these three as a preliminary to realizing the view.

Prior to meditating on special insight, engage in the same preliminaries described for calm abiding plus the additional ones mentioned here. The first is to listen to teachings on emptiness from your guru. For those practicing tantra, the second is to view your guru as inseparable from your special deity and make fervent prayers and supplications. Those who are not practicing tantra can engage in guru-yoga practice for the second of these special preliminaries. Third is to accumulate merit and purify negative karma extensively to help prepare you to realize special insight.

MEDITATION ON THE EMPTINESS OF PERSONS

Actual Session

1" How to meditate [on special insight], having determined the selflessness of persons

2" How to meditate [on special insight], having determined the selflessness of phenomena other than persons

    a" How to meditate [on special insight], having determined the lack of inherent existence of composite phenomena

        1: Matter

        2: Consciousness

        3: Nonassociated compositional factors

    b" How to meditate [on special insight], having determined the lack of inherent existence of noncomposite phenomena

1" How to Meditate [on Special Insight], Having Determined the Selflessness of Persons

Numberless proofs of selflessness are taught in the scriptures of the Conqueror. However, for beginners to understand, it is easiest to determine it from the perspective of the four vital points. The way you do that is as follows.

So regarding the actual teachings on special insight, there are two types of selflessness—selflessness of persons and selflessness of phenomena. *Easy Path* explains that there are numberless analyses and reasons given in the Buddha's teachings to prove emptiness, but the easiest way for beginners to progress is by meditating on four vital points. These four points are (1) identifying the object of negation, (2) understanding the entailment, (3) understanding that self is not the same as the aggregates, and (4) understanding that self is not different from the aggregates.

Identifying the Object of Negation

All the time, even in deep sleep, the mind clings tightly in the center of the heart to the thought "I, I." This is the innate misconception of a self. For instance, say that having done nothing wrong, you are accused falsely by someone, "You did such and such bad deed." There then arises tightly in the center of your heart the thought "I, I": "I did no such a wrong thing, yet I am being accused falsely." At that time the way that the "I" is conceived by the innate misconception of a self is clear.

Correctly, precisely identifying the object of negation is extremely important for meditation on selflessness. The Panchen Lama describes how you hold the thought "I, I" in the center of your chest, giving the example of how that feeling of "I" is intensified in your heart when you are falsely accused. This innate self-grasping is always there but appears more strongly and clearly when you are falsely accused.

"Object of negation" refers to the way you experience the self: as though it exists from its own side, without depending on the mind and body, the five psychophyscial aggregates. It is, in other words, an instinctive sense that the self exists from its own side. Such a self does not exist at all.

Lama Tsongkhapa explains in his *Concise Instructions* how this "self" that is the object of negation arises and appears experientially. It is not something that arises due to analysis. It spontaneously appears as though it exists from its own side, without having to depend on its basis of imputation—the five aggregates. Lama Tsongkhapa says that experientially, this self appears *solidly*. He uses the analogy of walking in pitch darkness, reaching out your hand, and suddenly touching a pillar. At such a moment, the pillar appears very solid to you. The pillar doesn't seem at all to depend on anything—on having been constructed, on its parts, or on the label "pillar." The experience of the self that is the object of negation is similar. Lama Tsongkhapa also says that that self appears *like a lingering thought*, always there in the back of your mind. This is likened to how when you touch a pillar in the dark, the pillar seems to you to have always been in that spot, primordially present. And he says that that self also appears *vividly* to you. Again this can be likened to the experience of suddenly coming upon a pillar in the dark and how that pillar appears to your mind. This analogy and these adjectives are intended to help you identify the object of negation in your own experience.

Shar Kalden Gyatso, a mahasiddha of the Geluk tradition sometimes called "a second Milarepa" due to his accomplishment of *siddhis*,[45] describes in detail how the object of negation appears. He begins with an analogy, like Lama Tsongkhapa's, of reaching out in the pitch darkness and touching a table. When you lay your hand on the table, you instinctually think and feel that the table exists from its own side and always has. It seems like you're touching something that's always been there, primordially. Although the existence of the table depends on many factors such as its component parts and your own imputation of "table" once you laid your hand on it, it ordinarily would never occur to you when you touch a table in the dark that it doesn't exist from its own side. You never think at such a moment that it only arises in dependence on many factors including its component parts and your own labeling! You instinctively think that it existed prior to your touching it, that it exists from its own side, and that it doesn't depend on its parts or your labeling. This is how you experience the object of negation. You instinctively think that the self existed in your mental and physical aggregates prior to your labeling it. You think it exists from its own side, and it doesn't occur to you that it's merely labeled by yourself. Your thought that a self exists from the side of the aggregates—that it exists there independently of your imputation—is the object that must be refuted.

Kalden Gyatso continues by explaining that there are actually two objects that must be refuted or destroyed. One is that object just described—the independently existent "I" on the aggregates—which is actually a totally nonexistent entity. That is like a hallucination—something that appears to you but has never existed at all. The other is the subjective self—the mind that clings and grasps at that hallucination as though it did exist. It's like a person with jaundice perceiving a Himalayan mountain as yellow. The yellow mountain doesn't exist, but the person with jaundice does exist. Just so, while the object of negation—the truly existent self—doesn't exist, the mind grasping at that false "I" does exist. This is important for your practice of meditation on emptiness. As you meditate on emptiness, you must come to see that the objective self doesn't exist. But the subjective mind grasping at that object is not capable of such insight or analysis. That mind of ignorance cannot become wisdom; when emptiness is recognized, that subjective mind grasping at true existence has its continuum severed. So you must employ another part of your mind to analyze whether the truly existent self exists. One part of your mind experiences grasping at the truly existent self while another part of your mind analyzes that self, looking at all the logical contradictions. This second part of your mind eventually refutes the existence of the objective self. This is what destroys the continuum of the subjective mind grasping it. What continues is a wisdom mind.

Kalden Gyatso concludes his discussion of the object of negation by offering to reveal the object of negation nakedly, just as it is. He then says that everything that appears to you is the object of negation! Your own body and mind as well as all external things appear to you as truly, inherently existent, and you then grasp and cling to that false mode of appearance. Although things do exist conventionally in mere name, ordinary beings have not yet realized emptiness and so cannot differentiate experientially between what's conventionally existent and what's the object of negation. Ordinary beings are always mistaken in actually believing in the false appearance of things existing from their own side. When you negate this false appearance, that simple negation induces the experience of emptiness.

> At that time, therefore, analyze with a subtle portion of the mind how that ["I, I"] mind conceives the self and where it conceives the self to be. When the analytical portion of the mind becomes too strong, the misconceiving mind disappears. Then nothing will come to mind except for a vacuity. Therefore, while the main mind is firmly and continuously generating the thought "I," analyze it with a subtle portion of the mind.
>
> When analyzing in that way, the locus where the innate conception of a self has apprehended an "I" is not somewhere other than your combined body and mind or your five aggregates. It

is also neither upon each of the five aggregates taken singularly, nor the body or mind taken singularly. However, an "I" that is able to set itself up from the beginning is conceived as existing without being merely designated by thought upon the mass that is either a mere collection of body and mind combined, or a mere collection of the five aggregates. This is the way that the innate misconception of a self conceives an "I." The "I" that is its object is the object of negation that will be refuted.

The way of identifying the object of negation must be realized nakedly in your own mental continuum without its being just an idea presented by others or a generic image evoked by words. This is the first vital point, ascertaining how the object of negation appears.

Here the Panchen Lama is describing a process like the one Kalden Gyatso taught of having the main part of your mind grasp at the objective, inherently existent "self" while another portion of your mind analyzes whether that self exists. In order to bring that self-grasping mind into your experience clearly and strongly, you imagine being falsely accused of something until you feel upset. A strong sense of grasping at a self in your heart will arise as you think, "I didn't do that!" When that clinging to a sense of self arises strongly, don't let it go. Sustain it with mindfulness. While most of your mind is engaged in grasping at the truly existent self, engage a small part of your mind in analyzing your experience of how that self-grasping mind is generated. Begin checking if it corresponds to something that exists in reality! If you engage most of your mind in such analysis, you will lose the vividness of the object of negation. Then your analysis won't be useful. You must keep most of your mind engaging in grasping at the inherently existent "I" in your heart.

The fact that you have a strong experience of self-grasping—the object of negation—doesn't prove it's valid any more than someone's experiencing a hallucination proves that the object of his or her hallucination exists. If it's valid, it must correspond to something in reality. If that inherently existent self actually exists, then it must exist in your mind or body. So you search your own body and mind, first checking each of the five aggregates one by one. When you search your body, feelings, consciousness, and so forth, you find it cannot exist in any one of them. Then you check whether it can exist in all five aggregates combined. But if you found that it didn't exist in any one, then it cannot exist in their collection. Through your own analysis, you'll discover that there is no truly existent self in the body, in the mind, or in the collection of those two. You then see how the mind imputes or labels a self on the basis of the aggregates. When you think that the self exists from its own side, independent of being merely imputed by the mind on the aggregates, this is the "self" that is the object of negation! By going though this step-by-step meditation process, you can come to see clearly that object of negation in your own experience.

Analyzing the Entailment

> Second is the vital point of ascertaining the entailment. The mind holds tightly in the center of your heart the thought "I." If the "I" that is conceived by that mind exists upon your five aggregates, then it must be either the same as or different from the five aggregates. No third way of existing other than those two is possible. Whatever exists must be either singular or plural. So think and decide that, "It is not possible at all to have a third way of existing other than those two ways of existing."

The second vital point is entailment, which is a point of logic recognizing that if the truly existent self you grasp at actually exists, then there are only two possibilities—it must exist as one with the aggregates or as separate from the aggregates. If such a self exists, it must either be identical with or separate from the aggregates. If something truly exists, it must be singular or plural—one or many. These points of logic must be understood for successful meditation. You analyze each of the aggregates, checking if the self exists in one of them. If the self existed in each of the five, then you would have five selves! If the self existed pervading all five, then those five would have to be inherently one thing, which of course they are not. You also check if the self could exist inherently apart from those five. For your analysis to have an impact, you must be convinced that you have exhausted all logical alternatives for how that self could exist.

The Self Is Not the Same as the Aggregates

> The third vital point is ascertaining the lack of true sameness. If you think that the "I" that has been conceived in that way [as able to set itself up from the beginning] is the same as the five aggregates, then there are many faults. For instance, just as one person has five aggregates, the "I" would also be five different continua. Or just as there is one "I," the five aggregates would also become a partless whole. Therefore think, "The 'I' that has been conceived in that way is not the same as the five aggregates."

The third vital point is that the self is not one with the aggregates. If you assert that the self is the same as the five aggregates, many absurd logical consequences ensue. As there are five aggregates, if each is the truly existent self, then you must conclude that you are five people! Or you'd have to assert that those five things are actually just one thing!

In meditation, you investigate which of the five is the self or where it exists on them. If the body were the self, you would be able to find it on the body. The body is likewise made up of many parts, so then you'd again have the problem of many selves. Also, the self you experience is a composite of mind and body, but the body alone is merely matter. So you can see that form alone is not the self.

Then you can check whether feelings are the self. Feelings are temporary and quite fleeting, whereas the self seems to be lasting and eternal. So self and feelings are not identical. You then analyze if discrimination is the self. Discrimination is mental in nature, but the self also has a physical component, so this is not the self. Then you can check compositional factors for a truly existent self. Through analysis, you can see that the self seems to have power over all the aggregates, but compositional factors do not. If you analyze consciousness, the last aggregate, you find that the self seems to have all the aggregates including form, but consciousness doesn't have form.

You might think that the collection of all five aggregates is the self, but that's not so because the self is singular while the aggregates are plural. Also the collection of the aggregates is nothing other than the basis of imputation for the self. The basis of imputation and the self are not identical.

> Furthermore, if the "I" that has been conceived in that way were the same as the five aggregates, then just as the five aggregates are produced and perish, so the "I," which is able to set itself up and which is conceived by that mind, would be produced and perish. In that case, the "I" that is produced and perishes would be established as either [inherently] the same as or [inherently] different from its former and later moments.
>
> If it is the same, the "I" of former and future lives and the "I" of this life would be one partless whole. If it is different, then the "I" of future and former lives and the "I" of this life would have to be different, without any connection at all. The reason is that although in general it's not necessary for mere difference to be a difference that is without any connection, it is necessarily so when it is an inherent difference. Therefore the former and later moments of such an "I" are not [inherently] different; for if they were, it would incur many faults, such as our meeting with actions that we had not done and actions we had done having no effect.
>
> Thus you should think, "The 'I' that has been conceived by the mind in that way [as able to set itself up from the beginning] is not the same as the five aggregates."

Furthermore, if the self and the five aggregates existed as one and the same thing, then just as the aggregates arise and perish, not going on to the next life, so also the self wouldn't connect to the next life. Similarly, if the self truly existed as one with the aggregates, which are always changing, then either the self of this present moment would have to be perfectly identical with the self of yesterday, or today's self and yesterday's would have to be totally unrelated. This same reasoning applies to previous lives and this current life, childhood and adulthood, or yesterday and today. If you assert that the self and the ever-changing aggregates are identical, you get stuck with the absurd conclusion that the self of the past and the self of the present are identical, contradicting your experience of change.

If you assert that the self and the ever-changing aggregates are inherently different, then you must accept that they are totally unrelated, which sticks you with the absurd consequence that your present experiences have nothing to do with your past experiences and karma. If two things are different, it doesn't generally mean that they're unrelated, but if things are inherently or ultimately different, then they can't be related. So if the "I" were truly existent, it would either have to be totally one with previous moments or would have to be totally unrelated to those previous moments. Neither of these positions is tenable. The self of today is indeed related to the self of childhood but is not identical to that self.

> Furthermore, if the "I" that has been conceived in that way is the same as the five aggregates, all its parts would have to be the same in all aspects, because it is a truly existent sameness. In that case, there would be many faults, such as that the "I" or "self" would not be that which appropriates the five aggregates and the five aggregates would not be that which is appropriated by the "I" or "self."

Also, if the "I" were the same as the aggregates, then they couldn't be appropriated by the person. Yet we naturally speak of "my body," "my mind," "my feelings," and so forth. Through analyzing your experience of the object of negation, checking if it is indeed identical to one or all of the aggregates of body and mind, you will come to the clear conclusion that it is not.

The Self Is Not Different from the Aggregates

The fourth vital point is ascertaining the lack of true difference. You might think, "Since the 'I' that has been conceived in that way is not the same as the five aggregates, it must be different from the five aggregates." After you have eliminated individually the aggregates—form and so on—you are able to identify separately, "This is the aggregate of consciousness." Just so, after eliminating individually the mental and physical aggregates, you should be able to identify the "I" as different: "This is the 'I' that has been conceived in that way." However, it is not so.

Therefore you should think, "The 'I' that has been conceived in that way is not different from the five aggregates."

The fourth vital point is ascertaining the lack of true difference—that the self does not truly exist as something separate from the five aggregates. If it did, then you should be able to eliminate all of the aggregates and then find an "I" there, existing as something real, separate from those aggregates. In that case, the self and the aggregates would be like a vase and a pillar—two separate things, either of which can be found in the absence of the other. You should be able to pinpoint something that is the "I" that is findable apart from the aggregates. But you cannot find anything apart from the aggregates of body and mind that corresponds to a truly existing self!

Space-Like Equipoise

Having depended on the analysis of the four vital points in that way, you ascertain that the "I" that has been conceived by the innate misconception of a self does not exist. Then you should sustain the continuum of that ascertaining consciousness one-pointedly, free of sinking and excitement.

Furthermore, if that ascertaining consciousness becomes a

little weaker, beginners rely on doing the analysis of the four vital points as above and induce an ascertainment of the lack of true existence.

Those of higher intelligence rely on doing an analysis of whether the "I" is established or not as it appears to the innate misconception of a self and induce an ascertainment of the lack of true existence similar to doing the analysis of the four vital points.

Since the logical entailment is valid, being unable to find a truly existent self as one with or different from the aggregates induces an experience of emptiness. Once you go through those four vital points to ascertain the lack of a truly existent self, you then sustain your awareness of that emptiness in meditative concentration without sinking or excitement as described earlier. For beginners, when your concentration wanes, it's good to again rely on the reasoning of the four vital points to re-establish your understanding. Those of higher capacity don't have to go through the four vital points again but can instead rely on a briefer reasoning or recollection to again bring a clear understanding of emptiness to mind to focus upon single-pointedly. I'll share some additional lines of reasoning below.

At that time you possess two attributes: subjectively there is a firm ascertaining consciousness that apprehends the lack of inherent existence of the self, and objectively there is the appearance of clear vacuity that is the mere negation of true existence, the object of negation. Sustaining these two one-pointedly is the way to practice space-like meditative equipoise.

Space-like meditative equipoise on emptiness has two important qualities. In terms of understanding, you are ascertaining with certainty that things lack inherent existence. In terms of appearance, a great, space-like emptiness or vacuity dawns to the mind. Dwelling in the mere negation of true existence with these two attributes is called "space-like meditative equipoise on emptiness."

> In post-meditation, you should view all phenomena—the self
> and so on—as being the sport of emptiness, like a magician's
> illusions. That is, in meditative equipoise you should rely on
> inducing a strong ascertainment of the lack of true existence.
> Then, after meditation, you should learn to understand what-
> ever appears, though appearing [to be inherently existent], as
> sport, like a magician's illusion—false, without truth.

When you come out of that equipoise, view everything as illusion-like.
As you go about daily activities, focus on seeing things as dependently
arisen like a magician's illusions.

If something truly exists, then when you search for its ultimate existence, you should be able to find it, but you cannot. This does not refute
things existing conventionally, as merely labeled. Conventional existence
is different from inherent existence. Conventionally, we can say that
things exist in the manner of illusions. They exist in dependence upon
many causes
and conditions, including mere imputation.

Take the example of walking. If walking existed inherently rather
than conventionally or like an illusion, then walking would have to exist
without relying on causes and conditions. But where can you find such an
inherently existent act of walking? Does it exist in the ground or in the
feet? It's clearly not in the ground. You cannot find truly existent walking
in the floor itself! Then if you search the feet, does it exist in the front
foot or the rear foot? The foot that has not yet taken a step isn't walking
yet, so it's not there. If you assert that walking exists on the front foot,
then you must check which part of the front foot it truly exists in. Does
it exist in the toes, the sole, or the heel? The heel hasn't yet reached the
spot where the toes are. So, relative to the tips of the toes, the heel hasn't
yet reached the destination. If it's in the tips of the toes, then can you
find walking in one of the atoms that make up the toes? Which atom
of which toe has taken the step? Search as you wish, you cannot ever
find anything that exists that is, inherently, the act of walking. No truly
existent thing can be found that ultimately corresponds with "walking,"
and yet walking does exist in an illusion-like, relational manner.

Whether you analyze the self or walking, if you search for something to point to as ultimately being that thing, you cannot find it! They exist like illusions, dependent upon many causes and conditions including your own imputation. You have to be satisfied with the self and all other appearances existing conventionally, depending on many factors, including mere mental imputation. If you search for something more than that, you cannot find it.

Additional Lines of Reasoning Establishing the Emptiness of Persons

All the lines of reasoning establishing the emptiness of the self of persons come down to identifying the object of negation in your own experience and then analyzing that. You must begin by clearly identifying just how you experience a self that exists inherently, from its own side, without depending on other factors such as the basis of imputation and imputation itself. You must see how you cling and grasp at that false appearance of an intrinsically existing self.

Having identified the object of negation, you investigate the four vital points as described to induce ascertainment of emptiness and then dwell in space-like meditative equipoise on emptiness. When the appearance of a truly existent self reasserts itself, you can use other lines of reasoning to refute it.

A second approach to investigating emptiness of persons is the sevenfold reasoning taught by Master Chandrakirti, which is usually illustrated using the example of a chariot. The seven points of reasoning are that the self is not one with aggregates, it's not other than the aggregates, it doesn't inherently depend on the aggregates, it's not a basis on which the aggregates inherently depend, it's not the owner of the aggregates, it's not the mere collection of the aggregates, and it's not the shape of the aggregates. Contemplating these reasons is a powerful means for establishing emptiness.

Another extremely profound contemplation to prove emptiness is the reasoning of dependent arising. Dependent arising is the most important line of reasoning proving emptiness. Self-grasping clings to an independent, inherently existent self. Recognizing dependent arising directly reveals that all phenomena lack such independent existence, since a thing cannot exist both independently and dependently. Also, all meditations on emptiness eliminate eternalism—the view of permanence. As you refute eternalism, you risk falling into nihilism, believing that even the conventionally existent self doesn't exist. The reasoning of dependent arising shows how things do exist as mere mental imputations. Through such reasoning, you must develop great certainty regarding how things do exist conventionally in that way while at the same time lacking any independent, inherent nature whatsoever.

Contemplation of dependent arising has two aspects. One is that things arise in dependence upon causes and conditions. The other, subtler reasoning is that things arise in dependence upon imputation or labeling. For the first of those, you reason, "The self doesn't truly exist because it arises depending on causes and conditions." In the *Sutra Requested by the Naga King Anavatapta*, the Buddha said:

> Whatever arises based on conditions is not arisen.
> That does not have the nature of arising.
> Whatever depends on conditions should be understood
>   as empty.
> Whoever understands emptiness is conscientious.

If things exist depending on causes and conditions, then they don't exist independently or truly. Regarding the second reasoning of dependent on mere imputation, you must begin by identifying the object of negation as described earlier. Then you refute that self that appears to exist from its own side and the mind that grasps at that false appearance. You do so by reasoning that such a self does not exist because the self is merely imputed by your own mind in dependence upon the component parts. How things dependently arise due to mental imputation is expressed in the *Sutra Requested by Upali*, where the Buddha said:

> Flowers of many colors bloom, bringing joy.
> Exquisite, brilliant mansions of gold please the mind.
> These do not have a creator, for they are imputed by thought.
> The world is imputed through the power of thoughts.

As you analyze, you can see that the "self" is imputed on the five aggregates. In his *Precious Garland*, Arya Nagarjuna also teaches a method of analyzing selflessness by seeing how "self" is imputed on the elements. He advises first clearly identifying the object of negation and then examining all the six elements to see that each of the elements is not the self. So you look at flesh and bones, which constitute the earth element; the blood and other bodily fluids, which constitute the water element; heat, which is the fire element; breath, which is the wind element; consciousness; and space within your body. You find that none of these is the self. Nagarjuna says:

> The person is neither earth nor water,
> not fire, wind, or space,
> nor is it consciousness or all of them together.
> What is a person separate from these?

If you analyze in this way, you will see that person or self exists as something merely imputed or labeled on the elements.

Thus you can say that the conventional self exists, but it doesn't have to exist within the basis of imputation—the body or the mind—to exist. Even the conventional self cannot be found anywhere in the body or mind. It exists as something merely labeled on the basis of the body and mind. The conventionally existent self does not exist from the side of the object; it's not something that can be pointed out anywhere. It exists merely as a mental imputation, but it doesn't exist from its own side.

When people bring up the object of negation in a visceral way and then meditate in the ways described on its emptiness, it's normal to experience intense fear at first, as though you were about to lose something you've felt was very precious for a long time. Some people experience such fear at the beginning. Others who've been seeking the meaning of emptiness for a long time may experience great joy, as though they've found something wonderful that they'd lost. Either of these emotional experiences is a good sign your meditation on emptiness is being effective, and both sorts of individuals will experience bliss and joy if they persist with their contemplation at such times.

MEDITATION ON THE EMPTINESS OF PHENOMENA

Easy Path next explains meditation on the emptiness of phenomena. "Phenomena" refers here to everything that exists other than persons. This includes produced phenomena—matter, consciousness, and non-associated compositional factors—as well as unproduced phenomena, such as space.

Matter

> Take the example of the body. This is the way that the object of negation appears: It appears to us undeniably as a whole, palpable, singular body that is able to set itself up without being merely designated by thought upon this body, a mere collection of five limbs—a mass of flesh and bones.
>
> If such a body exists upon this body that is a mere collection of five limbs—a mass of flesh and bones—it must be either the same as or different from this body that is a mere collection of five limbs—a mass of flesh and bones.
>
> This body that is a mere collection of five limbs—a mass of flesh and bones—comes from the sperm and blood of your parents. Therefore, if the [truly existent] body is the same as this body, even that drop of blood and semen that is the basis for the entry of the consciousness would have to be a body that is a mere collection of five limbs—a mass of flesh and bones. Or, just as there are five limbs, the body would also have to be five bodies that are collections of five limbs.
>
> If they are different, you would have to show "This is the body" after eliminating each of the limbs—the head and so on. However, it is not so. Therefore, having induced the ascertaining consciousness that thinks, "Such a body completely does not exist," sustain it.

When meditating on the emptiness of matter, take the example of your own body. Then, as you did when meditating on the emptiness of the self, identify the object of negation. The object of negation here is the way your body typically appears to you, as a truly existent whole that does not arise as something merely imputed on its parts. The "five limbs" the Panchen Lama refers to are the arms, the legs, and the head. You see your body as something singular and whole, but if the body were inherently one with its parts, then because there are many parts, you would have many bodies. If the body were inherently different from its parts, then those parts would be unrelated to your body; you'd have to be able to eliminate all the parts of your body and still point to something that is your body existing apart from its parts. Clearly this is impossible. Furthermore, if your body existed as inherently the same as its parts, then all the limbs you have now would have had to have already been present when you were an embryo. But at that stage your limbs and many other parts hadn't yet arisen. Such contemplations reveal that the body is produced based on its parts, which proves that it lacks inherent, independent existence.

Take the example of a vase. When we say that a conventional vase exists, we're not saying that we can find the vase on the base, the handle, the bulbous body, or the spout. It is not findable on any of those parts. It is merely imputed on that material basis. We feel that a truly existent vase does exist there, from the side of the object, but it's not findable on the basis of imputation. A merely labeled vase does not need to be findable from its own side, as it exists as something merely labeled! A truly existent vase or body should be findable as existing from its own side. But when you search you cannot find anything existing from its own side. It exists in mere name, labeled upon the basis of designation.

Consciousness

Take the example of today's consciousness. If there exists a consciousness of today that is established in its own right, without being merely designated by thought upon both the consciousness of the earlier and the consciousness of later parts of today, then it would have to be either the same as or different from both the consciousness of the earlier and the consciousness of the later part of today.

If it were the same, the consciousness of later part of today would have to already exist with the consciousness of the earlier part of today. And if it were different, you would have to show it, saying "This is today's consciousness" after eliminating individually the consciousness of the earlier part of today and the consciousness of the later part of today. However, it is not so. Therefore, having induced the ascertaining consciousness that thinks "Such a consciousness completely does not exist," meditate as before.

The basis of imputation for your consciousness today is the consciousnesses of the morning, afternoon, and evening. So analyze if it exists as one with or as different from those. If it's inherently one with both the morning's consciousness and the evening's consciousness, then you have to accept the absurd conclusion that the morning's consciousness exists in the evening and that the evening's consciousness already existed in the morning! These absurdities only arise if you hold to a view of true existence. If they are inherently different—if today's consciousness exists as something inherently separate from the morning's and evening's consciousnesses—then you must be able to find a consciousness of today that exists apart from those two. That's impossible. When you gain certainty regarding the emptiness of such an independent, inherently existing consciousness through such reasoning, sustain that awareness in your meditation.

Nonassociated Compositional Factors

Take the example of a span of time, such as one year. If there exists a year that is established in its own right, not merely designated by thought upon its basis of designation—the twelve months—it would have to be either the same as or different from the twelve months.

If it is the same, then just as there are twelve months, there would also be twelve years. If it is different, you would have to show it, saying "This is that year" after eliminating individually the twelve months. However, it is not so. Therefore, having induced the ascertaining consciousness that thinks "Such a year completely does not exist," sustain it as before.

Nonassociated compositional factors are produced phenomena that are neither matter nor consciousness. The example given here is one year. If a year exists inherently, then it must exist as one with or as separate from the twelve months that comprise it. The logic here is similar to that employed earlier. If it's inherently one with the twelve months, you come to the absurd conclusion that there are twelve years in one year; or you conclude that the twelve months are inherently one thing. If they inherently exist separately, then you must be able to find the year totally apart from the months that make it up! If there's one year that truly exists, then you should be able to find it on its basis of imputation. But can you find the year on the first month? The second month? The third? Of course you cannot. If you eliminate all the months, you cannot find a year existing apart from them. Therefore a year doesn't exist inherently in any of the months that make it up or apart from those months. Rather, a year exists as merely labeled on the twelve months that are its basis of designation.

Unproduced Phenomena

> The Way to Meditate [on Special Insight], Having Determined the Lack of Inherent Existence of Unproduced Phenomena
> Take space as an example. There are many parts to space—cardinal directions and intermediate directions. Examine whether space is the same as or different from its directions and induce an ascertainment of its lack of true existence, and then meditate as before.

Space is given as the example of an unproduced phenomenon. Such phenomena don't depend on causes and conditions as people or things do, so we may think that they exist inherently. But take the example of space. Within space there are four cardinal directions—front, back, right, and left—as well as intermediate directions, up, down, and so forth. In your meditation, contemplate whether space exists independently of the space in those different directions. If space were inherently one with the directions, then you'd be stuck with the absurd conclusion that space is many. Also "up" only exists in dependence upon "down" and so forth. If space existed apart from those directions, then you'd have to be able to take away all the space in all the directions and still have something to point to as being truly existent space.

These logical absurdities only apply to truly existent space. They don't apply when you accept that space just exists conventionally, as something merely imputed.

In short, there is the yoga of space-like meditative equipoise, which sustains in one point the ascertainment of the lack of existence in its own right, without being merely designated by thought, of even a mere atom of any phenomenon of samsara and nirvana—self, aggregate, mountain, fence, house, other dwelling, and so on. And there is the yoga of illusion, the subsequent attainment that knows that all objects and their appearances arise from depending on assemblages of causes and conditions but are naturally false and without truth. The definition of *special insight* is the meditative equipoise that is based on sustaining well those two yogas and is conjoined with the bliss of mental and physical pliancy induced by the strength of having analyzed.

Easy Path advises engaging in the yoga of space-like meditative equipoise on emptiness and then, between sessions, viewing everything as like a magician's illusion, as described earlier. Sustaining these two yogas leads to the attainment of special insight. When one first gains calm abiding in accord with the approach taught in the Sutra Vehicle, exceptional physical and mental pliancy and bliss arise through single-pointed absorption on an object of meditation that is not analyzed. Here one generates such bliss and pliancy in deep meditative absorption through analyzing the meaning of emptiness. When that happens, you've attained genuine special insight.

Conclusion
It is the same as before.

What to Do Between Sessions
It is the same as before—look at the scriptures and commentaries that present special insight and so forth.

Having trained ourselves in the general path in that way, we must certainly enter the Vajra Vehicle. Based on that path, we will accomplish easily both accumulations without having to persist for three immeasurable eons.

Furthermore, the best way to make the most of this life of leisure is to receive experiential instruction on [all the topics of the stages of the path, from] the way to rely on the spiritual teacher up to calm abiding and special insight, and then to practice them each day in four sessions—or at least one session—causing transformational experience of the stages of the path to arise.

The conclusion of the session and what to do between meditative sessions are just the same as described earlier except that for one meditating on special insight, the study of texts on the subject are recommended.

It's also advised that having trained yourself in the stages of the path as taught here, you must enter the Vajra Vehicle. To enter the Vajra Vehicle, you must receive initiation from a qualified guru and keep the vows and commitments you take during the initiation. Many essential points of tantric practice have been integrated throughout this discussion of the stages of the path, in accord with the unique approach of *Easy Path*, so I won't go into more detail here. If you practice taking guru yoga as the life of your practice along with visualizing the descent of five-colored nectars and lights in conjunction with the contemplations and meditations explained here, you'll find that it will strongly support your understanding and practice of tantra.

Finally, the Panchen Lama advises four practice sessions per day—or at very least, one session per day—of meditation on the stages of the path to enlightenment as they've been explained. Doing so is truly the best way to take the essence of your precious, brief human life.

Colophon
This arrangement of the concise stages of practice—
the import of the peerless Buddha's thought—
illuminated by the second Conqueror, Losang [Drakpa],
and Shri Dipankara and his disciples,
I, the so-called Chokyi Gyaltsen, composed well
as a means for the fortunate traveling to liberation.
By this virtue may all transmigrators, myself and others,
accomplish the practice of the beings of the three scopes.

This *Stages of the Path to Enlightenment: Practical Instructions on the Easy Path to Omniscience* was given directly to an ocean-like assembly of the spiritual community at the summer debating retreat by the Dharma teacher Losang Chokyi Gyaltsen. It is from notes taken from that presentation, which he reviewed and corrected. By this may it be a victory banner of the never-disappearing precious doctrine.

Appendix I

*An Extremely Brief Preliminary Practice
According to the Condensed Jewel Tradition*

*This preliminary practice is to be performed prior to engaging in a
direct meditation on the stages of the path to enlightenment. First
choose a topic and then proceed as described. This extremely brief
version is for those who find themselves too busy or distracted to
engage in longer versions of the preliminary practices. For citations
of those longer versions and some background on the condensed
jewel tradition, see the preface.*

Imagine your guru in his or her ordinary form atop your head.

Cultivate the conviction that in the space in front of you all your teachers are arrayed along with the lineage teachers, deities, buddhas, bodhisattvas, solitary realizers, arhats, dakas, dakinis, and Dharma protectors.

Recite three times:

> I go for refuge until I am enlightened
> to the Buddha, Dharma, and Sangha.
> Through the merits I create by practicing generosity and the
>   other perfections,
> may I attain the state of a buddha to be
> able to benefit all sentient beings.

May all beings have happiness and the causes of happiness.
May all beings be free from suffering and the causes of
    suffering.
May all beings not be separated from sorrowless bliss.
May all beings abide in equanimity, free of the biases of attach-
    ment and aversion.

All of those in front dissolve into Shakyamuni Buddha with Vajradhara
in his heart, who in turn has a *Hum* syllable at the center of his heart. He
dissolves into the root teacher on your crown, and they become inseparable. Your guru takes on the form of the three-tiered being: Shakyamuni
Buddha with Vajradhara in his heart, who in turn has a *Hum* syllable
in his heart. He embodies all objects of refuge. Focusing on him, recite:

Reverently I prostrate with my body, speech, and mind and
    present every type of offering actual and imagined.
I confess all my negative actions committed since beginning-
    less time and rejoice in the virtues of all holy and ordinary
    beings.
Please remain until samsara ends and turn the wheel of
    Dharma for sentient beings.
I dedicate my own and others' virtues to great enlightenment.

Then offer a short mandala offering:

The ground anointed with perfume, flowers strewn,
Mount Meru, four lands, sun, and moon—
I imagine as a Buddha land and offer to you.
May all beings enjoy this pure land.

Recite:

Unity of all objects of refuge, guru supreme deity,
to Shakyamuni Vajradhara I make requests.

With this supplication streams of five-colored nectars together with rays of light descend from the body of your guru deity seated upon your crown. These streams enter the bodies and minds of all sentient beings and yourself, thereby purifying all the misdeeds and obstructions accumulated from beginningless time. In particular they purify all the misdeeds, obscurations, sicknesses, and spirit possessions that prevent the ability to actualize the realization of [whichever meditation topic you are meditating upon]. Your and all others' bodies transform into the nature of pristine, luminous light. All your and others' good qualities, such as long lifespan and merit, are increased and expanded. In particular, think that these streams have produced in the minds of yourself and all others the special realization of [whichever meditation topic you are meditating upon].

Next engage in meditation on one or more topics from the stages of the path to enlightenment.

Appendix II

A Biographical Sketch of the First Panchen Lama

A FULL BIOGRAPHY OF Panchen Lama Losang Chokyi Gyaltsen (1570–1662), who lived for over ninety years and authored a great many works in addition to the text commented upon here, is beyond the scope of this book. But a general sense of his importance to the history of Central Asian Buddhism will put his writing into perspective. As a root teacher to both the Fourth and Great Fifth Dalai Lamas, an abbot of seven important monasteries, a peacemaker, and the most respected scholar of his time, the First Panchen Lama was a towering figure in the religious and political history of the seventeenth century.[46]

RE-BIRTH

It's difficult to know where to begin in discussing the life of the First Panchen Lama. His Tibetan biographies often begin at the end of the life of the great yogi Gyalwa Ensapa (1505–66), who was famous for having attained full enlightenment in one lifetime. When this master was close to the end of his life, he was together with his dearest student, Sangye Yeshe (1525–91), to whom he had passed the precious oral practice lineage stemming from Lama Tsongkhapa (1357–1419). Sangye Yeshe, himself already a great yogi and scholar, was unbearably sad to see his root teacher about to pass away. He wanted to request him to live longer but was so overwrought he couldn't speak. Reading his student's mind, Gyalwa Ensapa told him that he'd indeed pass away but would then return quickly in the form of a young boy.

After his teacher passed away, Sangye Yeshe dreamed that his teacher would reincarnate in the village of Drukgya. So he went to this village and met the young boy who would later become greatly renowned as the Panchen Lama. By the time the boy was five, Sangye Yeshe felt quite certain that he was indeed the reincarnation of Gyalwa Ensapa, but still he checked with a yogi famed for his clairvoyance, Je Langmikpa Chokyi Gyaltsen. This yogi told him that the boy was undoubtedly the reincarnation of Gyalwa Ensapa, suggesting that he name the boy Chokyi Gyaltsen after himself!

So in one sense the life story of Losang Chokyi Gyaltsen, a.k.a. Losang Chogyen, begins with the story of the master Gyalwa Ensapa. But other Tibetan biographers trace his lineage back to Sonam Chokyi Langpo (1439–1505) and to Khedrup Je (1385–1438), one of Tsongkhapa's foremost disciples. By this reckoning, Losang Chogyen is frequently attested as the Fourth Panchen, with the posthumous application of the Panchen title to these three earlier figures. He was, however, the first master to hold the title within his lifetime. Beyond that, Thuken Chokyi Nyima writes, he "was believed to be a single mental continuum with Master Padmasambhava, the noble lord Atisha, and the matchless Gampopa," adding that his prior incarnations also included Buddha's disciple "Subhuti and the clan chief Majushrikirti, who compiled the *Kalachakra Root Tantra* in Shambhala. He was also Abhayakaragupta . . . Go Lotsawa, Sakya Pandita Kunga Gyaltsen," as well as the other masters already mentioned.[47] And the Great Fifth Dalai Lama would come to identify his teacher as an emanation of Amitabha Buddha.

Putting aside his previous lifetimes, Losang Chokyi Gyaltsen was born, as Sangye Yeshe's dream predicted, in a village called Drukgya ("Six Hundred") in the Lhen Valley of the Tsangpo River north of Shigatse. Scholars differ on whether he was born in 1567 or 1570.

EARLY LIFE

All reports agree that he was a prodigy; he took to Dharma study and meditation as young Mozart took to music. He studied with his own father, brother, and other teachers, but the primary teacher of his youth was the great master Sangye Yeshe, who was then abbot of Tashi Lhunpo and Ensa monasteries. It's said that Losang Chogyen could often memorize texts such as the *Heart Sutra* and *Chanting the Names of Manjushri* by just hearing them once. By the age of five he engaged in daily recitations and meditations of a number of such prayers, including that of the seven Medicine Buddhas.

Before the end of his thirteenth year, during which he entered Ensa Monastery, he had already received numerous commentaries on the stages of the path to enlightenment along with many other commentaries on texts such as the *Four Tantras* of medicine and the Perfection of Wisdom sutras along with initiations and practice instructions on Tara, Ushnisha Vijaya, Hayagriva, Six-Armed Mahakala, Rahula, and many others. When Sangye Yeshe granted him his intermediate ordination vows, he also taught him all the vital points of the guru-yoga method and the complete four initiations of the glorious Guhyasamaja. By that spring, the teenager Losang Chokyi Gyaltsen was reciting from memory verses of praise by Lama Tsongkhapa and was also practicing daily the four Kadam deities (Shakyamuni Buddha, Avalokiteshvara, Tara, and Achala), some forms of Manjushri, Yamantaka, and Six-Armed Mahakala. While still thirteen, he had direct visions of Yamantaka and many protectors. It's said that he was able to recall thousands of his own and others' past lives, and he also had visions of future events based upon which he occasionally made predictions.

That winter, he spent his days and nights reading life stories of great Buddhist masters, generating great faith and determination to follow their footsteps. He vowed to emulate the deeds of great masters such as Milarepa, Tsongkhapa, and Gyalwa Ensapa. Observing the qualities of this teenager in their midst, the other monks at Ensa Monastery developed uncontrived faith that he was the reincarnation of Gyalwa Ensapa.

He remained at Ensa studying and progressing in his practice until he was eighteen, when he entered the Tsonam Ling college of Tashi Lhunpo. Through the remainder of his teens, he received countless teachings from Sangye Yeshe on the works of Buton Rinchen Drup, Milarepa, Tsongkhapa and his heart disciples, the First Dalai Lama, Baso Chokyi Gyaltsen, and others. He received hundreds of tantric initiations and commentaries during these years as well. He privately received the famed eight great commentaries belonging to the uncommon ear-whispered teachings of Lama Tsongkhapa. He completed retreats on White Manjushri and Yamataka. He excelled in studies of logic and epistemology and of Middle Way philosophy at Tashi Lhunpo.

When Sangye Yeshe died, Losang Chokyi Gyaltsen oversaw the funeral rituals. He took his full ordination in 1591 from Panchen Damcho Yarpel, abbot of Tashi Lhunpo.

Next he traveled to Lhasa to Ganden Monastery, the seat of the Geluk tradition founded by Tsongkhapa. While there he received many further teachings, oral transmissions, and initiations. He continued his studies with "a veritable army of teachers."[48] Not only did he receive vast numbers of teachings from his living gurus, he also received teachings and blessings in his pure visions. For example, in a vision of Tsongkhapa himself, while moving in a subtle dream body, he received infinite blessings and initiations and saw in detail the seminal commentaries on the core treatises of Maitreya, Nagarjuna, Aryadeva, Chandrakirti, and Shantideva, the root tantras of the four main highest yoga tantra deities, and many other works, reciting and memorizing each one.[49]

TEACHING

As a young man, Losang Chokyi Gyaltsen began splitting his time primarily between teaching and doing retreats. He did many different retreats, sometimes fasting or living on small herbal pills for extended periods. At one point, he did a retreat wearing only light cotton robes, following the tradition of Milarepa.

He also began teaching at Tashi Lhunpo and elsewhere as many disciples gathered. He taught great scholars and common people. He granted teachings on all aspects of Buddhist sutras and tantras. He had a reputation as a great scholar and yogi who was also extremely humble.

In the early 1600s, he was still quite young and not yet so widely known, particularly in Central Tibet. Thus some were surprised when he was selected to be the tutor to the young Fourth Dalai Lama, a Mongolian child who'd recently come to Tibet to study. The Panchen Lama granted him many teachings and initiations, mentoring him, and also gave him his novice and full monastic vows.

When the Fourth Dalai Lama died at the age of twenty-seven, it was only natural that Tibetans turned to Losang Chogyen to be the primary tutor to the next Dalai Lama, who would come to be known as the Great Fifth.

Losang Chokyi Gyaltsen was actually one of two lamas responsible for identifying the Fifth Dalai Lama from among three candidates, and he then served as the senior tutor to the young Dalai Lama. He granted the Fifth Dalai Lama both his novice and full ordination vows as a monk. He taught him logic and philosophy and also gave him hundreds of transmissions and tantric initiations, including those of Guhyasamaja, Chakrasamvara, and Yamantaka. It seems likely that the First Panchen Lama's wide-ranging approach to study and practice helped lead the Great Fifth Dalai Lama to a similarly nonsectarian approach.

At the age of twenty-five, the Great Fifth Dalai Lama became the first Dalai Lama to hold the position of spiritual and temporal ruler of Tibet. With the help of powerful Mongolian disciples such as Gushri Khan, he unified much of Tibet under the control of his new government and also initiated the building of the Potala in Lhasa.

The First Dalai Lama had founded Tashi Lhunpo Monastery, and late in Losang Chokyi Gyaltsen's life the Fifth Dalai Lama asked him to accept the monastery as his primary seat for lifetimes to come. He accepted his famous student's request, and so all the subsequent Panchen Lamas have been associated with Tashi Lhunpo. The Dalai Lamas are famed as being incarnations of Avalokitesvara, the bodhisattva of compassion, and the Fifth Dalai Lama declared that Losang Chokyi Gyaltsen was an incarnation of Buddha Amitabha, Avalokitesvara's celestial guru. After Losang Chokyi Gyaltsen passed away, the Fifth Dalai Lama oversaw the search for his reincarnation. He also bestowed the title Panchen, which means "great scholar," on the line of incarnations of his root guru. It was largely due to the stature of Losang Chokyi Gyaltsen that the Panchen Lamas became the second highest-ranking line of incarnations in Tibet and that the Dalai Lamas and Panchen Lamas developed a "father and son" relationship from life to life, with each often playing important roles in identifying and teaching the other.

His other students included many great scholars, abbots, reincarnate lamas, princes, and ordinary monks and lay practitioners. He taught repeatedly at every major Geluk monastery, and it is said that he ordained over fifty thousand monks. Among his other prominent students was Galdan Boshogtu Khan, a Mongolian prince who was also a reincarnate lama. Gene Smith notes that after the Panchen Lama sent this student back to Mongolia predicting great things for him, "It seems that the phenomenal rise of the Dzungars as a Central Asian political power can be attributed to the victories of Galdan Boshogtu."[50] He also taught the First Khalka Jetsun Dampa, an incarnation of Taranatha who plays a role in Mongolia analogous to the Dalai Lama. Overall, the First Panchen Lama was "the most prominent teacher of great incarnations of Tibet and Mongolia for almost fifty years."[51] He also taught many Bhutanese religious and secular leaders.

He was the principal holder of the Geluk mahamudra lineage during his time. The verses of praise and supplication for that lineage praise him, "Knowing everything with respect to the teachings of Gyelwa Je Losang [Tsongkhapa], you are indistinguishable from that very Refuge."[52] He was also the principal holder of the practice lineage of Yamantaka during his time and of the Luipa tradition of Chakrasamvara, both of which he passed on to Vajra Holder Konchok Gyaltsen (1612–87).

SERVING AS ABBOT

While in his early thirties, Losang Chokyi Gyaltsen was asked to assume the role of abbot of Tashi Lhunpo. By that time he was also already serving as abbot of Ensa Monastery and of Gangchen Chopel Monastery as well!

As abbot of Tashi Lhunpo, he taught extensively, initiated a tradition of annually celebrating the Great Prayer Festival there, oversaw the construction of new buildings and retreat facilities, had new stupas built on the grounds, had new statues and paintings done for the temples, and established a tantric college as part of the monastic university. In 1617, upon the death of the Fourth Dalai Lama, he was asked to also assume the abbacy of both Drepung and Sera monastic universities and, in 1626, the Jangtse college of Ganden. In 1642, he also became abbot of Shalu Monastery, the originally Kadam monastery in Tsang that reached its most illustrious period as a Sakya institution under the abbacy of Buton Rinchen Drup, who compiled the Tibetan canon there in the fourteenth century.

AUTHORING BOOKS

The First Panchen Lama's collected works fill more than 4,500 Tibetan folios. One of his most important and influential works is the *Guru Puja*,[53] which continues to be recited by thousands of practitioners of Tibetan Buddhism as part of their regular meditation practice. It is an extremely popular guru yoga ritual in the Geluk tradition, and it is frequently recited by thousands of monks together at the great Geluk institutions. This text is remarkable in encompassing the entire range of Buddhist practices in a single set of poetic verses. It put core elements of the oral tradition of Lama Tsongkhapa in writing for the first time, fully integrating them with the stages of the path tradition, the instructions of mind training, and Vajrayana practices, including core elements of Yamantaka, Guhyasamaja, and Chakrasamvara tantras.

Perhaps even more influential than the *Guru Puja* is his *Six-Session Guru Yoga*.[54] This text itself or later compositions based upon it is generally recited six times daily by those who take yoga or highest yoga tantra initiations from His Holiness the Dalai Lama or other teachers of the Geluk tradition. This practice allows one to preserve the commitments taken during the initiation, and an entire genre of spiritual literature has arisen around it.

The Panchen Lama's root text on mahamudra along with his auto-commentary have served as the most influential compositions on mahamudra within the Geluk tradition.[55] And, as has been discussed in some detail elsewhere in this book, *Easy Path* has been an extremely important text for meditation on the stages of the path. Many versions of the preliminary practices take significant sections of this text as their basis, and numerous later texts on the stages of the path borrow from the Panchen Lama's unique manner of integrating tantra and guru yoga into these practices. All of the texts mentioned thus far were unprecedented in presenting in writing for the first time essential elements of what had previously been a purely oral tradition.

The Panchen Lama also composed *Essence of the Five Stages*, an important commentary on the completion-stage practices of the Guhyasamaja tantra. He wrote quite extensively on tantric Buddhism, and a number of these works have been translated into English:

- *Essence of the Ocean of Attainments*, a commentary on the generation-stage practices of Guhyasamaja[56]
- The extensive *Sadhana Method of Attainment for the Glorious Chakrasamvara* in the tradition of Luipa[57]
- A commentary on the completion-stages practices of Chakrasamvara entitled *The Extremely Profound Commentary to the Five Stages of the Profound Tradition of the Powerful Siddha Ghantapa*[58]
- *Guru Yoga for the Five Stages of Completion of Ghantapa*[59]
- *The Golden Key: A Profound Guide to the Six Yogas of Naropa*[60]
- *An Aspiration to Fulfill the Stages of the Glorious Kalachakra Path*[61]

He also wrote *The Concise Essence Sutra Ritual of Bhagavan Medicine Buddha Called the Wish-Fulfilling Jewel*, which is now commonly practiced by Western practitioners as well.[62]

The First Panchen Lama wrote a book on Buddhist tenets most likely in response to a request by his famous student, the Fifth Dalai Lama, responding to the Sakya scholar Taktsang Lotsawa's eighteen points of criticism of the views of Tsongkhapa with regard to emptiness.[63] He also wrote other philosophical treatises, sadhanas, practice manuals, tantric commentaries, and biographies, including an extensive autobiography.

ACTIVITIES TO RESOLVE CONFLICTS

The First Panchen Lama lived during a time of great political and sectarian conflict. Tibet was not a unified nation through most of his life. Central Tibet was split into two regions—U, the ruler of which supported the Geluk tradition, and Tsang, whose ruler supported the Kagyupas. During the time of the Fourth Dalai Lama, the Tsangpa ruler defeated the king of U and declared himself king of all Central Tibet. Gelukpas then allied themselves with a number of Mongolian leaders, the foremost of whom was Gushri Khan. Thus military tensions between Mongolian forces and the Tsangpa ruler were closely related to sectarian tensions between some Gelukpa and Kagyupa leaders.

Given that political climate, it would not have been insignificant that the First Panchen Lama often referred to Milarepa—an important master in the founding of the Kagyu tradition; that he often quoted Marpa in his writings, including in his *Golden Key* and his *Essence of the Five Stages*; or that he engaged in a retreat wearing just cotton robes like Milarepa himself, a practice more common among Kagyupa practitioners. Also, given his acute awareness of the sectarian tensions of his time, it was perhaps no accident that he named one of his most important compositions *A Root Text for the Precious Geluk/Kagyu Tradition of Mahamudra*, also writing an autocommentary to that text. In those texts, he specifically names numerous Kagyu traditions of mahamudra practice along with the Dzogchen tradition of the Nyingmapas and the approach of the Gelugpas, then famously stating, ". . . when scrutinized by a yogi learned in scripture and logic and experienced [in meditation], their definitive meanings are all seen to come to the same intended point."[64]

So while, in the words of Thuken Chokyi Nyima, "his deeds on behalf of upholding and enhancing the tradition of Je Lama [Tsongkhapa] were as vast as space,"[65] both his words and his deeds reflected an attitude of utter nonsectarianism. In fact, despite his being the abbot of powerful Geluk monastic universities and the fact that the Tsangpa ruler was staunchly anti-Geluk, this very king was willing to work collaboratively with the Panchen Lama.

In the early 1600s when a war was about to break out between Kagyu and Geluk kings, the Panchen Lama advised the young Fourth Dalai Lama with regard to the situation, and tensions calmed. In 1621, when war was about to break out between the Tsangpa ruler and Mongolian forces that had come too close to Lhasa, the Panchen Lama went and negotiated a peace treaty between the two armies.

The Panchen Lama helped on numerous occasions to negotiate peace between Mongolian and Tibetan armies. In the 1650s the Panchen Lama also negotiated a peace between Tibet and Bhutan, also gaining agreements for the freeing of hostages and the trading of prisoners.

The First Panchen Lama died in 1662. Over the course of his lifetime, he saw his most famous student, the Great Fifth Dalai Lama, become both spiritual and temporal leader of Tibet—a position held by the Dalai Lamas until recently, when the Great Fourteenth Dalai Lama insisted on relinquishing political power in favor of a democratic system. He saw his student the First Khalka Jetsun Dampa begin the establishment of a similar system for Mongolia. And he helped Bhutan establish itself as an independent state under the rule of the Drukpa Kagyu. He played significant roles in all of these major political developments.

The Tibetan title Panchen includes *pan* from the Sanskrit term *pandita*, meaning "learned, wise scholar," and *chen*, the Tibetan word for "great." When one reads his writings and considers his actions teaching the greatest minds of three generations throughout Central Asia, it's clear that he was indeed one of the great Buddhist scholars of Tibetan history. In addition, when one considers the intensive retreats he engaged in, the experiential quality of the realizations expressed in his writings, and his many visionary experiences, it's quite clear that Losang Chokyi Gyaltsen did indeed fulfill his teenage aspiration to engage in meditative activities like those of Milarepa. Seeing that he accomplished such scholarship and yogic success while also eventually serving as abbot of seven important monasteries; serving important political roles between Tibet, Mongolia, and Bhutan; teaching two Dalai Lamas, other great scholars, and important political leaders; overseeing large-scale projects of sacred art; founding a tantric college; and writing so beautifully and extensively, one can only marvel at the truly remarkable qualities of this towering figure.

Appendix III

A Brief Biographical Sketch of
Gyumed Khensur Rinpoche Lobsang Jampa

KHENSUR RINPOCHE was born in 1939 in Nyakten, Tibet, which at the time was a suburb of Tibet's capital, Lhasa, and has since grown to be encompassed by the expanding city. His father, Sona, and mother, Tashi, both worked on a family farm and also as nomadic herders. The family had between thirty and forty yaks, making them a middle-class family by the standards of the time.

Rinpoche spent his first ten years happily living with his parents and his large extended family in the area. He and an older female cousin would often spend their days in the pastures, keeping watch over the family's sheep and yaks.

Sona, Rinpoche's father, had studied some Dharma but wasn't very serious about practicing. When Rinpoche was still just a baby, his mother took him to visit and be blessed by Pabongka Dechen Nyingpo Rinpoche—one of the most famous teachers of the time. Pabongka Rinpoche gave the young child the name Trinley Topgyal, by which he would be known for many years.

In 1947 at the age of ten, Rinpoche entered monastic life by being admitted to Sera Mey Monastic University. Sera was one of the three great seats of higher Buddhist studies in the Geluk tradition near Lhasa, the other two being Ganden and Drepung. Rinpoche was quite happy for the opportunity. Soon after arriving, Rinpoche had his first chance to see His Holiness the Dalai Lama—a child himself at the time. His Holiness was being celebrated by those three great seats of learning, and when His Holiness came to visit Sera, Rinpoche was naturally quite excited to be among the many monks in line to greet the Dalai Lama.

As his family home was nearby, Rinpoche often went home for visits during his first year at Sera. However, once he began his formal and rather demanding studies the following year, visits home became rare. As a young monk, Rinpoche shared a room with his maternal uncle, Kalsang Namgyal, who would later play an important role in Rinpoche's escape from Tibet, and the two would remain close until Namgyal's death in 2011. Namgyal was not a scholar monk; he worked as the manager of the kitchen store in their monastic house and sometimes went home to visit family.

As a young student, Rinpoche focused on memorizing texts and reciting them. A teacher named Geshe Ngawang taught Rinpoche how and what to memorize. Meanwhile, an administrator of Rinpoche's regional house, or *khangtsen*, at Sera Mey looked after his daily life and basic needs. Rinpoche began by memorizing the daily prayers for monks at Sera and later would focus on memorizing the texts that he was studying and debating. Since that time, Rinpoche has never stopped making efforts to memorize more Dharma texts.

In the monastery in Lhasa, Rinpoche spent a number of years studying Collected Topics for debate (*dura*), Awareness and Knowing (*lorik*), which encompasses psychology and phenomenology, and Logic (*tarik*). Then Rinpoche began his studies of the Maitreya's *Ornament for Clear Realizations*. At Sera Mey, the study of *Ornament* involves a total of six classes. Rinpoche had completed four when his studies were interrupted and he had to escape from Tibet to India. During Rinpoche's years as a monk in Tibet, his main teachers were Yeshe Wangchuk (who would later compose a long-life prayer for Rinpoche), Geshe Chodak, and Geshe Losang Rinchen.

In addition to these studies at Sera Mey, Rinpoche also attended his first teaching by His Holiness the Dalai Lama, a Kalachakra initiation at the Norbulingka Palace. While in Tibet Rinpoche also attended a number of teachings by Kyapje Trijang Rinpoche, the Dalai Lama's junior tutor. These included a commentary given over twenty-five days on the *Guru Puja* along with the First Panchen Lama's root text on mahamudra at Drib Tsechok Ling Monastery in Lhasa, an extensive teaching on the guru yoga called the *Hundred Deities of Tushita* at Sera Jey's Trehor Khangtsen, and the Hundred Initiations of Surka along with other rare initiations and practice permissions at Shidey Monastery.

Rinpoche received his novice monk vows in 1952 from Minyak Tashi Tongdu, the ninety-fifth Ganden Throne Holder, at which time he received the ordination name Lobsang Jampa. In 1959, he received the vows of a fully ordained monk from Kyapje Ling Rinpoche, the ninety-seventh Ganden Throne Holder and senior tutor to His Holiness the Dalai Lama.

During the early 1950s the Chinese Communist army had invaded Tibet and by 1959 were present in Lhasa as an occupying force. Deeply engaged in memorizing, studying, and debating, Rinpoche hadn't heard a great deal about the political and military situation in Tibet. But on March 10, 1959, the outside world suddenly and violently impinged on life in the monastery. March 10 is often referred to as Tibetan Uprising Day. On that day, the Chinese authorities had requested that His Holiness the Dalai Lama come with no bodyguards or other personnel to attend a theatrical performance and tea inside the army camp. The Tibetans feared the Chinese would kidnap the Dalai Lama, and so tens of thousands of Tibetans had surrounded the Norbulingka Palace in order to prevent the Dalai Lama from being taken. Among them were numerous monks from Sera Mey, though Rinpoche himself had remained at the monastery at that time. With the situation extremely tense and with those tens of thousands of Tibetans surrounding the palace, His Holiness the Dalai Lama secretly escaped to make his way into exile in India. Meanwhile, the Chinese army began shooting Tibetans in the streets and bombing the Norbulingka as well as many monasteries. Injured monks began returning to Sera Mey from the fighting nearby. The Chinese army followed them, and on the evening of March 10, they began shelling Sera Monastery. Some monks died and others were injured. That night Rinpoche and many other monks fled, taking refuge in the surrounding hills. Two days later the Chinese army would actually march into Sera, destroying many houses and buildings but leaving the main prayer hall standing.

On the night of March 10, Rinpoche's uncle Kalsang Namgyal found him in the hills and insisted that Rinpoche join him and some other monks in escaping Tibet. Rinpoche was quite concerned about his family; knowing that his mother would be very worried, he wanted to go reassure her. However, his uncle insisted that there wasn't time and that they had to flee directly. At his uncle's insistence, Rinpoche began traveling on foot toward India. Their party walked to Phenpo, where they paused to rest. Rinpoche again told his uncle that he wanted to go back to reassure and say farewell to his mother and other family members. Again, his uncle insisted that he continue with the party of monks on their journey to India following His Holiness the Dalai Lama. Rinpoche would never again see either of his parents. He would not see any of his siblings again until over fifty years later, when his sister would visit him in India.

There were seven or eight people in Rinpoche's party fleeing Tibet. They had no money, almost no food, and no books or other belongings from the monastery. All they had were the clothes they were wearing. They stayed for one night in Phenpo but then had to leave to avoid being found by the Chinese army. They eventually came to another small village, where they hid for three days in the home of a local family before again having to flee. There they got a small amount of barley flour to share between them. Later in their journey they came across a large house that had been abandoned by a wealthy family who'd also had to flee. Refugees were stopping there to gather some supplies, and so Rinpoche's party took a bit more barley flour and some butter. This was what they would have for the remainder of their journey on foot across the Himalayas. It had to last them fifteen days until they reached a border area called Mon in the Indian state of Arunachal Pradesh. They remained in this area for some time, receiving assistance from the Indian government.

From Mon, Rinpoche was sent to a temporary Tibetan refugee camp just south of there in Masamari, which is in the state of Assam, where he spent almost one year waiting to be relocated. Then Rinpoche was sent to a new refugee camp in Buxa in the state of West Bengal just south of Bhutan. Many Tibetan monks were sent there during this period. Buxa was a jungle-bound former prison where both Gandhi and Nehru had been detained by the British government during the Indian independence movement. Unfamiliar diseases along with the heat and humidity of the jungle environment led to the deaths of many Tibetan monks at Buxa from tuberculosis and other diseases. When Rinpoche arrived at Buxa, he was glad to resume his studies. After some time, though, he fell ill. Incorrectly diagnosed with tuberculosis, he was sent to a hospital for treatment where he remained for about a year. The hospital staff recognized that he didn't have tuberculosis but kept him there for a period of recuperation, as he'd become quite weak.

Rinpoche then returned to Buxa and focused on completing his studies of *Ornament for Clear Realizations* that he'd begun in Tibet. In addition to Maitreya's root text, Rinpoche particularly based these studies on Khedrup Tenpa Dargye's textbook, which is the standard textbook on this subject used by Sera Mey Monastic University. He also relied upon Lama Tsongkhapa's famous *Golden Garland* commentary, on Gyatsap Je's *Ornament of the Essence*, and on Khedrup Je's *Appearance of Logic*.

Next, Rinpoche turned the focus of his studies to Middle Way philosophy. The root text for these studies was Chandrakirti's *Entering the Middle Way*. Rinpoche also relied upon the two primary textbooks of Sera Mey on this topic, again composed by Khedrup Tenpa Dargye— one a general commentary and the second clarifying his personal views. Rinpoche also relied for these studies on Tsongkhapa's *Illumination of the Thought*, which provides his definitive commentary to Chandrakirti's text, and *Ocean of Reasoning*, Tsongkhapa's commentary directly upon Nagarjuna's *Fundamental Verses on the Middle Way*.

While residing at Buxa refugee camp, Rinpoche also took teachings from a number of the great teachers of the Geluk tradition. He attended quite a few teachings by Trijang Rinpoche, including the Chakrasamvara Body Mandala initiation and commentary as well as a commentary on the *Guru Puja*. He took many teachings from Ling Rinpoche, including a Vajrayogini commentary, a commentary on the *Guru Puja*, and a commentary on Shantideva's *Guide to the Bodhisattva's Way of Life*. He also took many teachings from Song Rinpoche—a highly respected teacher who was former abbot of Ganden Shartse Monastic University—

including commentaries on Tsongkhapa's *Great Treatise on the Stages of the Path*, Guhyasamaja practice, Chakrasamvara practice, and *chod* practice; he also received many initiations from Song Rinpoche, including Chakrasamvara, Yamantaka, Guhyasamaja, Vajrayogini, and Chittamani Tara.

After studying at the Buxa refugee camp for the better part of a decade, in 1970 Rinpoche moved south to the Mysore district of Karnataka state, where he and other monks began rebuilding Sera Monastic University in exile.

Farming in southern India was not easy for monks raised in Tibet. When the crops were young and low to the ground, wild boars would come and eat the plants. Insect damage to crops had to be controlled by monks who had vowed not to kill or harm any living creatures. And, as the crops grew tall, wild elephants would come eat them as well! While helping keep wild animals from eating their crops, Rinpoche and the other monks had to build a monastery from the ground up. Rinpoche's earliest experiences as a Himalayan nomad and subsequent years training as a Buddhist scholar were not the ideal training for farming and building in South India. At the same time, young Tibetan boys who had been born to refugee families in India or who had more recently themselves escaped on foot from Tibet began arriving at the ever-growing monastery. As a now mature young man, Rinpoche had responsibility to help provide for, look after, and educate these new monks. Life at Sera Mey was by no means quiet, simple, or cloistered!

All the while, Rinpoche energetically continued his study, contemplation, debate, and meditation on the great classics of Buddhist philosophy. At the newly created campus, Rinpoche completed his formal studies of Middle Way philosophy. He then undertook in-depth studies of Vinaya—the codes of ethics and discipline—and of Abhidharma, which includes teachings on Buddhist psychology, cosmology, and meditative states.

In 1986, Rinpoche completed the final exam for a geshe degree and received the esteemed honor of Geshe Lharampa (equivalent to a Ph.D. in Buddhist philosophy, psychology, cosmology, ethics, and practice), the highest level awarded. After earning his geshe degree, Rinpoche went to Gyumed Tantric College for one year to continue his studies in Buddhist tantra. After completing his studies there, he returned to Sera Mey. There Rinpoche continued his study, contemplation, and meditation practices while teaching other monks.

In addition to formal studies at the monastery, Rinpoche also attended many teachings during these years by His Holiness the Dalai Lama on important texts on the stages of the path, including all of the eight great treatises on the stages of the path, Pabongka Rinpoche's *Liberation in the Palm of Your Hand*, and many others. He also received many initiations from His Holiness, including the initiations and oral transmissions related to the Great Fifth Dalai Lama's *Secret Visions*. While at Gyumed Tantric College, Rinpoche received many other teachings from His Holiness, including the four interrelated Guhyasamaja commentaries by Tsongkhapa.

During his years in South India at Sera Mey, Rinpoche's main teacher was Khensur Ngawang Tekchok. He also studied in South India with Dhakpa Rinpoche—a former abbot of Sera Mey—and took initiations from him including the Hundred Initiations of Rinjung, the Hundred Initiations of Pari, the Initiations of the Thirteen Pure Visions of Tapuk Dorje Chang, and many others. While at Gyumed Tantric College, Rinpoche also received teachings from Denma Locho Rinpoche on an important commentary on Guhyasamaja by Jetsun Sherap Sengye, the founder of Gyumed Tantric College. Rinpoche himself notes that his closest lamas have been Trijang Rinpoche, Song Rinpoche, Ling Rinpoche, His Holiness the Dalai Lama, and then Dhakpa Rinpoche, Khensur Ngawang Tekchok, and Denma Locho Rinpoche.

In 1989, Rinpoche was appointed to the position of discipline master (*geku*) of Gyumed Tantric College for one year. Then in 1990, he received the advanced degree of Ngakrampa (the highest degree in Buddhist tantra studies) from Gyumed after extensively studying these secret teachings of the Mahayana tradition.

In 1993, monastic leaders submitted Rinpoche's name and that of eight other prominent geshes to the Dalai Lama as candidates for the post of ritual master *lama umzey* of Gyumed Tantric College. On January 7, 1994, His Holiness the Dalai Lama selected Khensur Rinpoche to serve in this role. Then on November 12, 1996, His Holiness the Dalai Lama appointed him abbot (*khenpo*) of Gyumed.

Khensur Rinpoche completed his three-year term as abbot with dedication and success, teaching tantric studies continuously and conducting many religious rituals and ceremonies. As abbot, Rinpoche was responsible for teaching the four interrelated Guhyasamaja commentaries. He also gave teachings on generation-stage practices of Guhyasamaja, Chakrasamvara, and Yamantaka. And he taught on Tsongkhapa's *Clarifying the Hidden Meaning of Chakrasamvara*. As a new set of geshes would come to Gyumed each year, Rinpoche taught all these topics each year of his term as abbot.

Upon completion of his term, Khensur Rinpoche returned to Sera Mey, where he continued teaching sutra and tantra to students and senior geshes. He also continued his active leadership and participation in all religious ceremonies of the monastery.

During his term as abbot of Gyumed, Khensur Rinpoche made his first visit to the United States and Canada to conduct various teachings and rituals at the request of the Gyumed College administrators and Western students. A considerable number of Westerners benefited from this initial tour. In 2003, he taught widely in Singapore and Malaysia.

In 2006, at the suggestion of Kyabje Ribur Rinpoche and at the request of Kyabje Lama Zopa Rinpoche, Khensur Rinpoche took up the role of resident teacher at FPMT's Guhyasamaja Center in the suburbs of Washington DC. It was in this capacity that Rinpoche gave the teachings on *Easy Path* that serve as the basis for this book. Since 2006, Rinpoche has spent a good deal of his time in the United States, where in addition to giving teachings in the capital area, he has also been invited with increasing regularity to Buddhist centers in many different states. Rinpoche has also become the spiritual director of Do Ngak Kunphen Ling Tibetan Buddhist Center for Universal Peace in Redding, Connecticut, where he also teaches regularly. In 2012, at Rinpoche's invitation, Do Ngak Kunphen Ling hosted teachings by His Holiness the Dalai Lama in conjunction with Western Connecticut State University.

Khensur Rinpoche is highly respected as both a scholar of great knowledge and a practitioner of the Mahayana Buddhist teachings in general and the Vajrayana teachings in particular. He has served as a teacher to many monks, scholars, and reincarnate lamas. Prior to his death, Kyabje Ribur Rinpoche requested that Khensur Rinpoche serve as the primary teacher to his next incarnation. Rinpoche also served as a close teacher to former Gyuto abbot Ngawang Jordan, who later also served as abbot of Segyu Monastery and who at this writing is abbot of Sera Mey.

This brief outline is intended to give the reader a general sketch of the external events of Rinpoche's life. Since the age of ten, however, Rinpoche's own focus has primarily been on inner transformation—on not only studying but also putting the teachings of the Buddha into practice. Thus the teachings in this book may be a truer account of Khensur Rinpoche's life than any narration of external events.

Notes

1. See Pabongka Rinpoche, *Liberation in the Palm of Your Hand*, trans. Michael Richards (Boston: Wisdom Publications, 2006), pp. 699–725. *Ornament for the Throats of the Fortunate* was actually composed by Pabongka Rinpoche's root guru, Jamphal Lhundrup.
2. See Jampal Lhundrup and Losang Chokyi Gyaltsan, *Lama Chöpa Jorchö* (Portland OR: FPMT, 2011).
3. For an English translation of this text with commentary, see Geshe Sonam Rinchen, *Atisha's Lamp for the Path to Enlightenment* (Ithaca: Snow Lion, 1997).
4. Lama Tsongkhapa's extensive text has been translated in three volumes:Tsong Kha Pa, *The Great Treatise on the Stages of the Path to Enlightenment*, trans. Lamrim Chenmo Translation Committee (Ithaca: Snow Lion, 2000–2004). Lama Tsongkhapa's medium-length text is available in translation with commentary as part of the Foundation for the Preservation of the Mahayana Tradition's Basic Program, and can be found online at www.fpmt.org. His brief text is available as "A Prayer for the Beginning, Middle, and End of Practice," in Tsongkhapa, *Splendor of an Autumn Moon*, trans. Gavin Kilty (Boston: Wisdom Publications, 2001), pp. 193–208. The Third Dalai Lama's text has been translated in Glenn Mullin, *Essence of Refined Gold* (Ithaca: Snow Lion, 1982).
5. Vajra Vehicle, Buddhist tantra, and secret mantra are all synonyms.
6. An *arhat* has attained the cessation of afflictive emotions, the state of *nirvana* for oneself, whereas a *buddha* has gone beyond this to attain omniscience and infinite manifestation for the welfare of others as well. "Eons" in this context refers to *countless great eons*. Descriptions of the length of countless great eons vary. In general, one *intermediate eon* is said to last sixteen million years. And a single *great eon* is said to be made up of eighty intermediate eons. A single countless great eon is said to be made up of 10^{60} great eons. So then a single countless great eon would be 128×10^{67} years.
7. The bodhisattva "Ever Crying," Sadaprarudita, was an extremely empathetic bodhisattva whose story is told in the sutras. See the translation by Edward Conze in *The Perfection of Wisdom in Eight Thousand Lines and Its Verse Summary* (Delhi: Sri Satguru Publications, 1973), pp. 277–99.
8. Khensur Rinpoche noted that this *Tushita Emanation Scripture* was also accessible during the twentieth century to Pabongka Dechen Nyingpo. For more on

the topic of this mystical scripture, see Janice D. Willis, *Enlightened Beings: Life Stories from the Ganden Oral Tradition* (Boston: Wisdom Publications, 1995).

9. If you do not have a spiritual teacher, you can still benefit from practicing the meditations taught in this book. However, if you wish to make meaningful progress on the path to enlightenment, then the Buddha himself and many later teachers of the Mahayana tradition agree that it is very important and beneficial to seek out a qualified teacher to guide you.

10. For example, see Pabongka Rinpoche, *Liberation*, pp. 28–52. For translations of biographical texts by Atisha and his Tibetan disciple Dromtonpa, see Thupten Jinpa, trans., *Mind Training: The Great Collection* (Boston: Wisdom Publications, 2006), pp. 27–70.

11. Pabongka, *Liberation*, p. 71.

12. For more details on these stories of the Buddha's sacrifices in his previous lives, see Stanley Frye, trans., *The Sutra of the Wise and the Foolish* (Dharamsala, India: Library of Tibetan Works and Archives, 1981).

13. This kind of patience is especially emphasized as arising at the patience level of the path of preparation. Another level of it arises on the path of seeing, and a third level arises at the eighth bodhisattva ground far along the path of meditation.

14. *The Exhortation to Wholehearted Resolve Sutra* describes two sets of twenty benefits of giving teachings—totaling forty benefits in all. See Lamrim Chenmo Translation Committee, *Great Treatise*, p. 63. Also Pabongka, *Liberation*, pp. 94–95.

15. There are two kinds of pure lands in this context. One is a place where nirmanakaya buddhas manifest, such as Bodhgaya for Shakyamuni or Sukhavati for Amitabha. The other is a place where sambogakaya buddha forms manifest, heavenly realms such as Akanishta.

16. A stupa is a traditional Buddhist monument, often a reliquary, and is said to represent the mind of a buddha. Buddhist scriptures are full of descriptions of the extensive benefits of making offerings before stupas. The vajra and bell are hand implements used in tantric practices.

17. *Emptiness* refers to the lack of true or inherent existence of entities. *Signlessness* refers to the lack of true or inherent existence of causes. *Wishlessness* refers to the lack of true or inherent existence of results.

18. Around the deities of highest yoga tantra are those of yoga tantra, then those of performance (*carya*) tantra, and then those of action (*kriya*) tantra.

19. The eight great bodhisattvas who were close heart sons of Shakyamuni Buddha are Manjushri, Avalokitesvara, Vajrapani, Maitreya, Kshitigarbha, Akashagarbha, Sarvanivaranavishkambin, and Samantabhadra.

20. The six ornaments are six great Buddhist masters from India: Nagarjuna, Aryadeva, Asanga, Vasubandu, Dignaga, and Dharmakirti, and the two supreme ones are Gunaprabha and Shakyaprabha.

21. When doing a short prostration, the five points that touch the ground are your forehead, palms, and knees.

22. See Geshe Jampa Gyatso, *Everlasting Rain of Nectar* (Boston: Wisdom Publica-

tions, 1996), or Lama Zopa Rinpoche, *The Preliminary Practice of Prostrations* (Portland OR: FPMT, 2010).

23. The eight auspicious symbols are the right-coiled conch, precious umbrella, victory banner, golden fish, Dharma wheel, auspicious knot, lotus, and treasure vase. The seven royal emblems are the precious wheel, wish-granting jewel, queen, minister, elephant, horse, and general.

24. He actually did one hundred thousand prostrations to each of those buddhas, thus completing 3.5 million prostrations while engaging in this practice.

25. For example, see *FPMT Retreat Prayer Book* (Portland OR: FPMT, 2009), pp. 104–15. Or see Pabongka, *Liberation*, pp. 706–9.

26. Rinpoche noted that some texts also teach what qualities the teacher and the student should have. Teachers of different levels of Buddhist subjects should have different qualifications. For a detailed explanation of this, see Lama Zopa Rinpoche, *Heart of the Path* (Boston: Lama Yeshe Wisdom Archive, 2009).

27. Paragraphs like this one on how to think while nectars and light rays descend appear with each major meditation topic. The sections in brackets are not written out explicitly in the Tibetan text, but that text indicates that they should be inserted each time.

28. If you have discussed Dharma with your friends or have attended a lecture on Buddhism with the motivation of simply gaining intellectual knowledge, then those need not be seen as establishing a teacher-student relationship.

29. As translated in Pabongka, *Liberation*, p. 239.

30. Pabongka, *Liberation*, p. 242.

31. Pabongka, *Liberation*, p. 242.

32. This story is from the *Gandavyuha Sutra*. Sudhana visits fifty-three spiritual teachers in all, culminating in Maitreya.

33. Nagarjuna in his *Letter to a Friend* lists these five: the luster of the body fades, their thrones are no longer pleasing, their flower garlands fade, their clothes pick up stains, and their bodies begin to sweat.

34. Some depictions of the wheel of life include a sixth section for the demigod realm, but often the demigods are included in the drawing of the god realm, shown battling with them.

35. The "and so on" here indicates that having requested your guru's blessings, you imagine five-colored nectars and light rays descending to bless you and all sentient beings as described earlier. Though we will not include "and so on" in subsequent verses, it should be understood that wherever it says "Please bless me, guru deity, to be able to do that," one continues visualizing the descent of five-colored nectars and light rays along with thinking that one has been purified, has received blessings for the realizations of the contemplation one is engaging in, and so on.

36. The Lord of Death became so angered by the new bodhisattva's compassion that he stabbed him with his trident, killing him in hell and causing him to be reborn in the Heaven of the Thirty-Three.

37. This verse was translated and kindly offered by Wilson Hurley.

38. The path of preparation is the second of the five paths traversed on the way to

enlightenment. These include the paths of accumulation, preparation, seeing, meditation, and no-more learning. The path of preparation itself has four stages: heat, peak, patience, and supreme mundane qualities.

39. These twelve are: sutras, songs (*geya*), prophecies (*vyakarana*), verses (*gatha*), aphorisms (*udana*), pragmatic stories (*nidana*), parables (*itivrittaka*), legends (*avadana*), birth stories (*jataka*), vast presentations (*vaipulya*), miracle stories (*adbhutadharma*), and profound teachings (*upadesha*).

40. The five greater sciences include arts and crafts, medicine, grammar, logic and epistemology, and the study of Dharma.

41. *Clarity* and *subjective clarity* are differentiated here in terms of the clarity of the object of meditation and the clarity of the subjective mind that apprehends that object.

42. The "ph" in *Phat!* here is not pronounced with an *f* sound but is rather a *p* sound with the *h* creating an aspirated, breathy quality.

43. You can accomplish this by swallowing and/or slightly tightening your stomach muscles, pushing downward a bit with them.

44. The "emptiness" of mind experienced here is not the mind's ultimate nature—its lack of inherent existence. Rather what's being referred to here is the mind's being empty of color or shape—its unobstructedness. Some scholars in the past have mistaken this emptiness that is part of the mind's conventional nature for its ultimate nature. Realizing the mind's conventional nature in meditation makes it easier to realize its ultimate nature, but these are different realizations.

45. *Siddhi* is a Sanskrit term for "powers" or "attainments," typically supernatural or spiritual in nature. The ultimate siddhi is enlightenment itself. A *mahasiddha* is one who has attained great siddhis for the welfare of others, usually through tantric practice. Milarepa is the most famous of the Tibetan mahasiddhas. Kalden Gyatso, whose life spanned the seventeenth century, was the founder of Labrang Monastery and had many disciples.

46. For a wonderful account of his life, see Willis, *Enlightened Beings*, pp. 84–96.

47. Thuken Losang Chökyi Nyima, *The Crystal Mirror of Philosophical Systems*, trans. Geshe Lhundup Sopa et al. (Boston: Wisdom Publications, 2009), p. 293.

48. Willis, *Enlightened Beings*, p. 213.

49. Willis, *Enlightened Beings*, p. 91.

50. E. Gene Smith, *Among Tibetan Texts: History and Literature of the Himalayan Plateau* (Boston: Wisdom Publications, 2001), p. 122.

51. Smith, *Among Tibetan Texts*, p. 127.

52. Willis, *Enlightened Beings*, p. 102.

53. Numerous English translations of this text have been done, including Losang Chokyi Gyaltsen and Jamphal Lhundrup, *Lama Chopa Jorcho* (Portland OR: FPMT, 2011). For the text with a commentary, see Dalai Lama, *The Union of Bliss and Emptiness*, trans. Thupten Jinpa (Ithaca: Snow Lion, 2009).

54. Available in English translation: Alexander Berzin, "Original Panchen Lama Version of An Extensive Six-Session Guru Yoga," at www.berzinarchives.com.

55. Available in H.H. the Dalai Lama and Alexander Berzin, *The Gelug/Kagyü Tradition of Mahamudra* (Ithaca: Snow Lion, 1997).

56. Translated by Yael Bentor and Pema Dorjee in a forthcoming volume in the AIBS Treasury of the Buddhist Sciences series.

57. Translated by Alexander Berzin, available from www.berzinarchives.com.

58. Ngulchu Dharmabhadra and the First Panchen Lama Losang Chokyi Gyaltsen, *Source of Supreme Bliss: Heruka Chakrasamvara Five Deity Practice and Commentary*, trans. David Gonsalez (Ithaca: Snow Lion, 2010), pp. 123–51.

59. Ibid., pp. 209–19.

60. Glenn Mullin, *The Practice of the Six Yogas of Naropa* (Ithaca: Snow Lion, 1997), pp. 141–53. Mullin notes that this brief text presents both the yogas of inner fire and of transference of consciousness in detailed and profound ways.

61. Glenn Mullin, *The Practice of Kalachakra* (Ithaca: Snow Lion, 1991), pp. 281–86.

62. Panchen Losang Chokyi Gyaltsen, *The Concise Essence Sutra Ritual of Bhagavan Medicine Buddha Called The Wish-Fulfilling Jewel*, trans. David Molk (Portland OR: FPMT, 2009).

63. This work of the Panchen Lama, not yet published in English, is called *Lion's Roar of Scripture and Logic: A Response to the Critiques of Drapa Sherap Rinchen*. See Jeffrey Hopkins, *Maps of the Profound: Jam-yang-shay-ba's Great Exposition of Buddhist and Non-Buddhist Views on the Nature of Reality* (Ithaca: Snow Lion, 2003), p. 15, and José Cabezón, "On the *sGra pa Shes rab Rin chen pa'i brtsod* of Panchen bLo bzang chos rgyan," *Études Asiatiques* 49.4 (1995): 643–69.

64. Dalai Lama and Berzin, *Gelug/Kagyü Tradition*, p. 98.

65. Thuken, *Crystal Mirror*, p. 293.

Index

About the Authors

A student of the Dalai Lama, GYUMED KHENSUR RINPOCHE LOBSANG JAMPA was born in Tibet in 1939. A geshe from Sera Monastery and former abbot (*khensur*) of Gyumed Tantric College, both in South India, he now spends most of his time in the United States, with active centers in Washington DC, New York City, and Connecticut, and he also teaches annually in the Silicon Valley. His center Do Ngak Kunphen Ling in Redding, Connecticut, hosted a visit from the Dalai Lama in 2012. This is his first book in English.

LORNE LADNER, Ph.D., is a clinical psychologist in private practice in the suburbs of Washington DC, where he also directs and teaches at the Guhyasamaja Buddhist Center. Dr. Ladner has produced a training video on *Mindful Therapy* and provides workshops on the psychology of positive emotions, the integration of meditation and psychotherapy, and on Buddhist psychology. He is the author of *The Lost Art of Compassion* and editor of *The Wheel of Great Compassion*.

About Wisdom Publications

Wisdom Publications is dedicated to offering works relating to and inspired by Buddhist traditions.

To learn more about us or to explore our other books, please visit our website at www.wisdompubs.org.

You can subscribe to our e-newsletter or request our print catalog online, or by writing to:

Wisdom Publications
199 Elm Street
Somerville, Massachusetts 02144 USA

You can also contact us at 617-776-7416, or info@wisdompubs.org.

Wisdom is a nonprofit, charitable 501(c)(3) organization, and donations in support of our mission are tax deductible.

Wisdom Publications is affiliated with the Foundation for the Preservation of the Mahayana Tradition (FPMT).